Spice Islands

Sultan Sayfoedin of Tidore (r. 1657–89) (Bridgeman Art Library/Czartoryski Museum, Kracow)

Spice Islands

Ian Burnet

ROSENBERG

First published in paperback in 2013
by Rosenberg Publishing Pty Ltd
PO Box 6125, Dural Delivery Centre NSW 2158
Phone: 61 2 9654 1502 Fax: 61 2 9654 1338
Email: rosenbergpub@smartchat.net.au
Web: www.rosenbergpub.com.au
Copyright © Ian Burnet 2011

National Library of Australia Cataloguing-in-Publication entry

Author: Burnet, Ian.

Title: Spice Islands / Ian Burnet.

Print ISBN: 9781922013989 (pbk.)
Print ISBN: 9781921719110 (hbk.)
Epdf ISBN: 9781925078091
Epub ISBN: 9781920578107
MOBI ISBN: 9781925078114

Notes: Includes bibliographical references and index.

Subjects: Spice trade–History

Spices--History. Cooking (Spices)–History. Trade routes–History.

Dewey Number: 380.141383

Set in 12 on 14 point Arno Pro

Printed in China by Everbest Printing Co Limited

Contents

This book is dedicated to the memory of Paramita Abdurachman (1920–88),
Indonesian patriot and historian,
who first introduced me to the history of the Spice Islands

Gold chain belonging to the Sultan of Ternate, weighing approximately 750 grams
(Rijksmuseum, Amsterdam)

ACKNOWLEDGMENTS

It has been 10 years since I first started the research for this book and I would like to thank my wife Yusra Zahari Burnet, my daughters Miranda and Melissa, and family and friends who have supported me through the highs and lows of this journey. I would also like to thank Yul and Wati Chatab who provided help in Indonesia. Thanks to Greg Lund and Michelle Sirkedjian who read early versions of the manuscript, Xavier Waterkeyn and Carl Harrison-Ford who provided valuable input along the way, and Peter Meredith who worked overtime on the final edit. My thanks also to the librarians of the British Library, the Oriente Museum in Lisbon, the KITLV/Royal Netherlands Institute of South East Asian Studies Library in Jakarta, the Australian National Library, and the State Library of New South Wales.

MAPS

Prologue

In the Moluccas, when the clove trees are in blossom,
They are treated like pregnant women.
No noise may be made near them,
No one may approach them with his hat on,
All must uncover in their presence.
These precautions are observed lest the tree should be alarmed
And bear no fruit, or should drop its fruit too soon,
Like the untimely delivery of a woman who has been frightened in her pregnancy.

—James Frazer, *The Golden Bough*, 1890

Sitting in the dim and dusty libraries of the world doing the historical research necessary for this book, I would dream of the fabled Spice Islands. Images of palm-fringed tropical islands backed by towering volcanoes filled my imagination and I saw myself arriving on their sandy shores by sailing boat, like the explorers, adventurers and traders that had gone before me. As I started writing this story of the Moluccas and the Spice Islands I realized that it would be impossible for me to finish until I had reached that destination.

My boat was the *Bintang Laut*, a Bugis phinisi that had left the port of Ambon in Eastern Indonesia heading north towards the island of Ternate with a cargo of goods and myself the only passenger. The Bugis phinisi is a classical looking two-masted schooner of all wood construction, usually built in the island of Sulawesi using traditional methods and a design that has lasted centuries. In their heyday, several thousand of these vessels connected all the islands in the Indonesian Archipelago. Even today, they carry a significant portion of the inter-island trade in what is still the largest fleet of sailing traders in the world, although now fitted with diesel engines as well as sail. Even in the capital city of Jakarta, a visitor to the harbour of Sunda Kelapa will find dozens of Bugis phinisi lined up along the quay, loading and unloading their traditional cargoes such as rice, copra, sago and spices as well as television sets, motorcycles and mobile phones. This work is still done by human labour, with shirtless and barefoot labourers carrying sacks and boxes down the narrow gangplanks to waiting handcarts and battered trucks.

The best accommodation on the *Bintang Laut* was a straw mat on deck, away from the fetid smells of bilge water, engine oil and humanity below. Meals were simple: squatting on our haunches, the crew and I ate a regular diet of rice and fresh or salted fish with some vegetables and chilli paste. I was pleased to have brought some extra rations to vary the menu.

'Captain Sam' with his long lank hair and wispy beard, only needed a gold earring and a buccaneer's hat to get a part in a Hollywood movie. A man of few words, he communicated with the crew by gestures and brief commands. The crew were hard-working, lean, and blackened by the sun. I could sense that they were at one with the vessel and the sea, and had an innate sense of what had to be done in any given situation. When they were not busy with their shipboard duties, we amused ourselves by trawling for fish or smoking kretek, the pungent clove-flavoured cigarettes smoked throughout Indonesia, all the time carrying on a friendly banter in a mixture of Bahasa Indonesia and fractured English.

Awake since before dawn, my body felt stiff from a wakeful night dozing to the rhythmic splash and hiss of the bow wave slapping against the boat, accompanied by the creaking of the wooden hull, the straining of ropes and the rattle of pots and pans in the galley. I welcomed the morning sun as it revealed a sea like glass stretching away to the horizon and warmed my stiffened joints. We were four days out from Ambon when we first sighted Bacan, the biggest and tallest of all the Spice Islands with its cloud-wrapped peak rising 2110 metres out of the sea.

Sailing through the strait separating Bacan from the southern arm of the island of Halmahera we headed for the main port of Sayoang, on the east coast. Here I had a chance to explore the tiny port and recover my land legs while the crew helped unload goods for the local stores. Leaving Bacan later that evening, we sailed north, passing several small tree-covered islands with the dim outline of the coast of Halmahera in the background.

Sometime during the night the *Bintang Laut* crossed the equator and the first pink light of dawn revealed two more volcanic islands, which the nautical chart confirmed were Makian and Moti. We were sailing along the narrow Patinti Strait, between the large four-fingered island of Halmahera and a chain of offshore volcanic peaks rising directly out of the sea. Makian was once the most prolific producer of cloves in all the Spice Islands, and sailors have described how, with the wind in their faces, they could smell its sweet, spicy fragrance from far out at sea. The map by Jan Janssonius has north oriented to the right and shows the Patinti Strait separating the Spice Islands from the main island of Gilolo or Halmahera.

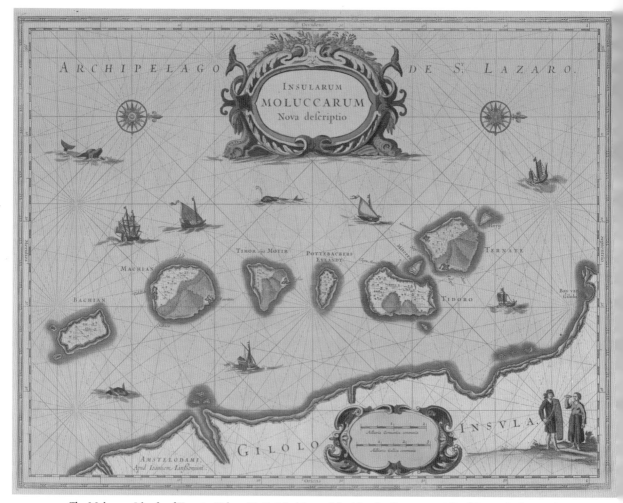

The Moluccan Islands of Ternate, Tidore, Motir, Machian and Bachian, Jan Janssonius, 1651 (National Library of Australia, nla.map-rm267)

This journey is one of the most beautiful sea voyages in all of Indonesia, and to make it even more spectacular we were accompanied by a school of dolphins welcoming the *Bintang Laut* by diving out of the crystal clear waters beside our vessel. The wind had picked up, and by mid-morning these islands were receding in our wake and the twin islands of Ternate and Tidore were in view, with wisps of cloud starting to build up around their volcanic peaks.

The Ring of Fire is the name given to the belt of 400 active volcanoes that circle the Pacific Ocean. More than 155 of these volcanoes are in Indonesia, making it the most tectonically active region on the earth. The cataclysmic explosion of the Krakatoa volcano in 1883 echoed around the world, the huge tsunami wave generated by a submarine earthquake off North Sumatra in 2004 devastated Banda Aceh and engulfed coastal villages as far away as Thailand and Sri Lanka, and every year there are new earthquakes and new volcanic eruptions.

The jigsaw puzzle of continental and oceanic plates that make up the earth's surface is in constant motion. Driven by the circulation of molten rock within the earth's core and moving only centimetres per year, the earth literally quakes as these plates collide and grind past each other. When they collide, the heavier oceanic plates sink under the lighter continental plates, subducting marine sediments deep into the interior of the earth. Here, these subducted rocks become superheated and the resultant steam, gas and molten lava can erupt explosively at the earth's surface.

The great arc of the Indonesian Archipelago starts north of the island of Sumatra and curves south and east until it reaches the northern part of the Australian continent. This arc of islands is defined by a string of active volcanoes, in Sumatra, Java, Bali, Lombok, Sumbawa and Flores, that erupt as the Indian Ocean plate is subducted under the Asian continental plate. Further east, the island arc is pushed to the north by the Australian continent, which has been relentlessly marching northward since it separated from Antarctica 45 million years ago. The continuing collision of the Australian continent and the Pacific Ocean plate has thrust the Papuan mountains up to a height of 5000 metres above sea level, where a tropical glacier still exists only four degrees south of the equator. The huge Pacific Ocean plate is moving westward pushing the island arc back on itself and rafting segments of Papua hundreds of kilometres towards the west.

Eastern Indonesia represents a unique part of the Earth's surface because it is here that four of the earth's great tectonic plates—the Indian Ocean, the Asian Continent, the Australian Continent and the Pacific Ocean—are in collision with each other.

Three million years ago in the Moluccan Sea, these powerful forces fused together volcanic island arcs, seafloor sediments and coral reefs to create new land, forming the unusually shaped island of Halmahera. A subduction zone then formed along the western side of Halmahera, causing the volcanoes that lay before me to erupt out of the sea and spreading a thick layer of volcanic ash across the adjacent islands.

We know that Nature abhors a vacuum, and the rich volcanic soils of these newly emergent islands were quickly populated by coconut trees grown from coconuts washed up on these shores, by plants whose seeds blew with the winds, by birds and butterflies able to fly from island to island, and by animals and insects drifting on floating trees and branches. Tropical temperatures and monsoonal rains provided the environment for a diversity of plant, bird and animal species to thrive and evolve in unique ways. The profusion of islands allowed for a separation in the evolution of different species and became an ideal natural laboratory for scientific study. The British naturalist Alfred Russel Wallace spent five years trekking through the tropical forests of the Moluccas, collecting and studying the birds, butterflies, insects and animal life of eastern Indonesia. He made Ternate his headquarters and it was a letter he wrote to Charles Darwin in 1858, elegantly arguing his own theory of the evolution of species by natural selection, that precipitated the publication by Darwin of his landmark work, *On the Origin of Species by Means of Natural Selection*, before Wallace's return to England.

Luxuriant tropical vegetation similar to that of the rest of the archipelago now covers these islands. However, a botanical miracle occurred when two new species of plant life developed. Did God throw a few seeds left over from the Creation into this tropical hothouse? For the Moluccas, or Maluku, are famous for two trees that grew only in this part of the world and the spices they produce—cloves and nutmeg.

The clove tree is indigenous to only five small volcanic islands off the west coast of Halmahera, namely Ternate, Tidore, Moti, Machian and Bacan. The nutmeg tree is indigenous to the equally small and even more remote islands of Banda, Lontar, Ai and Run, which lie 700 kilometres away in the Banda Sea. The exact location of these islands was long shrouded in myth and mystery, and together they became known as the Spice Islands.

In the 1670s the naturalist Georg Rumphius described the clove tree as the most beautiful, the most elegant and the most precious of all known trees. Like most understory trees, it is unable to regenerate under the full tropical sun and its seed is only viable for a short period, which may explain why its worldwide distribution was limited to these few tiny islands. A member of the Myrtle family, the clove tree grows to a height of ten metres and is covered with glossy and powerfully aromatic leaves, but it is the flower bud that is valued. The clove buds grow in clusters and change colour as they mature, from green through yellow to pink and finally a deep russet red. In order to retain the maximum amount of their aromatic oil, the buds are harvested before they flower, then spread out on mats to dry. The buds harden and blacken as the heat of the tropical sun seals in their fragrant oil. As the clove bud and stem dries, it takes on the characteristic nail-like appearance that gives the spice its name, which is derived from the Latin word clavus for nail. Cloves are called cravo in Portuguese, clavo in Spanish, clou de girofle in French, chiodo di garofano in Italian, and the Dutch term is kruidnagel, or spice nail. The Indonesian word is cengkeh, derived from the word zhen ka, which in the Fujian dialect of south-east China means scented nail. In Sanskrit cloves are called katuka-phala, meaning strong scented plant: this became the Arabic word karanful, which then became caryophyllon in Greek. Cloves were used by the ancients not just for their unique flavour and aroma, but also for their antibacterial and analgesic properties, which made them highly valued in a world without modern medicine. The fact that it takes more than 3000 flower buds to produce one kilogram of dried cloves may also explain why they are so valuable.

The nutmeg tree is also a member of the Myrtle family and its fruit is the size of a small

Botanical drawing of a clove branch and flowers, Georg Rumphius, 1690 (University Library, Leiden)

peach. When ripe, the fruit opens to reveal the seed surrounded by a red web known as mace, these are then separated and dried in the sun. The dried seed is broken to reveal the nut, which is best when freshly grated and added as flavouring to various dishes and desserts.

From earliest times, traders sailed from the Spice Islands across vast oceans in leaky boats to bring these clove buds and nutmegs to markets in East Africa, the Middle East, India and China. Loaded onto the backs of recalcitrant camels, they were transported across the deserts of Egypt, Arabia and Central Asia before finally reaching the Mediterranean Sea and markets in Europe. The length of this journey halfway around the world and the profits and taxes extracted at each stage meant that when demand was highest these simple buds and seeds were said to be worth their weight in gold.

After the expansion of Islam across the Middle East in the seventh century, the spice trade was monopolized by the Muslims who were by now the sworn enemies of Christian Europe. The Pope and the Kings of Europe supported those explorers willing to sail into unknown seas in search of a direct route to the Spice Islands. The voyages of European exploration such as those made by Bartholomeu Dias, Christopher Columbus, Vasco da Gama, Ferdinand Magellan and Juan Sebastian Elcano were an attempt to find a new route to the Indies and the Spice Islands, and it was these epic voyages of 'The Age of Discovery' that allowed mankind to put a definite shape to the continents and oceans of our planet for the first time in human history.

Like those who had ventured before me, I wanted my first sight of Ternate and Tidore to be from the sea, a sight I had imagined countless times over the years. Rising from sea level were the volcanoes that form the centre of these two almost symmetrical islands, their slopes covered in lush tropical forest. As we sailed closer, I could see the groves of clove and nutmeg trees. Mount Kiematubu dominates the island of Tidore, its symmetrical volcanic cone rising to a height of 1730 metres. Mount Gamalama, at 1720 metres, dominates the island of Ternate, which exists under almost constant threat—the volcano has erupted more than 60 times since the start of record-keeping in 1538, with the most recent eruption occurring in 1994. The sight was awesome in the true sense of the word. I felt elated at the prospect of reaching my destination, but also anxious as to what lay ahead and whether the communal fighting that had made the headlines over the last few years was now over.

After sailing through the narrow strait that separates the islands of Ternate and Tidore, the *Bintang Laut* tied up at the main dock in Ternate and the process of unloading and loading goods began. Now largely a forgotten part of the world, Ternate is only reached by inter-island boat or small plane and sees very few travellers or tourists. The town is the provincial capital for North Maluku and it seems as if every government department known to the sprawling Indonesian bureaucracy has an office here. Other than at these

View of the Spice Islands from Ternate (Ian Burnet)

offices, most of the daily activity of the town seems to be at the port or the airport, as Ternate is a transportation hub connecting to other parts of eastern Indonesia, such as North Sulawesi, Halmahera and Papua.

I found my hotel, which is very plain but in a nice garden setting. You couldn't say the staff were friendly, but they are not unfriendly either, just indifferent. I ask a question at the front desk and the girl goes away to get the answer (I think) and never comes back. Perhaps it's a language problem. Anxious to get out and explore the town before dark, I leave my luggage in the corner of the room and head off into the street without any idea of where I am going.

The people on the streets are mainly of Malay origin, but there are also Papuans, some Indonesian Chinese and some Alfurus, who seem to be a mixture of Malay and Papuan. Certainly there are no other 'round eyes' like myself, and I am greeted by large smiles, and lots of giggles and 'Hello Misters' from the children, who describe me as being an 'Orang Belanda' or Dutchman. My exploration of the town inevitably leads to the seafront market. It seems that every evening half the population of Ternate meets along the waterfront, socializing, enjoying the cool sea breeze, shopping for street-side bargains and eating local delicacies being cooked at the food stalls. This is the durian season, and workers are busy unloading boatloads of this prized but pungent tropical fruit onto the waterfront and preparing to sell them to their happy customers thronging the market. The darkness of the tropical evening quickly closes in; hurricane lamps are fired up and hiss behind the vendors shouting their wares; the smell of coconut oil frying up martabak, dumplings or spring rolls permeates the air. It is time for dinner.

The extraordinary story of these forgotten islands and the clove buds and nutmegs that made them wealthy is a story of exploration, of adventure, and of our yearning for distant and exotic places. The early explorers, adventurers and traders risked fate and fortune and suffered the ravages of scurvy and tropical disease in an attempt to gain a share of and ultimately a monopoly over, these simple buds and seeds.

The history of the Spice Islands can partly be told by the decaying Sultan's palaces and the crumbling Portuguese, Spanish and Dutch forts which dot the islands, but perhaps we should start this story from somewhere near the beginning.

1   *The First Spice Traders*

… by equinoctial winds
Close sailing from Bengala, or the isles
Of Ternate and Tidore, whence merchants bring
Their spicy drugs.

—John Milton, *Paradise Lost*, 1667

A black strip of road stretches across the Syrian Desert to the horizon and the ancient city of Palmyra. As its name suggests, Palmyra was surrounded by palm trees, and the friezes carved on the Temple of Bel show the variety of palms that grew in the oasis as well as its abundant animal and bird life. A former stopping point for caravans travelling the Silk Road and the Spice Route between the Euphrates River and the ancient Mediterranean ports of Antioch and Tyre, the springs that fed the oasis dried up centuries ago and the Greco-Roman ruins of the city and its Great Colonnade now lie abandoned in the desert.

The ancient city of Terqa lies another 200 kilometres beyond Palmyra, on the banks of the Euphrates River, near the town of Ashara and in the heart of the once Fertile Crescent. Surrounded by an outer moat and three concentric rings of massive walls twenty metres wide and six metres high, the ancient city covers 24 hectares. Inside the walls, excavations by archaeologists from the International Institute for Mesopotamian Studies (sponsored by the University of California at Los Angeles, Johns Hopkins University, the University of Arizona and l'Université de Poitiers in France) have unearthed numerous temples, storage kilns and ovens, as well as residential areas.

Across the street from the main temple, excavations revealed a small private home with three main rooms clustered around a central courtyard. Carefully sifting through the material in the house, the archaeologists were astounded to discover a few clove buds preserved in one of the ceramic jars found in the pantry. We know that Puzurum, the owner of the house, was a successful land developer, since the cuneiform script on the clay tablets found in the house records in detail his loans from the temple treasury and land transactions. A reference to the reign of King Yadikh-Abu allowed historians to date the tablets to 1721 BC. The archaeologists also discovered eight Egyptian scarabs in the main temple, indicating that there was some contact between this site and Egypt.

Since we know that cloves only grew half the world away in the Spice Islands of Indonesia, a long-distance trade in these spices must have existed almost 4000 years ago. Exactly how these cloves reached Syria remains a mystery. However, we do know that at the time of the Egyptian Pharaohs there was an ancient trade route using the oceanic currents that circulate around the Indian Ocean from Indonesia to East Africa.

Opposite Luxor, in Southern Egypt, and set below the towering cliffs near the Valley of the Kings, is the mortuary temple of Queen Hatshepsut. Sculpted and painted tableaux on the walls of the temple depict history's first documented spice trading mission. In 1493 BC, a fleet of five Egyptian ships travelled down the Red Sea to the Land of Punt, believed to be in Ethiopia or Somalia, in search of myrrh, frankincense and exotic spices. The sculpted tableaux, still bearing some of their original colour, depict in detail the departure of the expedition, its arrival at the mysterious land and the preparations for the return voyage. Inscriptions on the temple walls describe the goods the Egyptians loaded for the return journey, including cassia or cinnamon:

> Loading of the ships very heavily with marvels of the country of Punt; all goodly fragrant woods of God's-Land, heaps of myrrh resin, with fresh myrrh trees, with ebony and pure ivory, with green gold of Amu, with cinnamon wood, khesyt wood, with two kinds of incense, eye-cosmetics, with apes, monkeys, dogs, and with skins of the southern panther, with natives and their children. Never was brought the like of this for any king who has been since the beginning.

In the Old Testament, the Book of Exodus describes how the Lord spoke to Moses on the top of Mount Sinai and gave instructions that the children of Israel should build a tabernacle that he might dwell among them. They were told to bring an offering of oil for light, spices for the anointing oil, and sweet incense for the tabernacle. For the anointing oil, with which they were to anoint the tabernacle, they were told to use cinnamon and cassia, along with other substances:

> Take thou also unto thee principal spices of pure myrrh five hundred shekels, and of sweet cinnamon half so much, even two hundred and fifty shekels, and of sweet calamus two hundred and fifty shekels,
> And of cassia five hundred shekels, after the shekel of the sanctuary, and of olive oil:
> And thou shalt make it an oil of holy ointment, an ointment compound after the art of the apothecary, and it shall be a holy anointing oil.

The Egyptians used cassia as incense and in their embalming process because of its antibacterial properties, but it does not grow in Africa and could have only come from Asia.

Early Austronesian traders gathered cassia and other spices in Java and Sumatra, before sailing thousands of kilometres across the Indian Ocean from Indonesia to the ancient port of Raphta, on the East African coast. Local traders then transported these spices from Raphta via the ports of East Africa to the Red Sea and Egypt.

These Austronesian traders originated from a group of people who crossed the straits from China to Taiwan around 7000 years ago. Here they adapted to island living, learnt to build outrigger boats and survived by fishing and shifting cultivation. A thousand

Allegorical scene of cloves being harvested in the Spice Islands (Leyden Atlas)

years later they fled their coastal villages as sea levels rose at the end of the last Ice Age, migrating first to the Philippines and then to Indonesia.

The Austronesians became the masters of the sea, their outrigger boats and navigation skills allowing them to populate almost a third of the earth's surface. In the last and the greatest act in the history of human migration, they sailed from Indonesia as far east as Easter Island, as far north as Hawaii, as far south as New Zealand, and as far west as East Africa.

Travelling on rafts and double-outrigger canoes across vast oceans, they brought plants such as coconuts, yams, taro, sugarcane, breadfruit and rice to new lands. Linguists have used the roots of their common language to mark the extent of these incredible voyages across the great oceans of the world, and today the people we know as the Malays, the Micronesians, the Polynesians, the Maoris and the Malagasy are their descendants.

After crossing the Indian Ocean to East Africa, the Austronesians left remnants of their culture on the island of Madagascar, including the cultivation of dry and wet rice, and ceremonies associated with its planting and harvesting. Their presence is reflected in the features of the Malagasy people and in their language, which has Austronesian roots. DNA analysis has found that the closest living ancestors of Madagascar's Malagasy people are on the island of Kalimantan (Borneo) in Indonesia. This matches the linguistic evidence that the languages spoken around the Barito River in southern Kalimantan are the closest extant relatives of the Malagasy language. After their settlement on Madagascar, the pressure of later migrants from mainland Africa forced these ancient seafarers to move into the highlands of the interior of the island. Here they lost their maritime skills, but terraced rice fields evoking images of their Indonesian homeland.

The Greek philosopher Pliny the Elder, in his 37-volume *Naturalis Historia*, written around AD 77, expressed his admiration for these intrepid Austronesian seamen who voyaged across the Indian Ocean:

> They bring spices over vast seas on rafts which have no rudders to steer them or oars to push … Or sails or other aids to navigation … instead only the spirit of man and human courage … These winds drive them on a straight course, from gulf to gulf. Now cinnamon is the chief object of their journey, and they say that these merchant sailors take almost five years before they return and that many perish.

In 2003, expedition leader Phillip Beale, ex-Royal Navy, maritime historian and investment fund manager, sought to follow this ancient trading route using a vessel constructed to match the carved stone image of a ship from the walls of the eighth-century Borobudur Monument in Central Java.

The largest Buddhist monument in the world, Borobodur has been built around a hill on the plains of Central Java and is surrounded by green terraced rice fields and 3000-metre volcanic peaks. Constructed from over one million blocks of stone, the monument consists of four terraces lined with 1460 carved stone panels illustrating five

Buddhist scriptures. By circumambulating each successive terrace, the dedicated pilgrim could hope to physically and spiritually reach a level of enlightenment reflected by the stone Buddhas housed within their stupas on three concentric circles at the highest level of the monument.

On the lower level of the monument are several stone panels showing the images of sailing vessels of the period. From its stone image, the Borobodur vessel is estimated to be about twenty metres long and has two tripod masts with lug-sails, a foresail and a side rudder, as well as outriggers that provided stability in rough seas and a place for paddlers to propel the vessel in calm weather.

The building of the replica of the Borobodur vessel required using tools, materials and construction techniques from first millennium South-East Asia, which meant no use of nails or iron. The hull construction used edge-dowelled planks fitted together, with supporting ribs lashed to lugs on the inboard side of the planking.

In August 2003 the vessel, renamed the *Samudra Raksa* (Defender of the Seas) when officially launched by President Megawati Sukarno, left the port of Jakarta with a crew of fifteen men and women. Sailing west through the Sunda Strait that separates Java from Sumatra, it passed the circle of islands that form the remnant crater of Krakatoa. The eruption of Krakatoa in 1883 and the resulting tsunami caused huge loss of life. The

The Borobodur vessel (Ian Burnet)

volcano ejected millions of tons of volcanic ash into the atmosphere, causing temperatures to drop and harvests to fail around the world. In 1928, the aptly named Anak Krakatoa, (Child of Krakatoa), emerged smoking from the sea, extruding ash and lava as it built a new volcanic cone inside the remnant crater of its infamous parent.

The *Samudra Raksa* used the oceanic currents and monsoonal trade winds to sail the 6000 kilometres across the Indian Ocean to the Seychelles in only 26 days. The ship's log describes the replica eighth-century vessel surfing along the crest of ocean swells at speeds of up to eight knots, and it averaged a speed in excess of five knots as it rode the oceanic currents towards Africa. The next leg of the journey, south-west to Madagascar, was against the prevailing winds and took another fifteen days, but the Borobudur Ship Expedition had proved the feasibility of this ancient trade route, now known as the Cinnamon Route. A special hall has now been built in the grounds of the Borobodur Monument to house the *Samudra Raksa* and to document its voyage across the Indian Ocean to Africa.

These Austronesian seafarers also reached China, where history's earliest written record of cloves dates from the third century BC. The annals of the Han Dynasty describe how the Emperor would not allow his courtiers to approach him without first chewing a clove bud to sweeten their breath. Considering the lack of oral hygiene in early times, cloves were invaluable. Their antibacterial properties killed oral bacteria and imparted their unique scent as a 'breath freshener'. The Chinese also valued the analgesic effects of clove oil. A small amount of the oil applied to an aching tooth deadened the nagging pain, and rubbed into the forehead or temples relieved a throbbing headache.

Because of its antibacterial properties, traditional Chinese physicians have long used cloves to treat internal parasites and intestinal infections, as well as athlete's foot and other fungal infections. India's traditional Ayurvedic healers used cloves to treat respiratory and digestive ailments; ground cloves mixed into a paste and applied to the skin helped to heal wounds and skin infections, and clove tea was a useful household remedy for all sorts of stomach ailments.

Although little is known about these masters of the oceans, the early Austronesian seafarers were the world's first long-distance traders, and the spices they carried helped establish the first segments of what was to become a global trading network.

2 *The Spice Route*

If you come hoping for merchandise,
The riches of the sumptuous Levant,
Cinnamon, cloves, ardent spices,
Or potent, health-giving drugs,
Or if you hope to find precious stones,
The exquisite ruby, the precious diamond,
If these are the luxuries you treasure,
Here is your journey's end, by any measure.

—Luis Vas de Camões, *The Lusiads*, 1572

It is known that Austronesian seafarers brought cinnamon, cloves and nutmeg to India, since the island of Java is mentioned in the earliest written versions (300 BC) of the Indian Ramayana epic. From India, sailors traded these and other spices along the Arabian coastlines in exchange for gold, silver, metal utensils and weapons.

The Red Sea and the Persian Gulf, together with the great rivers of the Nile, the Tigris and the Euphrates, provided natural trade routes for spices and other commodities to move from the Indian Ocean to the Mediterranean Sea. These trade routes or geographic highways became part of the Spice Route, which extended halfway around the world, and shaped the history of people and commerce for the next 1500 years.

Wishing to avoid the pirate-infested coastlines, a Greek navigator known as Hippalus learnt to use the monsoonal winds to make the first direct crossing of the Indian Ocean from Arabia to the coast of India. Risking his vessel and crew to the waves and storms of the open ocean, he sailed to India with the south-west monsoon, which blows from June to October, and returned with the north-east monsoon, which blows from December to March. According to *The Periplus of the Erythraean Sea,* dating from AD 50:

Hippalus was the pilot who by observing the location of the ports and the conditions of the sea, first discovered how to lay his course straight across the ocean. For at the same time when with us the Etesian winds are blowing, on the shores of India the wind sets in from the ocean, and this southwest wind is called Hippalus, from the name of him who first discovered the passage across.

The word monsoon comes from the Arabic word mawsim, meaning season. The monsoon seasons are powered by the warming and cooling of the air over the Asian continental land mass. From spring through summer, the warmer air over the Asian continent rises, pulling in moist oceanic air from the south-west and bringing life-giving rains to the plains of India. From autumn through winter, the system reverses as the warmer air over the ocean rises, bringing cool dry continental air from the north-east. Since the timing of these monsoonal winds controlled the movement of trading vessels across the oceans, they became known as the trade winds.

The Egyptian port of Alexandria was established and ruled by the Ptolemys, who were remnants of the armies of Alexander the Great. The port city became the economic and cultural centre of the classical world, and from here the Ptolemys ruled Egypt like Pharaohs. Cleopatra was the last of the Ptolemys and it was after her unfortunate dalliance with the Roman General Marc Antony, and then the poisonous asp, that the Romans inherited this trade.

Most of the goods traded between the Mediterranean and India crossed the bustling docks of Alexandria, manhandled by Greeks, Egyptians, Phoenicians and Nubians. From here the trade route extended down the Nile by boat to Aswan, across the desert by camel caravan to the ancient Red Sea port of Berenice, by boat down the Red Sea to Aden and from there directly across the Arabian Sea to the pepper-growing Malabar Coast of south-west India.

Excavations at Berenice have uncovered teakwood and sailcloth from ancient ships, stores of peppercorns, and goods indicating trade with places as far away as Thailand and Java. Inscriptions and other written material in Greek, Hebrew, Latin, Coptic and Sanskrit attest to the cosmopolitan mix of people who lived in or passed through Berenice on their way to and from India.

The golden age of Greco-Roman trade between Egypt and India extended from 50 BC to AD 96, and the Roman chronicle *The Principat of Augustus* reported 120 ships per year trading across the Arabian Sea. Huge quantities of pepper harvested in the Kerala hills were exported from the ports of the Malabar Coast of south-west India, as evidenced by the large numbers of Greek and Roman coins that have been found there. One hoard consisted of 83 gold and silver coins dating from 123 BC to AD 117 spans almost the entire period of Greco-Roman trade with India.

The Periplus of the Eyrthraean Sea, a sailing manual compiled by a Greek shipmaster, is the only first-hand account of the spice trade to survive from classical times. The manual includes descriptions of the ports, sailing conditions and trade commodities from Berenice to the mouth of the Indus River, to the Malabar Coast, to the island of

Sri Lanka, to the Coromandel Coast and as far as the Ganges River in the Bay of Bengal.

The opulence of Rome contributed to the rising demand for spices, and the centre of the Empire imported huge quantities of pepper and cinnamon. The Romans loved the taste of pepper, and the only cookbook to survive from Roman times, *De Re Coquinaria* uses pepper in 349 of its 468 recipes. A recipe for pepper sauce was to 'pound pepper, steep overnight in wine and then add fish sauce to form a smooth, muddy fluid'. The Romans did not commonly use cloves in their cooking. Pliny the Elder refers to them in his *Naturalis Historia*, although their origin in the Spice Islands was still unknown:

> There is also in India another grain which bears a considerable resemblance to pepper, but is longer and more brittle; it is known by the name of caryophyllon. It is said that this grain is produced in a sacred grove in India; with us it is imported for its aromatic perfume.

Odour impressions have always fascinated mankind. For our ancestors the smoke from incense made of resins, woods, barks and aromatic plants had magical properties and their perfumed scents were sent heavenward to honour the gods. The Greeks were experts at extracting the essential oils of plants for use in perfuming their rooms and their bodies. Aristotle noted that pleasant odours contribute to the wellbeing of mankind, and Pliny reminded his followers that perfumery was the most necessary luxury. The practice of aromatherapy had begun, for the Romans believed that the use of sweet-smelling perfumes was the most effective remedy against illness.

The demand for incense, perfumes and spices was such that Pliny believed Rome was beggaring itself by exporting hard currency in the form of gold and silver in order to import these luxuries. He wrote:

> And by the lowest reckoning India, Seres [China] and the Arabian Peninsula take from our empire 100 million sesterces a year—such is the sum that our luxuries and our women cost us; and what fraction, pray, of these imports now goes either to the gods, or the powers of the underworld?

He was particularly referring to the quantity of spices burnt in their funerary pyres, since the Romans favoured the sweet smell of cinnamon to accompany the soul on its journey to the gods. According to Pliny, when the Emperor Nero's consort died, he had her body cremated in a colossal funerary pyre that consumed a year's supply of cinnamon.

Spices were so precious in Europe they even became a form of currency. In AD 330, the Emperor Constantine presented the Bishop of Rome with gifts of gold and silver vessels containing incense and spices, including 300 kilograms of cloves. In AD 408, Alaric the Visigoth besieged Rome for six months and finally received a ransom of gold, silver, silk and 6000 kilograms of pepper to lift his grip on the city.

The centre of learning during this period was the famous Library of Alexandria, which had accumulated all the knowledge of Greek civilization. Here Greek geographers and astronomers studied the earth and the heavens, producing maps and star charts. As early as 235 BC, the Greek scholar Eratosthenes sought to determine the circumference of the earth. He knew that the town of Syene, in southern Egypt, was near the Tropic of Cancer, since at midday during the summer solstice the sun was directly overhead and cast no shadow at the bottom of a deep well. He also deemed Syene to be on the same north-south meridian as Alexandria. Using a measurement of the angle of the sun from Alexandria at the time of the summer solstice and the estimated distance between the two towns, Eratosthenes calculated that the circumference of the earth was 250,000 stadia, or 39,000 kilometres, surprisingly close to the actual circumference of around 40,000 kilometres.

Claudius Ptolemy headed the Library of Alexandria from AD 127 to 150 and his monumental work *Geographia* was the founding text of modern geography. Ptolemy combined the principles of mathematical geography with knowledge of the wider world he gathered from the shipmasters and merchants travelling through Alexandria. *Geographia* consists of eight volumes, including an index of 8000 place names, with their coordinates and a topographical description. Most importantly, it included a map of the known world from Europe to Asia, complete with lines of latitude and longitude, showing that the Greco-Romans knew as much about the Malay Peninsula as the British Isles.

Ptolemy, like Eratosthenes before him, sought to determine the circumference of the earth. He used star observations to calculate a circumference of 32,000 kilometres, compared with his predecessor's 39,000. This error became relevant more than 1300 years later when both Christopher Columbus and Ferdinand Magellan used Ptolemy's smaller circumference of the world in their maps and calculations, and it was this shrinking of the estimation of the world's circumference that convinced Christopher Columbus a westward journey to the Indies was possible.

After the collapse of the Roman Empire, the accumulated knowledge of the Library of Alexandria was scattered, and Ptolemy's writings lay dormant in libraries throughout Byzantium and the Muslim world. In Europe during the Dark Ages, the collective knowledge of the Greeks was forgotten, but the Muslim world stored and translated the Greek manuscripts and continued intellectual excellence in every field of scholarly endeavour. Fortunately, a copy of Ptolemy's work translated from the original Greek into Arabic had made its way to Toledo, in northern Spain, and was rediscovered after the capture of the city from the Muslims by the Spanish forces of Castile in 1085. Gerard of Cremorna, the most prolific of the Christian translators, laboured from 1140 to 1187 translating 90 works from Arabic into Latin. They included works on mathematics, medicine, science, astronomy, philosophy and logic, as well as the Greek Classics. The translation into Latin of Ptolemy's *Geographia* allowed medieval Europeans to rediscover the world of the Indian Ocean, 1000 years after the decline of the Roman Empire.

A 1466 woodcut of Ptolemy's map shows a grid of longitude of 180 degrees representing half of the earth's sphere, as well as a grid of latitude extending north and south of the Tropic of Cancer, which runs through southern Egypt. The map extends as far east as the Malay Peninsula and as far west as the British Isles. The size of Sri Lanka is grossly exaggerated, southern Africa and China are still unknown, and the Indian Ocean is represented as a lake.

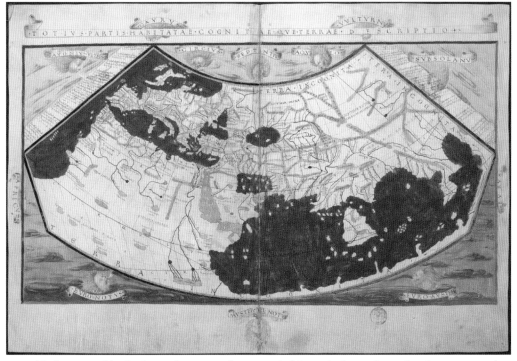

Map of the known world , Claudius Ptolemy, second century AD (National Library of Australia, nla.map-rm2988)

The Florentine geographer Francis Berlinghieri eloquently described the map in the introduction to his translation of Ptolemy's *Geographia* in 1482:

> We can leap up within ourselves, without the aid of wings, so that we may view the earth through an image marked on a parchment. Its truth and greatness declared, we may circle part of it, pilgrims through the colour of a flat parchment, around which the heavens and stars revolve.

The Persians expanded the trade in spices and other goods from India into the Persian Gulf. Shallow boats and rafts carried goods up the Tigris and Euphrates Rivers, then across the desert by camel caravan to Palmyra in Syria and on to the ancient ports of Antioch and Tyre on the Mediterranean coast. A key desert oasis midway between the

Euphrates and the Mediterranean, Palmyra had the geographic good fortune to lie on both a segment of the Spice Route bringing goods by sea from India and the Silk Road bringing goods overland from China, and grew exceedingly wealthy.

As the wealth and power of the city increased, Queen Zenobia declared her independence from Roman rule in AD 269 and sent her armies out from Palmyra to conquer Syria and Palestine. The Roman general Aurelian had his first victory against her forces at Antioch in AD 272, and advanced until Palmyra capitulated and Queen Zenobia surrendered to his armies. During the Emperor's triumphal parade through Rome, the once-proud Queen suffered the indignity of being forced to march behind his chariot, a captive in golden chains.

In the Indian Ocean, the main entrepôt for east–west trade moved from the Malabar Coast of India to the island of Sri Lanka. Cosmas Indicopleustes, a Greek known as the India Sailor, reached Sri Lanka and provides this description from his work entitled the *Christian Topography of Cosmas* which dates from AD 548:

> This is a large oceanic island lying in the Indian Sea. By the Indians it is called Sielediba, but by the Greeks Taprobane … The island is a great market for the people in these parts … Being, as it is, in a central position, it is much frequented by ships from all parts of India, and from Persia and Ethiopia, and it likewise sends out many of its own. And from the furthest east, I mean China and other trading places, it receives silk, aloes-wood, cloves, sandalwood and other products.

Indian traders sailing east from Sri Lanka established trading centres in Burma, Malaya, Sumatra and Java. A fresco painting from the early sixth century, found in the caves of the Ajanta Range in south central India, reveals an Indian vessel of the period. A four-masted vessel with tall rectangular sails, it has a billowing spinnaker and is steered by a oar-like rudder. On the prow is painted a watchful human eye, and the captain is at the helm, surrounded by large earthenware pots that contain his precious cargo of spices.

These Indian traders brought the Hindu and Buddhist religions with them, and Sanskrit inscriptions found in Indonesia dating from the fourth century are evidence of the early commercial and cultural links between India and Indonesia. The Indian-influenced South-East Asian civilizations flourished, reaching their peak during the construction in Java of the great temple of Borobodur in the eighth century and the temples of Angkor Wat in Cambodia in the twelfth century.

In Arabia, a new trade route developed from Jeddah on the eastern Red Sea coast to Medina, then across the desert to Petra in Jordan and onwards to the port of Gaza on the Mediterranean coast. The hidden city of Petra, carved out of solid rock and made famous by the film *Indiana Jones and the Last Crusade* was the capital of the Nabateans, who were the masters of this caravan trade.

It was in Mecca that the Prophet Mohammed grew up as a member of a merchant family involved in the spice trade. Orphaned as a young boy, he made several journeys with trading caravans, travelling from Mecca to Damascus in the company of his uncle. Mohammed became a skilled manager of these trading caravans and his first wife, Kahidja, was the widow of a wealthy spice merchant. After the revelation of the Holy Qur'an to Mohammed in AD 600, the rapid expansion of the Islamic religion united the Arab world from Alexandria to Baghdad under the Umayyad Dynasty in Damascus, leading to Muslim control of the spice routes across the Arabian Peninsula.

Over centuries, Arab camel drivers had used the stars shining brilliantly in the night sky to help them navigate across trackless deserts and were easily able to adapt these skills to navigation at sea. The Arab camel caravaneer and the Arab shipmaster used the same stars to guide them on their journey, and the Qur'an refers to their use in navigation:

> He it is, who hath appointed for you the stars that ye guide yourselves thereby in the darkness of land and sea, and we have made the signs distinct for people who have knowledge.

Of all the great world religions, Islam is the most supportive of trade. The Qur'an and the Hadith heap praise upon the merchant who trades profitably for the benefit of himself, his family and worthy causes. Arabian merchants whose ancestors had profited from the incense trade in frankincense and myrrh across the Arabian Peninsula redirected their skills towards the spice trade, sending their sons to trade in India, East Africa and as far away as Indonesia.

In AD 750, the accession of the Abbasid Dynasty to the caliphate resulted in the capital of the Islamic world moving from Damascus to Baghdad. Small craft could carry commodities from the Persian Gulf ports up the Tigris River to Baghdad, and then through canals that connected Baghdad to the Euphrates River.

To gain an insight into the world of the Muslim traders one has only to read *The Seven Voyages of Sinbad the Sailor*, which tells of merchants and foreign ports, shipwrecks and survival, fortunes won and lost, beautiful women and devious swindlers. As written in the fifth voyage of Sinbad:

> I was again seized with the longing to travel and see foreign countries and islands. Accordingly I bought costly merchandise suited to my purpose and making it up into bales repaired to Bassorah [Basra], where I walked about the river quay till I found a tall ship, newly built with gear unused and fitted ready for sea. She pleased, so I bought her and embarking my goods in her, hired a master and crew … A number of merchants also brought their outfits and paid me freight and passage money, then after reciting the Fatihah we set sail over Allah's pool in all joy and cheer, promising ourselves a prosperous voyage and much profit.

Trading continued eastwards, and in AD 671 there is evidence from Chinese sources of the first Arab and Persian traders to arrive in China. According to the Caliph of Baghdad,

'This is the Tigris and there is no obstacle between us and China, everything on the sea can come to us'. From the earliest days of coastal trading along the Arabian Peninsula, the development of the Spice Route from the Red Sea and the Persian Gulf all the way to Southern China was a remarkable achievement.

Even more remarkable was the construction of Arab trading vessels. Boat builders sewed the planks and ribs of the hulls together with cord made from coconut husks. An illustration from the 1237 manuscript of Al-Hariri's *Maqāmāt* shows an Arab trading vessel at sea, and you can see the stitching joining the planks of the hull. The ship is steered

Arab trading ship, Al-Hariri's *Maqāmāt*, 1237 (Bibliothèque nationale de France)

by a stern rudder, and the captain is trimming the sails aided by two seamen. One is also working the bailing pump. An anchor hangs from the bow, a lookout boy is at the top of the mast and below decks the merchants are looking anxiously out from their cabins.

Vessels departed from Basra at the head of the Persian Gulf in November and December with the north-east monsoon, and after six months of sailing and trading eventually reached Guangzhou (Canton). Cargoes of silk, camphor, porcelain and spices imported from the Moluccas were loaded, and the vessels would depart on the long and dangerous journey back to the Persian Gulf ports.

The adventurer Tim Severin sought to recreate this voyage in an Arab sewn ship he constructed in Oman, using timber from the Indian Malabar Coast and coconut fibre from the Laccadive Islands, where fishing boats are still built using these traditional methods.

The keel piece of the vessel was 52 feet long and cut from a single tree trunk selected from the Indian forest. Shipwrights from the Laccadive Islands stitched together the planks that formed the hull with cord made from coconut fibre before inserting the supporting ribs. Workers swabbed the stitching with fish oil to provide waterproofing and plugged the stitching holes with putty made from heated tree resin.

Launching the vessel, the Sultan of Oman named it the *Sohar* after the ancient trading port that was the point of departure for many Arab ships making the journey to India and China. Departing Muscat in November 1980, the *Sohar* sailed with the north-east monsoon to Calicut in India and then on to Galle in Sri Lanka. Off northern Sumatra the vessel entered the doldrums and floated for a month, waiting for the change in the direction of trade winds, which would take them to China. Stopping at Malacca and Singapore, the *Sohar* reached Guangzhou after seven months at sea, a similar time to that taken by the ancient Arab traders.

Trade with Guangzhou ceased in AD 878 when the forces of the rebel Huang Cha'ah sacked the city and many of the foreign trading community were killed. This coincided with the rise of the Buddhist kingdom of Srivijaya located near Palembang in South Sumatra, which became the principal commercial centre between India and China. Sumatran and Javanese traders voyaged from here east to the Moluccas, to collect cloves and nutmeg, returning to South Sumatra to trade these spices with Chinese, Indian and Arab merchants.

Commercial trade between the Middle East and the Far East, which had developed over 1000 years, was to continue for another 500 years without significant interruption. This trading network not only carried spices and other goods westward but also religion and culture eastward, bringing Hinduism, Buddhism and then Islam to the Far East and the Orient.

On the docks along the Spice Route, sailors and sea captains swapped fanciful stories about the origins of the clove buds and nutmegs loaded onto their ships. The exotic and the rare demand a high premium, but the mysterious and the dangerous demand an even higher one, and these sailors told outrageous lies about the already legendary Spice Islands and the people who occupied them.

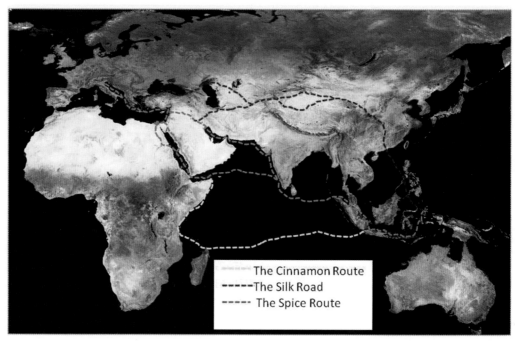

Map of the Cinnamon Route, Spice Route and Silk Road (Ian Burnet)

3 The Silk Road

I believe it was God's will that we should return, so that men might know the things that are in the world, since as we have said in the first chapter of this book, there was never man yet, Christian or Saracen, Tartar or Pagan, who explored so much of the world as Messer Marco, son of Messer Nicolo Polo, great and noble citizen of the city of Venice.

—Marco Polo, *The Description of the World*, 1307

The early Austronesian traders brought Moluccan spices and other goods to the southern ports of the Chinese mainland such as Guangzhou (Canton). Here, these traders bartered cloves, nutmeg and aromatic tree resins for Chinese goods such as cloth, silk and rice. Internal trade routes connected the ports of southern China to the capital of the Han Dynasty at Chang'an (Xian) in north-western China.

Surrounding the inner city of Chang'an and its elaborate palace compound was an outer city with hundreds of temples and two enormous markets—an eastern market that sold goods from within the borders of China and a western market that specialized in exotic goods from Europe, Persia, India and the Spice Islands. Down the narrow winding streets of the western market one could inhale all the scents and aromas of the spice trade. Sandalwood from Timor to burn as incense, cloves from the Moluccas to freshen the breath and treat intestinal disorders, nutmeg from the Moluccas to flavour foods, frankincense from Arabia to perfume the air, pepper from India for food preservation and flavouring, mustard from Tibet and camphor from Sumatra for use in balms, as well as numerous other spices and natural medicaments.

Today Chang'an is famously home to the army of 8000 life-size terracotta soldiers, complete with horses and all their equipment, that stood silent guard for two millennia over the tomb of the First Emperor before their discovery in 1974.

It was at Chang'an that the caravans assembled to load their trade goods and supplies for the first stage of the journey across the Silk Road. Crossing the remote steppes and deserts of Central Asia, merchant caravans traded silk along with furs, lacquer, jade, bronze and spices for Western goods including gold, silver, amber, glass, woollens and linen. This trade was dependent on the hardy two-humped Bactrian camels native to the steppes of Central Asia, which carried both men and goods. Able to scent water from great distances, these remarkable animals could drink up to 120 litres at a time and withstand both the scorching heat of the Gobi Desert and the frozen winters of Mongolia.

The caravans comprised hundreds of camels and their drivers, accompanied by an armed escort and the owners' agents, usually family members. No single caravan would cross the entire Silk Road, and along the route trade goods were exchanged from Chinese merchants to Central Asian merchants, then to Persian merchants, and then to Armenian or Arab merchants, until the goods finally reached the Black Sea or the Mediterranean Sea.

Silk came to dominate the trade. This shimmering symbol of luxury was not only a desirable and colourful textile but became a form of currency, used to pay for goods as well as debts and dowries. Most importantly, silks and spices were lightweight, highly valuable and did not deteriorate.

The oasis towns along the Silk Road provided welcome sanctuary from the desert for men and camels wanting to recuperate for the next stage of their journey, usually in a caravanserai. Built around a large courtyard, the caravanserai provided rooms for travellers, secure storage areas for their goods, and space in the courtyard for their animals to be fed and tethered. The large commercial towns at the crossroads of the Silk Road, such as Lanzhou, Anxi, Kashgar, Samarkand, Balkh, Merv, Hamadan and Palmyra, were crowded with men, markets, camels, horses and all the food, forage and water necessary for their survival.

From 1206 the Mongols, led by Ghengiz Khan, his sons and grandsons, conquered the vast plains of Central Asia, bringing stability to trade along the Silk Road. In 1227, Mongol invaders attacked northern China forcing the Song Dynasty to move their capital from the north to the port city of Huangzhou, south of the Yangtze River. With half of his income-producing lands now in the hands of the Mongols, the Song Emperor turned to seaborne trade to finance the state, and more importantly, to rebuild the army. When the southern capital of the Song Dynasty fell to the Mongol forces in 1276, Kublai Khan became the master of a huge empire that stretched 6000 kilometres from the coast of China to the Black Sea.

In Western minds, the Silk Road has been immortalized by the adventures of Marco Polo. He came from a family of Venetian merchants with a business in Constantinople and a trading post on the Crimean peninsula. In 1260, two of the Polo brothers, Mafeo and Nicolo, decided to travel north from their trading post to the Volga River, bringing with them jewels of great beauty to trade with a relative of Kublai Khan. With their return journey cut off by conflict, they then travelled east around the Caspian Sea and south to Bukhara in Uzbekhistan. Here they met an envoy of Kublai Khan, who promised them an opportunity that would change their lives, saying:

Sirs, if you will trust me, I can offer you an opportunity of great profit and honour, I assure you that the Great Khan of the Tatars has never seen any Latin and is exceedingly desirous to meet one. Therefore, if you will accompany me to him, I will assure you that he will be very glad to see you and will treat you with great honour and bounty. And you will be able to travel with me in safety without let or hindrance.

Travelling east along the Silk Road, the Polo brothers reached the court of Kublai Khan in 1266. The Great Khan was a shrewd and intellectually curious ruler interested in the world around him. He questioned them about life in the Latin world, about the Christian Kings of Europe, about the maintenance of justice, about the Pope and the practices of the Roman Church. He asked them to return to Italy bearing a letter to Pope Clement requesting he send to China 'One hundred theologians learned in the Christian religion, well versed in the seven arts and able to demonstrate the superiority of their own beliefs'. He even promised that if the theologians could prove by force of argument and the performance of miracles that other religions were false, he and all those under him would become Christians. He authorized the Polo brothers to receive food, lodgings, horses and guides for their return journey and issued them with a special gold 'passport' enabling them to travel under his protection.

Returning along the Silk Road, they reached Venice in 1269 after a nine-year absence and rejoined their families. Arriving home, Nicolo found that his wife had died during his travels and that his son Marco had grown to be a fine young lad of fifteen. The death of Pope Clement delayed their return to China and the brothers stayed two years in Venice waiting for the election of a new Pope. Lesser men would have stayed at home, but Mafeo, Nicolo and young Marco travelled with the Venetian trading fleet in 1271 to the coastal town of Ayas (Antioch) in Turkey, as described by Marco Polo in his manuscript *The Description of the World*:

On the sea coast lies the town of Ayas, a busy emporium. For you must know that all the spices and clothes from the interior are brought to this town and all other goods of high value, and merchants of Venice, Pisa, and Genoa and everywhere else come here to buy them. And merchants and others who wish to penetrate the interior all make this town the starting-point of their journey.

As they began their long overland journey, they were joined by two Dominican friars sent by the newly elected Pope Gregory X to honour Kublai Khan's request for 100 Christian theologians. The friars carried sacred oil from the Holy Sepulchre in Jerusalem and other gifts from the Pope to the Great Khan.

Detail from the Catalan Atlas of 1375 shows a party of European traders with their fully loaded Bactrian camels, accompanied by a military escort on horse travelling east along the Silk Road. The script to the right of the detail probably provides a traveller's guide for their journey.

Unfortunately, the Dominican friars were not prepared for the hardships of their

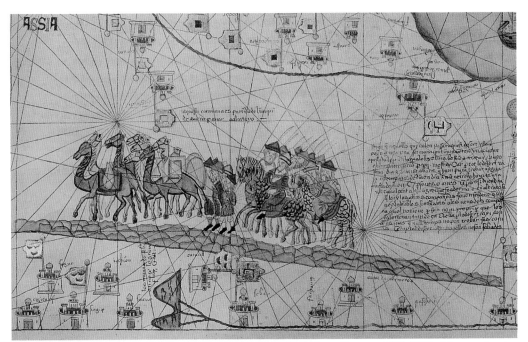

Detail from the Catalan Atlas showing travellers on the Silk Road, Abraham Cresques, 1375 (Bibliothèque nationale de France)

mission and turned back after encountering the dangers of war in Armenia. Not so easily deterred, the Polos continued their eastward journey to the Persian city of Tabriz. While drinking tea in the local bazaar, they overheard Persian traders talking of their sea voyage to China along the Spice Route. Telling of their experiences, the traders convinced the brothers that it would be quicker and easier to travel by sea. Making a considerable diversion from their overland route, the party travelled south to Hormuz on the Persian Gulf. The sea route would certainly have been quicker but they also had to weigh the potential risks, and on reaching the port and inspecting the ships that would carry them to China Marco Polo wrote:

> Their ships are very bad, and many of them founder, because they are not fastened with iron nails but stitched together with thread made of coconut husks … This makes it a risky undertaking to sail in these ships. And you can take my word that many of them sink, because the Indian Ocean is often very stormy.

Changing their minds, they retraced their steps from Hormuz and continued their travels through Persia, visiting the Central Asian trading centres of Kerman, Herat and Balkh. Reaching northern Afghanistan, they rested in the mountains to allow Marco time to recover from an illness. He describes streams full of trout and air so pure and salubrious that it would banish any malady. With his health restored, the party now faced the most difficult stage of the journey—crossing over the high passes of the Pamir Mountains.

Slowly climbing precipitous paths, they crossed the mountain passes surrounded by glaciers and towering 7000 metre peaks. Marco describes their journey:

> When the traveller leaves this place, he goes three days journey towards the north-east, through mountains all the time, climbing so high that this is said to be the highest place in the world. And when he is in this high place, he finds a plain between two mountains, with a lake from which flows a very fine river. This plain, whose name is Pamir, extends fully twelve days journey. In all these twelve days there is no habitation or shelter, but travellers must take their provisions with them. No birds fly here because of the height and cold; fire is not so bright here nor of the same colour as elsewhere and food does not cook well.

Descending from the mountains they reached the oasis of Kashgar, on the western edge of the Tarim Basin. Marco describes the oasis as having beautiful gardens, vineyards, and flourishing estates. He tells us that from here many merchants went forth about the world on trading journeys but unfortunately gives no details of the merchants they met on their travels, their caravans or the goods they were carrying.

Travelling along the southern margin of the Tarim Basin, the party eventually had to turn north and cross the shifting sands of the Taklamakan Desert, which covered and uncovered the skeletons of the beasts and men who had died in the desert crossing.

After more than three years of travel and hardship, the Polos reached Inner Mongolia in 1275 and presented themselves and the young Marco to Kublai Khan at his summer capital of Shangdu (Xanadu). The Polos knelt before the Great Khan as he sat surrounded by his courtiers and armed bodyguards all clad in colourful silks. They made obeisance before him with the utmost humility, he then bade them rise, receiving them honourably and entertaining them with good cheer. They presented him with the letters and privileges from Pope Gregory X as well as the sacred oil from the Holy Sepulchre in Jerusalem. They had not brought the 100 learned theologians that he had requested, or even the two Dominican friars sent by the Pope, and an opportunity to bring Christianity to China was lost forever.

Marco Polo rapidly learned the language and customs of this new civilization. By his own account he became an adviser to Kublai Khan and carried out various missions on his behalf that took him all over the Mongol Empire. On one of these missions Marco Polo visited the city of Kaidu in south-west China, where he described cloves, although he is under the impression they grew in this region:

> The province is a great source of cloves, which grow on a little tree with leaves like laurel but slightly longer and narrower, and little white flowers like clove-pinks. There is also ginger in abundance and cinnamon, not to speak of spices that never come to our country.

In the Moluccas, primitive harvesting techniques consisted of breaking and exporting the clove-bearing branches rather than individually picking the clove buds, and perhaps it was these branches that led Marco Polo to believe cloves grew in south-west China.

Kublai Khan became known as the 'Ruler of Rulers', but his hunger for power remained unsatisfied. He sent emissaries to Sumatra, Sri Lanka and southern India to establish political influence in these areas, and by the early thirteenth century Chinese traders had gained control of a large part of the lucrative sea trade from the Arabs.

After visiting the port of Quanzhou on the Fujian coast, Marco Polo gave the following description of Chinese vessels developed for the long-distance maritime trade with India:

> They have one deck; and above this deck in most ships are at least sixty cabins, each of which can comfortably accommodate one merchant. They have one steering oar and four masts ... The entire hull is of double thickness; that is to say, one plank is fastened over the top of another, and this double planking extends all the way around. It is caulked outside and in, and the fastening is done with iron nails. Some of the ships have bulkheads or partitions made of stout planks dovetailed into one another. This is useful in case the ship's hull should chance to be damaged in some place by striking on a reef or being rammed by a whale.

Depending on their size, these huge Chinese ships carried 150 to 300 people, with up to 120 tons of cargo. It is remarkable that western shipbuilders did not construct similar ships with double hulls and bulkheads for another 600 years.

By the end of their seventeen years in China, Kublai Khan was already an old man and the Polos feared that upon his death their favoured position within the court would be in jeopardy. Knowing it was time to leave, they grasped at the opportunity to escort a young Mongol princess betrothed to the Arghun Khan of Persia, the grandnephew of Kublai Khan. Together with the seventeen-year-old princess and her royal entourage of 600 courtiers, they joined a fleet of fourteen Chinese vessels that was to follow the routes the Chinese traders had established in the South China Sea and the Indian Ocean.

Departing from the port of Quanzhou in 1293, the fleet sailed down the South China Sea and through the Strait of Malacca to North Sumatra. Here, Marco Polo witnessed the spread of Islam to Indonesia:

> You must know that the people of Ferlac [Perlak] used all to be idolaters, but owing to contact with Saracen merchants, who continually resort here in ships, they have all been converted to the law of Mahomet. This only applies to the inhabitants of the city. The people of the mountains live like beasts.

The voyagers stopped here for many months while awaiting the arrival of the monsoon winds that would take them to India and built a stockade around their encampment. Marco thought the fish caught in the bay were the best in the world, and knowing the benefits of medicinal alcohol, he enjoyed the local palm wine, which he considered an excellent remedy for dropsy, consumption and the spleen.

On finally reaching Calicut and the pepper-growing Malabar Coast of south-west India, he describes the commerce of this city:

> When merchants come here from overseas they load the ships with brass, which they use as ballast, pepper, cloth of gold and silk, sandalwood, gold, silver, cloves, and other such spices that are not produced here. You must know that ships come here from very many parts, notably from the great province of Manzi [China], and goods are exported to many parts. Those that go to Aden are carried thus to Alexandria.

From Calicut, the Chinese fleet crossed the Arabian Sea to the strategic port of Aden, located at the entrance to the Red Sea. Aden commanded the trade between India and the Mediterranean coastal ports of Alexandria and Gaza, and in Marco Polo's words:

> Aden is the port to which all the ships from India come with their merchandise. It is a great resort of merchants. In this port they transfer their goods to other small ships which sail for days along a river [the Red Sea]. At the end of this time they unload the goods and pack them on camels and carry them thus for about thirty days after which they reach the River of Alexandria [the Nile] and down the river they are easily transported to Alexandria itself … And I assure you the Sultan of Aden derives very large revenue from the heavy duties he levies on the merchants coming and going in his country. Indeed thanks to these he is one of the richest rulers in the world.

The Chinese fleet then re-crossed the Arabian Sea to the port of Hormuz at the entrance to the Persian Gulf. The Polos, the princess and her royal entourage all disembarked at Hormuz and travelled overland to Tabriz in northern Persia. Here the Polos safely delivered the princess, not to the Arghun Khan, who had recently died, but to his son who had succeeded him. Marco tells how they had guarded the princess like their own daughter and how she wept with sorrow at their parting. As a reward, the Polos were given four tablets of gold, one cubit in length and five fingers across, as well as an escort of 200 horsemen to ensure their safe travel across the kingdom. Travelling north, they reached the Black Sea port of Trebizond, in Turkey, and finally returned to Venice in 1295.

Their families long believed them dead and failed to recognize the strangers dressed in foreign clothes that arrived at their doorstep. Myth has it that the homecoming ended happily at a splendid banquet when the travellers tore open the seams of their garments and a shower of rubies, diamonds and emeralds fell to the floor.

The Polos claimed to have seen more of the world than any other men, and Marco wrote that God's will had allowed their return so that men might know the things that were in the world.

The brothers' incredible journey provided an insight into a world previously unknown to Europeans and would have passed into myth, except that three years after his return to Europe the Genoese captured Marco Polo during a naval battle. While imprisoned, he dictated his memoirs to an Italian writer named Rustichello with whom he shared a cell.

Marco Polo told him of his travels but very little of himself, for we rarely see any revelations about Marco Polo as a person. After his release from prison, Marco was finally able to marry, have three children and lead a more sedentary life. Various versions of his manuscript *The Description of the World* exist but the most famous is that presented to the Duke of Burgundy in 1307, which is lavishly illuminated and held in the Biblothèque nationale de France.

The position of Venice at the centre of a vast mercantile empire allowed it to collect and systematize geographical information collected from sailors and travellers. Fra Mauro, a Camaldolese monk working from the monastery of San Michel in the Venetian lagoon, incorporated Marco Polo's descriptions of the world into the huge world map, or Mappa Mundo, he created in 1459. On display in the Biblioteca Nazionale Marciana in Venice, the map is nearly two metres in diameter and is a magnificent example of cartographic art, with its parchment surface decorated with gold leaf and lapis lazuli. Detail of the Chinese capital Khanbalik (Beijing) shows Mongol tents pitched in front of the Great Khan's palace, with a bridge described by Marco Polo in the background. The map shows remarkable detail of the coast of China, which is believed to have come from Chinese maps brought back to Venice by an Italian adventurer and traveller, Nicolo de Conti, who visited Calicut in 1421 and observed the sixth of the Chinese Treasure Fleets.

The text on the Mappa Mundo includes Marco Polo's description of how spices reached China and Arabia, although the location of the Spice Islands is still a mystery:

> Java minor, a very fertile island, in which there are eight kingdoms, is surrounded by eight islands in which grow the spices. And in the said Java grow ginger and other fine spices in great quantities, and all the crop from this and the other islands is carried to Java Major [Sumatra], where it is divided into three parts, one for Zaiton [Quanzhou], the other by the sea of India for Hormuz, Jeddah and Mecca, and the third northwards by the Sea of Cathay [to Beijing].

The volume of spices traded along the Silk Road varied according to political and economic conditions, but it was probably of greatest significance during the Tang Dynasty (618–907), after which it began to decline as the Spice Route across the Indian Ocean became increasingly more important.

Mappa Mundo, Fra Mauro, 1459 (Biblioteca Nazionale Marciana, Venice)

4 Zheng He

We have traversed immense water spaces
and have beheld in the ocean waves like mountains,
and we have set eyes on barbarian regions
hidden in a blue transparency of light vapours,
while our lofty sails unfurled like clouds.

—From a tablet erected by Zheng He at Changle on the Fujian coast of China, 1432

After Marco Polo, another great traveller of the period was Ibn Battutah. Born in Tangier, he studied Islamic Law as did his father and grandfather before him. Leaving Morocco in June 1325 at the age of 21 to make the obligatory pilgrimage to Mecca, he just kept travelling. Eloquently describing his departure in his manuscript *The Travels*, he wrote:

I departed with the objective of making the Pilgrimage to the Holy House at Mecca and of visiting the tomb of the Prophet, God's richest blessing and peace be upon him, at al-Madinah. I set out alone, having neither fellow-traveller in whose companionship I might find cheer, nor caravan whose party I might join, but swayed by an overpowering impulse within me and a desire long-cherished in my bosom to visit these illustrious sanctuaries. So I braced my resolution to quit all my dear ones, female and male, and forsook my home as birds forsake their nests.

His travels continued for almost 30 years and took him to Arabia, Persia, India, South-East Asia and China. There may have never have been a record of his travels if the Sultan of Morocco had not commissioned a young writer to take down his memoirs. The result was *A Gift to those who contemplate the Wonders of Cities and the Marvels of Travelling* or as it became known for short, *The Travels*.

After completing his pilgrimage to Mecca, Ibn Battutah travelled through Persia and India for many years while also acting as an adviser on Islamic law to the Sultans and other notables that sought his counsel. Intending to travel to China, he reached the port of Calicut at the centre of the pepper-growing areas of the Malabar coast:

The town of Calicut is one of the chief ports of the Malabar. It is visited by men from China, Java, Sri Lanka, the Maldives, al-Yemen and Fars [Persia], and in it gather merchants from all quarters. Its harbour is one of the largest in the world. We entered it in great pomp, the like of which I have never seen in those lands … There were at the time thirteen Chinese vessels in the harbour and we stayed there three months as the guests of the infidel sultan, awaiting the season of the voyage to China.

After many adventures and misadventures in the Maldives, Sri Lanka, Bengal, Sumatra and Java, he reached the China coast at Zaitun (Quanzhou) around 1335. In *The Travels,* Ibn Battutah describes such marvels as the Chinese use of paper money and the manufacture of porcelain. Over centuries the Chinese had perfected the art of making porcelain with hard translucent glazes that brilliantly reflected the sunlight. These were coveted throughout the world as both precious decorative objects and functional utensils. They included plates, bowls, cups and jars for the storage of foodstuffs, spices, balms and perfumes. After silkworms and the secrets of silk production were smuggled out of China to Central Asia and Persia, porcelain replaced silk as the main Chinese export item.

Ibn Battutah was in Khanbalik (Beijing) when news arrived of the death of Kublai Khan's successor. He describes in detail the lavish funeral for the Emperor, including the walling up of six of his courtiers, four of his favourite slave girls, as well as gold and weapons in his burial chamber. After his death, the Yuan Dynasty fell into disarray and the Mongols were toppled in 1368 by a peasant revolt, with the remnants of its armies defeated by the Ming in 1382.

Zheng He was born into a Muslim family in the western province of Yunnan and was only ten years old when Ming forces invaded. After his father was killed, the young Zheng He was captured and castrated as was the custom with many young boys who were destined to become imperial slaves. Eunuchs castrated before puberty usually show feminine characteristics, but Zheng He is described as being tall, strong and courageous. Given military training, he fought in several battles before becoming the trusted bodyguard of Prince Yan Zhu Di. This prince staged a court revolt in 1402 and, after storming Nanjing, declared himself the third emperor of the Ming Dynasty, Emperor Yongle.

The new emperor was far-sighted as well as ambitious. He saw that the Middle Kingdom, which the Chinese perceived as being at the centre of the universe, could expand its power and prestige by engaging with foreign rulers. These rulers and their lands were expected to pay tribute to the emperor and subject themselves as vassal states to China. The purpose of the tribute missions was to bring goods and ambassadors to China in return for imperial gifts and imperial patronage, as the Celestial Ruler stated:

We rule all under heaven, pacifying and governing the Chinese and the barbarians with impartial kindness and without distinction between mine and thine. Extending the way of the ancient sage emperors and the enlightened kings so as to accord with the will of heaven and earth, we desire all distant countries and foreign domains to each achieve its proper place under heaven.

To achieve this aim, Emperor Yongle issued orders to begin construction of an imperial fleet of trading ships, warships and support vessels to visit the barbarian domains in the South China Sea, Java Sea and the Indian Ocean. He mobilized material and craftsmen from all over China to build the many ships that would eventually become the world's largest ocean-going fleet. The emperor entrusted his former bodyguard with the responsibility for the huge Nanjing shipyards on the Yangtze River, for Zheng He was intelligent, experienced in politics and war, and had already distinguished himself in his service.

Hundreds of immense Chinese junks ranging from 40 metres up to 70 metres in length were built; they were easily the largest vessels on the seas and became known as the Treasure Fleets. The ships were specialized. Some carried only food and had large tubs in which to grow fresh vegetables. Some ships carried only fresh water, others carried animals for fresh meat and others carried horses, troops and weapons. The dimensions of these ships were always thought to be subject to exaggeration in comparison with other ocean-going vessels of the time, which were usually less than 30 metres long. However in 1962 a rudder post was excavated at the site of the former shipyards confirming the size of the treasure ships.

As part of the planned diplomatic exchanges, seven epic Chinese naval expeditions were sent to South-East Asia and the Indian Ocean from 1405 to 1433 under the command of Admiral Zheng He. The first expedition (1405–07) is believed to have consisted of 300 ships and visited Vietnam, Singapore, Sumatra, Sri Lanka and Calicut. The sixth voyage (1421–22) is purported to have rounded the Cape of Good Hope and sailed into the Atlantic to explore the coasts of Africa and America. Knowledge of these voyages might have lapsed into mythology had not physical evidence been unexpectedly discovered during the excavation of a culvert in the city of Galle on the south coast of Sri Lanka in 1911. Workers dug up a large stone marker decorated by two facing dragons, below which is essentially the same text engraved in three different languages, Chinese, Tamil and Persian. The stone marker is dated 1409 and was probably engraved in China before the departure of the third expedition. The Chinese text on the trilingual stone declares:

> His majesty the Emperor of the great Ming Dynasty has dispatched the eunuchs, Zheng He, Wang Jinghong and others to set forth his utterances before Lord Buddha, the World Honoured One ... Of late we have dispatched missions to announce our mandates to foreign nations and during their journey over the ocean they have been favoured with the blessing of your beneficent protection. They escaped disaster or misfortune, and journeyed in safety to and fro.

The text describes how the Chinese voyagers had bestowed special offerings of gold and silver, including incense burners, flower vases and lamps, together with gold-embroidered silk banners and silks of many colours, before the image of the Lord Buddha.

One of the tallest mountains on the island of Sri Lanka is Adam's Peak, which rises like a spire above the lush jungle. The Blessed Footprint found on a black rock on the mountain is venerated as the footprint of Buddha, and the precious stones found in the ravines around the mountain, the rubies, sapphires and yellow topaz are said to be his crystallized tears. Sri Lanka was obviously a special place of worship for the Chinese, and the Buddhists of the island who still believe they have a special destiny as defenders of the faith.

The third Treasure Fleet commanded by Admiral Zheng He included in its voyage a stop in the tiny port of Malacca, on the Malay Peninsula. Its leader, Parameswara, had cleverly sent an envoy to the Ming court in 1405 to swear his allegiance to Emperor Yongle, for which he was rewarded with a Chinese Seal of Investiture recognizing the fledgling city state of Malacca as an independent kingdom. This offered powerful patronage and protection from his Sumatran, Javanese and Thai rivals. Malacca's independent status was confirmed during the visit of Zheng He, when he presented Parameswara with two silver seals, an official hat, a royal girdle, and a robe as official recognition of his position. Zheng He also set up a stone marker stating that Malacca would be treated as a subject state of the Middle Kingdom in order to excel and be distinguished from the barbarian domains, but unlike the stone marker in Galle it remains undiscovered.

The Treasure Fleets stopped in Malacca on all

Statue of Admiral Zheng He, Stadhuys Museum, Malacca

their subsequent voyages. Ma-Huan, an interpreter on several of the voyages, describes the port in his *Description of the Coasts of the Ocean* in 1451:

> When this place is visited by Chinese merchant vessels, the inhabitants erect a barrier for the collection of duties. There are four gates in the city wall, each furnished with watch and drum towers. At night men with hand bells patrol the precincts. Inside the walls a second small enclosure of palisades has been built where warehouses have been constructed for the storage of spices and provisions. When the government ships were returning homewards, they visited this place in order both to repair their vessels and to load local products. Here they waited for a favourable wind from the south, and in the middle of the fifth month they put out to sea on their return voyage.

With its political survival secured, Malacca's future now depended on trade. For this it had an ideal location, a protected anchorage that lay midway between the South China Sea, the Java Sea and the Indian Ocean. Traders only required a single voyage from east or west with the appropriate monsoonal winds to reach Malacca. Chinese traders arrived with the northern monsoon in January or February and the Indian, Arab and Persian traders arrived with the south-west monsoon between April and August. Cargoes were bought and sold as the traders waited for the winds to change so they could embark on their return journeys. In the bustling markets, pepper, cinnamon, cloves, nutmeg and mace, as well as sandalwood and camphorwood, were exchanged for gold, silver, metal objects, Indian textiles, and Chinese silks and porcelains.

By the end of the fifteenth century Malacca had become one of the greatest trading ports of the world. At any one time there were hundreds of boats at anchor in the harbor, loaded with goods from all over the region; its markets were crowded with traders and merchants. There is no better description of Malacca than by the early Portuguese resident Tomé Pires, who wrote:

> Men cannot estimate the worth of Malacca, on account of its greatness and profit. Malacca is a city that was made for merchandise, fitter than any other in the world; the end of monsoons and the beginnings of others. Malacca is surrounded and lies in the middle, and the trade and commerce between different nations for a thousand leagues on every hand must come to Malacca.

In 1424 Emperor Yongle died and was succeeded by his son, Zhu Gaozhi. A strict follower of the Confucian tradition, he was more inward-looking and disdainful of foreigners. His first decree as emperor was that all voyages of the Treasure Fleet should be stopped, stating that he did not care for foreign things. He died a few years later and the grandson of Yongle was able to initiate the seventh and final voyage of the Treasure Fleet.

This was to be not only the last but also the largest expedition, with more than 300 ships. It left for South-East Asia, India and Africa in 1432. Knowing that this might be the last expedition, and aware of his advancing years, Zheng He erected a stone tablet at

Changle on the Fujian coast that documented the achievements of each expedition, the geographic knowledge acquired, and secured his place in history.

This final expedition (1432–33) visited southern Vietnam, Surabaya, Palembang, Malacca, Sumatra, Sri Lanka and Calicut. From Calicut, the great fleet divided and made separate voyages to East Africa, Jeddah and Hormuz. During the voyage home from Calicut, the great admiral died, and like all sailors, was buried at sea.

With such a formidable fleet, Chinese power and influence could have spread around the world, but the decline of the Treasure Fleet had already begun. By 1440 the number of ships had been reduced by half, China was turning its back on the world, and a subsequent imperial edict authorized the destruction of the remaining ocean-going ships. Incredibly, one of the greatest seagoing fleets ever known disappeared from the world's oceans.

By the end of the fifteenth century, the Spice Route had become specialized and segmented. The route was divided into six distinct areas: the South China Sea, the Java Sea, the Bay of Bengal, the Arabian Sea, the Red Sea and the Persian Gulf. As a consequence, the trading centres at the end points of these segments, such as Malacca, Calicut, Cambay, Hormuz and Aden, became even more important, and as long as they paid their taxes and respected the local rulers, the merchant communities in these ports had complete freedom in the Indian Ocean trade.

Significantly, the majority of these merchant communities were Muslims, of Arab, Persian, Indian, Malay or Javanese origin. In Islam, merchants are honoured, and it is written in the sayings of the Prophet Mohammed that 'The honest merchant is on a level with the prophets and the truthful ones and the martyrs'. Islam also placed emphasis on the administration of law and rules that governed commerce and all aspects of life, thus providing stability and a common legal system wherever it spread.

Close links developed between the merchant communities in these port cities. Sons were trained in bookkeeping, languages and other skills before taking up apprenticeships in the family businesses and travelling with their cargoes to other ports.

Voyaging with the trade winds, sailors spent several months in port waiting for the winds to change for their return journeys. From the early days of Islam, the religious practice of muta allowed sailors to enter into temporary marriages and set up semi-permanent homes in the foreign ports they visited. The children born of these unions perpetuated the Islamic faith. Their knowledge of boats, ports and local languages equipped them for careers related to the sea and trade. Although they rarely attained other government positions they were often appointed as the shahbandar or harbourmaster in control of the activities of the ports and the collection of taxes for the local rulers.

During the fourteenth century, trade between India and Cairo came under the control of the Karim, an Egyptian version of the later British or Dutch East India Companies. The wealthy merchants of Cairo joined together, pooling their resources to provide capital and protection against losses due to storms, pirates, desert raiders or excessive demands by local rulers. The activities of the Karim extended into finance, transportation, warehousing, marketing and politics at all levels, such that by the end of the fourteenth century the Karimi, as the merchants were known, controlled trade throughout the Middle East and Muslim India.

According to Islam, usury or the lending of money to earn interest without sharing in any business risk, is forbidden. Instead, the law prescribes an agreed sharing of profits from the trading voyage or venture between the capitalist and his debtor. The capitalist also shares the risk of catastrophic loss, if for example there was a shipwreck or other loss through no fault of the debtor.

Credit was established between the members of the Karim, as well as the dynastic trading 'families', and the faith-based networks such as those of the Jews and Armenians, with final payment expected in either gold or silver. The Chettia Hindus of the Coromandel coast of south-east India became known as the moneychangers, bankers and brokers to the merchant community, as they developed a system of letters of credit that reduced the risks involved in moving capital in the form of gold or silver between the port cities. The picture shows an Indian moneychanger, with clients of all different nationalities.

Indian moneychanger (Biblioteca Casanatense, Rome)

In 1490, Martin Behaim, a German cloth merchant based in Lisbon as well as a geographer and cartographer, received a commission from the city fathers of Nuremburg to make a terrestrial globe. Returning to that city, he spent over two years preparing the globe and his attempt to project a map of the known world onto a sphere was a breakthrough in cartographic science.

Now housed in the Germanisches Nationalmuseum in Nuremburg, the globe is annotated with the existing European knowledge of the commodities, commercial practices and trade routes at that time. The annotation over the Indian Ocean reads:

> Be it known that spices pass through several hands in the islands of Oriental India before they reach our country.
> 1. Firstly, the inhabitants of the island called Java Major buy them in the other islands where they are collected by their neighbours, and sell them in their own island.
> 2. Secondly, those from the island of Seilan [Sri Lanka] where St Thomas is buried, buy the spices in Java and bring them to their own island.
> 3. Thirdly, in the island of Seilan they are once more unloaded, charged with customs duty, and sold to the merchants of the island of Aurea Chersonesus [Malaya], where they are again unladen.
> 4. Fourthly, the merchants of the island of Taprobana [Sumatra] buy the spices there and pay the customs duties and take them to their island.
> 5. Fifthly, the Mohammaden heathen of Aden go there, buy the spices, pay the customs and take them to their country.
> 6. Sixthly, those of Cairo buy them, and carry them over the sea, and further overland.
> 7. Seventhly, those of Venice and others buy them.
> 8. Eighthly, they are again sold in Venice to the Germans and customs are paid.
> 9. Ninthly, at Frankfurt, Bruges and other places.
> 10. Tenthly, in England and in France.
> 11. Eleventh, thus at last they reach the hands of the retail traders.
> 12. Twelfthly, those who use the spices buy them of the retail dealers, and let the high customs duties profits be borne in mind which are levied twelve times upon the spices, the former amounting on each occasion to one pound out of every ten. From this it is to be understood that very great quantities must grow in the East and it need not be wondered that they are worth to us as much as gold.

At the end of the fifteenth century, European knowledge of the spice trade outside of the Mediterranean was still very limited. The annotation on the map is geographically confused and shows that knowledge of the Spice Route only extended as far as Cairo and Aden.

This was soon to change dramatically and with far-reaching consequences for both the Europeans and those in the region.

5   *Venice and Lisbon*

Should I go to church
And see the holy edifice of stone,
And not bethink me straight of dangerous rocks,
Which touching by my gentle vessel's side
Would scatter all her spices on the stream,
Enrobe the roaring waters with my silks,
And, in a word, but even now worth this,
And now worth nothing?

—William Shakespeare, *The Merchant of Venice*, 1597

Venice competed with other Italian states, such as Genoa, Pisa and Naples, to control trade in the Mediterranean Sea and eventually became the major commercial centre for the importation of silks, spices and other eastern goods into Europe. The splendid architecture of the city has become a lasting monument to the riches derived from the spice trade, and the facades and interiors of its marble palaces are inspired by the cities of the Near East, where the merchants of Venice traded for centuries.

Merchants and their goods crowded the open space at the foot of the Rialto Bridge, and nearby under the portico of the Church of San Giacomo moneychangers and bankers carried out their transactions.

A description of Venice by Canon Pietro Casola in 1494 paints an impressive picture of this cosmopolitan commerce:

Indeed it seems that the whole world flocks here, and that human beings have concentrated there, all their force for trading ... Who could count the many shops so well furnished that they almost seem like warehouses, with so many cloths of every make—tapestry, brocades, and hangings of every design, carpets of every sort, camlets of every colour and texture, silks of every kind; and so many warehouses full of spices, groceries and drugs, and so much beautiful wax! These things stupefy the beholder.

Medieval Europe could not grow enough feed to keep all its cattle alive during winter and much of the herd were slaughtered during the autumn harvest festivals. Spices such as pepper, cinnamon and cloves not only helped disguise the flavour of salted or rancid meat, but their antibacterial properties helped preserve meats that would otherwise putrefy. After the Crusades, demand for spices increased even more as the knights returned home from their occupation of the Holy Lands with an acquired taste for the exotic flavours and aromatic scents of the East.

From Venice, spices were distributed throughout Europe. Germany, Flanders and England produced gold, silver and textiles that were in demand in the East and could afford to buy the quantities of spices needed to satisfy a new taste for seasoned food.

The Venetians carried out this trade using fleets of galleys powered by both sail and oar, and always travelling in convoy. The fleet could act as a fighting unit: if one vessel came under attack the others quickly manoeuvred to come to its rescue. Each galley accommodated as many as 200 oarsmen, allowing for increased speed and manoeuvrability over sail and providing a formidable fighting force to protect the precious cargoes from attack by competitors and marauding pirates.

A mixture of state enterprise and private capital, the fleets generally consisted of fifteen to twenty trading galleys escorted by fighting ships. The Republic of Venice provided the naval escort, private enterprise provided the capital and made most of the profit. Every aspect of the voyage was meticulously regulated, from the choice of commander, to the fleet navigator, to the captain in charge of each vessel and the master in charge of its cargo. Every man in the fleet had an investment in the success of the enterprise since each was entitled to do his own trading on the side.

At least two fleets would leave Venice each year and sail together as far as Methoni, in southern Greece. From there one would turn north to Constantinople and the Black Sea ports of Tana and Trebizond to trade for goods coming along the Silk Road, while the other would continue east to the Mediterranean ports of Antioch, Tyre, Gaza and Alexandria to trade for goods coming along the Spice Route.

At the peak of its maritime power, Venice possessed a trading fleet of around 3000 small merchant galleys, 300 large merchant galleys and 45 war galleys, all manned by some 36,000 seamen. Venice's predominance over rival Italian cities owed much to the regularity and security of its fleets' operations, which followed a strict sailing schedule to take advantage of the prevailing winds and the demands of the market.

Over time, the Venetian merchants established homes in these port cities, maintaining permanent warehouses to store goods until the arrival of the next fleet. The diary of the Venetian merchant Girolamo Priuli gives us an idea of the increasing cost of these spices:

The spices that come to Venice pass through all of Syria, and through the entire country of the Sultan and everywhere, they pay the most burdensome duties. Likewise, in the state of Venice they pay insupportable duties, customs and excises. Thus with all the duties, customs and excises between the country of the Sultan and the city of Venice I might say that a thing that cost one ducat multiplies to sixty and perhaps to a hundred.

Spices became the most extensively traded of all commodities, and the wealth of Venice became the envy of all Europe. Traders distributed the spices from the great trading markets or 'fairs', such as at Frankfurt, Bruges, Champagne and Medina del Campo, to the spicers' shops of the cities and the weekly markets of the smaller towns. In France today a grocer's shop is still called an épicerie, or spicery. In England the Guild of Pepperers was founded in 1180, changing its name to the Company of Grossers (Grocers) in 1373 and adopting a crest that shows a fully loaded camel over a shield emblazoned with nine clove buds.

The Crest of the Worshipful Company of Grocers, Grocers' House, London

The consumers were the upper half of the social and economic hierarchy, and spices made their way into apothecaries, shops and kitchens all over Europe. An apothecary combined the roles of chemist, druggist, herbalist and spice merchant. In the kitchens, spices were used in abundance, especially if there were guests to impress. No respectable household would be without them. For a banquet of 40 guests, one household account book lists the following quantities of spices required: one pound of columbine powder, half a pound of ground cinnamon, two pounds of sugar, one ounce of saffron, a quarter pound of cloves, an eighth of a pound of pepper, and an eighth of a pound of nutmeg.

Spices were also used as currency, rents were sometimes paid in pepper, and 'judges' spices' were used to thank (or bribe) a judge for a favourable court decision.

The abysmal state of sanitation and personal hygiene in the overcrowded towns of medieval Europe meant that anything that could mask the pervading stench was welcome. A room freshener called Queen's Delight consisted of powdered cloves soaked in rosewater, which vaporized when sprinkled onto a hot pan.

> So smell these odours that do rise
> From out the wealthy spiceries:
> So smells the flowre of blooming Clove;
> Or Roses smother'ed in the stove.

Cloves inserted into an orange made a traditional pomander, which is still good for keeping clothes smelling fresh and repelling moths. Upper-class ladies of the period wore a silver pomander filled with expensive spices on a neck chain or attached to their girdle to ward off pestilence and bad odours.

The plague of 1348–50 caused the death of 30 percent of Europe's population and killed great numbers in its squalid and overcrowded cities. Fleas spread the disease but pestilent air was believed to be the problem and a healthy aroma such as that from spices was the cure. A pomander filled with a powder of cinnamon, aloes, myrrh, saffron, mace and cloves was considered highly effective in warding off the plague.

Long before the advent of the bottle and cork, the addition of spices masked the taste of what was either bad or spoiled wine, and is the origin of the spiced or mulled wine we now usually drink in winter. Cloves are described as amending the wine, rendering it both healthy and pleasant at the same time. In fact a lot of wine was probably undrinkable without the addition of spices, and what began as a necessity became an acquired taste.

Spiced ale was also common in the Middle Ages. Spices overcame the taste of ale that was already long past its use-by date. Nutmeg was the preferred spice and again it became an acquired taste, to be used, according to Chaucer, 'Whether the ale be moyste or stale'.

Many people considered the aromatic spices such as cloves, cinnamon, nutmeg and mace carried the tastes and smells of paradise. The vision of a biblical paradise somewhere in the mysterious East came to fascinate the Medieval imagination and the scent and taste of these exotic aromatics conjured up an imaginary paradise on earth.

Powerful and pleasurable aromatics such as cloves and nutmeg were also considered to have erotic powers and could aid conception. An old English guide to women's health suggests that three ounces of powdered cloves with four egg yolks would help a woman conceive. Men used cloves as aphrodisiacs to enhance their performance, and four drams of cloves drunk with milk were considered sufficient to fortify a man and restore his libido. Newlyweds were often served a posset of wine, milk, egg yolk, sugar, cinnamon and nutmeg before retiring to the wedding chamber. This is the origin of the eggnog now drunk as a Christmas treat. The author accepts no responsibility should readers try this at home, but the following recipe for a posset is from the courtier and alchemist Sir Kenelm Digby, published in 1669:

> Take a large pot of Cream, and boil in it a little whole Cinnamon, and three or four flakes of Mace. To this proportion of Cream put in eighteen yolks of eggs, and eight of the whites; a pint of Sack [sherry]; beat your eggs very well, and then mingle them with your Sack. Put in three quarters of a pound of Sugar into the Wine and Eggs, with a Nutmeg grated, and a little beaten Cinnamon; set the Basin on the fire with the Wine and Eggs, and let it be hot. Then put in the Cream boiling from the fire, pour it on high, but stir it not; cover it with a dish, and when it is settled, strew on the top a little fine Sugar mingled with three grains of Ambergris, and one grain of Musk, and serve it up.

On the Iberian Peninsula, the Spanish and the Portuguese were envious of the wealth and power of Venice, and wondered if there was a sea route to India and the Spice Islands that would break the stranglehold the Venetians and the Muslims had on the spice trade. This required a great deal of imaginative thinking and the risk of sailing into uncharted waters, or even off the edge of the world—as some still believed it to be flat.

The expansion of Islam from the Middle East across North Africa had extended to the Iberian Peninsula. The Muslim occupation of Portugal lasted more than 500 years and it was only in 1249, after the struggle known as the Reconquest, that the Portuguese expelled the Muslims from all of their land. This victory had united the people behind their king, giving them enormous pride and a sense of religious mission in their confrontations with Islam and the people they called Moors.

Relying on Atlantic fishing for a large part of their livelihood, the Portuguese were skilful and self-reliant sailors, experienced in the rigours of the Atlantic Ocean. They developed a new type of vessel that was a cross between the European single-masted and square-rigged sailboat and an Arab dhow—the lateen-rigged caravel. The Portuguese also added a fixed stern rudder and modified the hull, shaping it to turn downward at the keel and widen from the bow to the stern—all radical departures from the design of other European vessels.

Prince Henry, the third son of King John of Portugal, did not expect to attain the throne and dedicated his life to the religious Order of Christ and to what came to be called the Voyages of Discovery. Known as Prince Henry the Navigator, he founded a school of navigation at Sagres, on Cape St Vincent, and lived there for the next 40 years, far removed from the luxuries and intrigues of the royal court. The location of his school on the southernmost point of Portugal was symbolic as the rugged wind-blown cliffs of

Cape St Vincent jutting aggressively into the Atlantic Ocean seemed to be pointing the way to new lands.

During the Muslim occupation of the Iberian Peninsula, the Portuguese had inherited the navigational skills and maritime technology of the Arab world, such as the astrolabe, sextant, quadrant and compass. Prince Henry invited leading astronomers and geographers of the period to Sagres. Here they developed solar tables and star charts for navigation out of sight of land. The astrolabe was replaced by the much simpler cross-staff, which, aligned to the horizon, could measure the angle of the sun's elevation at midday in order to calculate latitude. The gimbal compass replaced the box compass and allowed for the pitch and roll of a ship on the open ocean. These improvements allowed the Portuguese to sail far out into the Atlantic Ocean, where they colonized the island of Madiera, discovered the islands of the Azores in the mid-Atlantic and began exploring down the coast of West Africa.

Ship's logs and maps recording details of latitudes, estimated longitudes, coastlines, winds and currents were updated in Sagres at the end of each voyage. Prince Henry the Navigator spent long evenings with his captains reliving their adventures on the high seas, for he himself never ventured out of sight of land.

By 1444 the Portuguese had sailed down the coast of Africa, past the red desert coasts of the Sahara and the unexpected fogs that engulfed them, reaching as far south as the tropical forests of the Senegal River on the western bulge of Africa and then into the Gulf of Guinea.

In 1454 Prince Henry and his nephew, Affonso, now King of Portugal, lobbied the Pope for the right to claim all lands discovered, as far as India. The Portuguese hoped to outflank the Muslim power that extended across the Middle East and establish a new trade route connecting Europe directly with India and the Spice Islands. The Papal Decree reads:

> Our joy is immense to know that our dear son, Henry, Prince of Portugal, following the footsteps of his father of illustrious memory, King John, inspired with a zeal for souls like an intrepid soldier of Christ, has carried into the most distant and unknown countries the name of God … If by his effort the Ocean can be made navigable as far as India, which it is said is already subject to Christ and if he enters into relations with these people, he will induce them to come to the help of the Christians of the West against the enemies of the faith … By our apostolic letter we wish the same King Affonso, the Prince, and all their successors, occupy and possess in exclusive rights the said islands, ports and seas undermentioned, and all faithful Christians are prohibited without the permission of the said Affonso and his successors to encroach on their sovereignty.

Thus, incredibly, the Papal Decree gave the Portuguese exclusive rights to the islands, ports and seas of India, a region of the world of which they had almost no knowledge. They were also given the responsibility of finding the Christians the Pope expected to be in India and enlisting their support against the enemies of the Faith.

The Crusaders had succeeded in wresting the Holy City of Jerusalem from Muslim control in 1099. For over 100 years, an alliance of European Kings ruled the Holy Land but it proved impossible to defend. Jerusalem fell to Saladin in 1244 and Acre was lost in 1291. The Third Crusade, led by Richard the Lionheart, had failed and the Christian Church was desperately looking for an ally to help reconquer Jerusalem; it was their hope this would be the legendary Prester John and the 100,000 soldiers of his Christian armies.

During the Middle Ages, the idea developed that Christian kings and communities in the East had been cut off from contact with their Christian brethren in Europe after the expansion of Islam through the Middle East and across North Africa. In 1165 a lengthy letter circulated among the churches of Europe reinforcing this idea. Supposedly sent by Prester John, the legendary Christian King and High Priest of India, it was addressed to the Emperor of Byzantium:

> If indeed you wish to know wherein consists our great power, then believe without doubting that I, Prester John, who reigns supreme, exceed in riches, virtue and power all creatures who dwell under heaven. Seventy-two kings pay tribute to me. I am a devout Christian and everywhere protect the Christians of our empire, nourishing them with alms. We have made a vow to visit the Sepulchre of our Lord with a great army, as befits the glory of our majesty, to wage war against and chastise the enemies of the cross of Christ, and to exalt his sacred name. Our magnificence dominates the Three Indias, and extends to Farther India, where the body of St Thomas the apostle rests.

This was a powerful image and all of Christendom was in awe at the possibility of a powerful ally in the East, ready to help recapture the Holy Sepulchre in Jerusalem.

In 1460 Prince Henry the Navigator died and the momentum of the voyages of discovery down the coast of Africa slowed. King John II then acceded to the throne after the death of King Affonso. A powerful force, one of the new king's first acts was to execute a rival duke who was plotting against him and then murder a brother-in-law he suspected of conspiracy, telling his queen that if she objected he would try her for treason.

In 1482, King John II dispatched a fleet of twelve ships and 600 men to build the first permanent European presence in sub-Saharan Africa. The fortress of São Jorge da Mina, on the Gold Coast of Ghana, received much of the African gold that had previously crossed the Sahara to the Muslim ports of North Africa, enriching the Portuguese crown at the expense of the Moors. Human gold, in the form of thousands of African slaves, also passed through the portals of the fortress on their way to forced labour in the sugarcane fields of Madiera.

It was from São Jorge da Mina that King John II sent a vessel with orders to seek a passage to India. Reaching further south than any previous voyage, its commander erected a stone pillar at Cape Cross on the coast of Namibia to mark the extent of his voyage:

In the year 6685 of the World, and in that of 1486 since the birth of our Lord Jesus Christ, the most serene, most excellent and potent prince King John II of Portugal did order this land to be discovered and this stone pillar to be set up by Diogo Cão, a knight of his household.

In preparation for the voyage to India, King John II decided to send a Portuguese spy on a mission to reach Calicut. Pero da Covilhão learnt Arabic in Andalusian Spain and had been sent twice as an ambassador to Morocco. He left Lisbon in May 1487 disguised as an Arab merchant and travelled via Rhodes to Alexandria and Cairo. In the bazaars of Cairo he traded the jars of honey he had brought from Europe and befriended a group of merchants who were preparing to travel with their trade goods to Aden on the Red Sea. From there he crossed to India in an Arab dhow, arriving in Calicut in 1489.

Pero da Covilhão stayed there several months exchanging his trade goods while awaiting the trade winds that would take him on his return journey. In the markets of Calicut he found an astonishing array of oriental goods and spices, and he carefully recorded their origins and value, as well as the type of trade goods the merchants sought in exchange. He learnt of the relationship between the ruling Hindu Zamorin and the large community of Arab and Gujarati merchants that lived in the city. He saw the bejewelled Zamorin leading a procession of richly decorated elephants through the streets of the city. Seated astride a gilded platform on his royal elephant, he was flanked by his palace guard with their razor-sharp scimitars flashing in the sun. But he found no evidence in Calicut of Prester John or his armies and was told that his kingdom now lay in ruins.

Returning to Cairo, Pero da Covilhão met Rabbi Abraham, an agent of the Portuguese king, and handed him his maps and report which the Rabbi would arrange to send by trusted courier to Lisbon. In return, the Rabbi gave Covilhão a letter from King John II commanding him to undertake a new mission. The Portuguese now believed the legendary kingdom of Prester John lay in the mountains of Ethiopia, for there was an apocryphal belief that St Matthew had converted the Ethiopians to Christianity. The early Greek traveller, Cosmas Indicopleustes, visited Ethiopia about 525 and described the palace of the Ethiopian King at Axum as having four great towers topped by statues of unicorns. He marvelled at the tame elephants and giraffes in the palace courtyard. He witnessed the formation of an army under King Ellesbaas to invade Yemen and end the persecution there of Christians by the Jewish kings. It may have been this visit that created the legends of a Christian king and vast Christian armies in the East. Thus, although the remote mountain region of Ethiopia was virtually unknown, it was of great interest to the Medieval church.

Covilhão travelled down the Red Sea to the Ethiopian port of Massawa; his journey then took him inland until he reached the capital of Axum in 1493. There Emperor Eskandar—the Lion of the Tribe of Judah, and the King of Kings—received Covilhão in his mountain capital and the Portuguese envoy handed him letters from King John II.

Wishing to protect his isolated kingdom from further intrusions from the outside world, the Ethiopian Emperor never allowed Covilhão to leave the country and there was no more news of him for almost 30 years. Detail from the 1558 map of Africa by Diogo Homem shows the Christian king Prester John in his mountain kingdom.

In August 1487, three ships set off from Lisbon on the next Portuguese expedition down the coast of Africa. The commander was Bartholomeu Dias, a knight of the king's household and superintendent of the royal warehouses. His orders were exceedingly

Detail of the Christian king Prester John, Diogo Homem, 1558 (James Ford Bell Library, University of Minnesota)

broad, as he was instructed to 'sail southwards and then on to the place where the sun rises and to continue as long as it is possible to do so'. When he reached as far as the Orange River in South Africa, a fierce storm drove him and his ships far to the south, and for two weeks they struggled to stay afloat. When the storm finally blew itself out they steered east for several days without sighting land; turning north, they eventually made landfall east of the Cape of Good Hope. Dias was keen to continue further into the Indian Ocean but his exhausted crew would sail no further.

The rounding of the Cape by Dias vastly extended geographical knowledge. European maps that had hardly changed in 1500 years had to be updated. The 1490 map by Henricus Martellus, a German cartographer working in Florence, started out as a traditional map of the world based on Ptolemy. It then had to be extended outside the original border to include the new information brought back by Bartholomeu Dias. The map also shows the distortion of the west coast of Africa caused by his cumulative errors in estimating longitude.

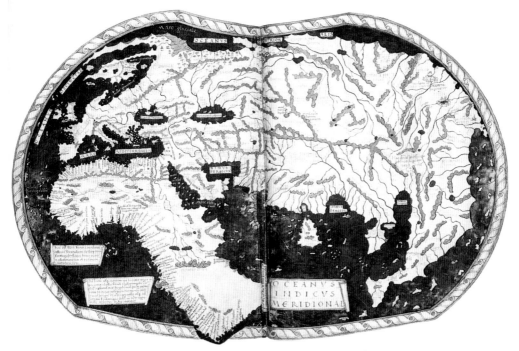

Map showing the Cape of Good Hope, Henricus Martellus, 1490 (British Library)

After their rounding of the Cape, Dias and his men named it the Cape of Storms because of the fierce storm that had driven them south and the dangers they had suffered. After their triumphant return to Lisbon, King John II renamed it the Cape of Good Hope because it promised the long-awaited discovery of a sea route to India. He knew that the nation which could open up this route would become the richest and the most powerful in all of Europe.

The route to India now lay before him, yet King John II hesitated. Information obtained by the Portuguese spy Pero da Covilhão about conditions in Calicut would be critical for the planning of the next expedition. His report should have already reached Lisbon and it remains unknown whether the King or his successor ever saw the report before the da Gama expedition sailed for India.

6   *Christopher Columbus*

According to the philosophers and to Pliny, the ocean which lies between Spain and Africa on the west, and India on the east, is not of very great extent and doubtless could be navigated in a few days with a fair wind. Therefore the beginnings of India in the East cannot be very far from the end of Africa in the West.

—Julius Capitolinus, Roman writer and historian, AD 300

Christopher Columbus, the Genoese ship captain and navigator, is said to have first reached Portugal by swimming ashore after his merchant fleet was attacked by French corsairs and his ship caught fire. Remaining in Portugal, he sailed with merchant fleets down the west coast of Africa as far as the Portuguese fortress of São Jorge da Mina in Ghana, bringing back gold, ivory and slaves. In Lisbon he married Dona Felipa Moniz, whose father was one of the discoverers of the Madeira Islands and had been granted the governorship of Porto Santo on the islands.

Columbus started a correspondence with a Florentine physician, mathematician and geographer, Paolo dal Pozzo Toscanelli, who shared his enthusiasm for undertaking a voyage westwards to India and the Spice Islands. We have no record of the letter that Columbus wrote, but his son Ferdinand quotes a letter that his father received from Paulo Toscanelli:

I have received your letter together with the things you sent me, and take great pleasure in them. I perceive your great and noble desire to sail from east to west by the route indicated on the map I sent you, a route which would appear still more plainly upon a sphere. When that voyage shall be made, it will be a voyage to powerful kingdoms and noble cities and rich provinces, abounding in all sorts of things that we greatly need, including all manner of spices and jewels in great abundance. It will also be a voyage to kings and princes who are very eager to have friendly dealings and speech with the Christians of our countries, because many of them are Christians.

Paulo Toscanelli had sent the same map to the Canon of the Lisbon Cathedral to present to the Portuguese King. His map showed the islands which he believed lay on the westward route to the Indies, which he describes as that place most fertile in all sorts of spices, jewels and precious stones. In his letter to the Canon, Master Paulo wrote: 'do not marvel at my calling west the regions where the spices grow, although they are commonly called east; because whoever sails westward will always find those lands in the west, while one who goes overland will always find the same lands in the east'.

Columbus had made his own calculations of the possible distance westward to the Indies, using the smaller circumference of the earth as calculated by Ptolemy, combined with an overestimation of the size of Asia from Marco Polo's *Description of the World*. This led him to believe that the Indies lay only 5000 kilometres westward across the Atlantic, when in fact the distance was four times greater and the still unknown continent of America lay in between.

In 1484 Columbus obtained an audience with King John II and presented his proposal to sail west across the Atlantic to reach India and the Spice Islands. But the King rejected his idea in favour of continuing the voyages of exploration down the west coast of Africa. Columbus was present at the Portuguese court four years later when Bartholomeu Dias returned with news of his rounding of the Cape of Good Hope, as he recorded:

> Note that in this year 1488 in the month of December arrived in Lisbon, Bartolomeus Didacus, captain of three caravels which the most serene King of Portugal had sent out to try the land of Guinea. He reported that he had reached a promontory which he called Cabo de Boa Esperanca [Cape of Good Hope], which we believe to be Agesinha [Abyssinia]. He says that in this place he discovered by the astrolabe that he was 45 degrees below the equator. He has described his voyage and plotted it league by league on a marine chart in order to place it under the eyes of the said king. I was present in all of this.

After Dias's success, there was no further reason for Columbus to remain in Lisbon and he decided to take his plan to the Spanish crown. The marriage of Queen Isabella of Castile and King Ferdinand of Aragón in 1469 united Spain against the Muslims, who still occupied Al-Andalus (Andalusia), including the cities of Seville, Córdoba and Granada. Columbus obtained an audience with the King and Queen but they were preoccupied with the war against the Moors and delayed any decision in the time-honoured way—by organizing an investigative commission to consider his proposal. For the next four years, Columbus was retained in the service of the Spanish crown but no decision was made. Fearing another failure, he sent his brother Bartholomew to England to try to solicit support for his proposed voyage from King Henry VII. As his son Ferdinand relates in his biography of his father:

> Christopher Columbus, fearing lest the king of all Castile in like manner should not condescend unto his

enterprise, he should be enforced to offer the same againe to some other prince, and so much time should be spent therein, sent into England a certaine brother of his, whose name was Bartholomew Columbus, who, albeit he had not the Latine tongue yet nevertheless was a man of experience and skilfull in sea causes, and could very well make sea cards and globes ... At length he began to deal with King Henry the seventh unto whom he presented a map of the world ... After he had seene the map, and that which my father Christopher Columbus had offered unto him, he accepted the offer with joyfull countenance, and sent to call him into England. But because God had reserved the said offer for Castile, Columbus was gone in the meane space, and also returned with the performance of his enterprise.

Almost immediately after the Moors surrendered Granada in January 1492, King Ferdinand and Queen Isabella agreed to provide Columbus with the 2500 ducats he needed to finance the voyage. Having reconquered their lands and united Spain, the crown could no longer resist the temptation of capturing the market in spices, silks, jewels and other exotic products from India. The crown appointed Columbus viceroy and governor-general of any land discovered, giving him rights to one-tenth of all merchandise shipped, including pearls, precious stones, gold, silver and spices.

There was also a religious aspect to his voyage and in the prologue to his journal Columbus wrote:

Your Highnesses, as Catholic Christians and as princes devoted to the holy Christian faith and propagators thereof, and enemies of the sect of Mahomet and all idolatries and heresies, took thought to send me, Christopher Columbus, to the said parts of India, to see those princes and peoples and lands ... and to bring about their conversion to our holy faith.

Columbus had three ships under his command, the flagship *Santa Maria*, the *Niña* and the *Pinta* with his captains and 90 men on board. In August 1492, his small fleet departed from Palos, in southern Spain, for the Canary Islands before embarking on their momentous voyage across the Atlantic, carrying letters from King Ferdinand to the Kings of India and Kublai Khan.

After a month in the open ocean, the crew grew ever more restless and afraid of the unknown that lay before them. But by early October the expedition sighted land birds and drifting branches. On the night of 11 October, Columbus on the *Santa Maria* claimed to have seen a light or torch that appeared and then disappeared a number of times. At two o'clock the next morning as the moon appeared, the night watchman on the *Pinta* fired the signal indicating land. The expedition had reached the island in the Caribbean that Columbus named San Salvador. He described the natives in his journal:

They all go naked as their mothers gave them birth, men and women ... their hair was almost as coarse as horses tails ... they are the colour of the inhabitants of the Canaries, neither black nor white, and some paint themselves white, some red, some whatever colour they find.

This must have been confusing for Columbus, as these natives and their ramshackle huts did not represent the fabulous wealth of the Orient or India that Marco Polo described. Columbus convinced himself that they had arrived at some islands off Cipangu, the name used by Marco Polo for Japan. Some of the natives wore small gold nosepieces and indicated that further to the south there was an island that possessed much gold. Columbus wrote in his journal:

> I wish to leave for another large island, which I believe must be Cipangu, according to the signs which these Indians whom I have with me make … The other islands we shall see in passing, and according to wether I shall find a quantity of gold or spices, I shall decide what is to be done. But I am still determined to proceed to the mainland and to the city of Quisay and to give the letters of your Highnesses to the Great Khan, and to request a reply and return with it.

Columbus immediately set sail in search of the gold, jewels and spices he expected to find. In the race to find these riches, the *Pinta* separated from the fleet and then the flagship *Santa Maria* ran aground on a reef off the island of Española (Hispaniola). Columbus and his crew were rescued by the *Niña*, but his flagship was abandoned. Reduced to a single vessel, he was forced to halt his search for the riches of the Indies. He decided instead to return to Spain carrying the news of his discoveries to King Ferdinand and Queen Isabella, leaving behind those members of his crew who chose to be the first settlers in the New World.

Reunited with the *Pinta*, the two vessels sailed into one of the worst Atlantic storms in recorded history. Fearful they would perish and the knowledge of their discoveries perish with them, Columbus and his men placed a sealed record of their voyage inside a wooden barrel which they cast into the raging seas, hoping beyond hope that the barrel would wash up on some European shore and its message tell the world of their momentous voyage. The *Niña* and *Pinta* were separated again as both struggled to survive the terrible Atlantic storm that raged around them. When the crew of the battered *Niña* finally sighted land, Columbus had no option but to seek refuge in the nearest port. Slowly the *Niña* struggled to make her way into the mouth of the Tagus River and towards the safety of Lisbon—the last place he wanted to make landfall since there were many in Portugal who considered him a dangerous rival, if not a traitor.

The Grand Captain of the Port of Lisbon went out in a longboat to inspect the papers of the battered vessel that had limped into harbour and interview its captain. Bartholomeu Dias stepped off the longboat to find that the captain of the caravel was none other than Christopher Columbus claiming to have discovered the Indies by sailing westward across the Atlantic Ocean.

This news quickly spread, and within days the Portuguese king asked Columbus join him at court. Columbus had already sent a messenger to the Spanish sovereigns asking for their protection; he feared treachery but had no choice but to submit to the request of the King.

Columbus demanded to be introduced in court as the Admiral of the Ocean Sea, a title promised him by the crown of Spain. He brought with him several natives whom he called 'Indians' and some native goods, including gold jewellery, but none of the spices, silks and exotic goods expected from a voyage to the Indies. Columbus had long been considered an eccentric by the Portuguese court, and after their meeting the King concluded he was a 'braggart' full of fancy and imagination, and wished him a safe voyage back to Spain.

Despite the lack of goods he was able to bring back to Spain, Columbus wrote in his first report to King Ferdinand and Queen Isabella:

> In Española there are many sources of spices, as well as large mines of gold and other metals. I shall give your Highnesses spices and cotton at once, as much as they shall order to be shipped, and as much as they shall order to be shipped of mastic [native gum] … and aloes as much as they shall order to be shipped, and slaves as many as they shall order to be shipped, and these shall be from idolatrous peoples. And I believe I have found rhubarb and cinnamon.

Columbus particularly wanted to find pepper, which was the spice in highest demand throughout Europe. It was not until his second voyage that he was able to bring back a spice that he called 'Pepper of the Indies'. Unrelated to the pepper grown in India, this was capsicum or what we now call chilli pepper and native to the West Indies. It has now became an essential ingredient in the hot and spicy curries of India and Indonesia since its introduction to the East Indies.

On his fourth and last voyage in 1502–04, Christopher Columbus reached the coast of Central America. Although he was never able to find Kublai Khan or the Kings of India, he remained convinced he had reached the Indies. A conviction which denied him a lasting legacy—the naming of the New World he discovered in his honour.

The return of Columbus caused a diplomatic storm in Europe, the Portuguese accusing the Spanish of breaking the Papal Decree issued to Prince Henry and King Affonso in 1454 that guaranteed a Portuguese monopoly on all discoveries beyond Guinea. The confrontation between the two Iberian Kingdoms obliged Pope Alexander Borgia to play an active part in the negotiations that led to the signing of the Treaty of Tordesillas in 1494.

In what today might seem to be the height of arrogance, Spain and Portugal, with the blessing of the Pope, divided the world in half along a pole to pole meridian in the middle of the Atlantic Ocean close to longitude 46 degrees 30 minutes west. This was halfway between the Portuguese-claimed islands of the Azores and the Spanish-claimed island of Hispaniola. Spain could claim any new territory discovered to the west of the line of demarcation and Portugal could claim any new territory discovered to the east.

Spain got the territories discovered by Columbus and what it believed was a western route to the Indies, while the Portuguese protected their African discoveries and what they believed was an eastern route to the Indies. The decision to position the line in the mid-Atlantic was intended to reduce any further disputes over territory, conveniently forgetting that a line cannot be drawn on water and that neither country had the ability to measure longitude accurately. As we shall see later, an even bigger problem was trying to determine where this line lay on the other side of the globe.

The result of the Treaty of Tordesillas is shown on the Portuguese map known as the 1502 Cantino Planisphere, which shows the islands discovered by Columbus in the Caribbean or 'Western Ocean' and the line of demarcation drawn in the central part of the North Atlantic. The map was smuggled out of Lisbon in 1502 by an Italian spy named Alberto Cantino, masquerading as a dealer in purebred horses. Cantino had acquired the map on behalf his client, the Duke of Ferrara, who wanted the latest map of the world for his personal collection, and it remained in the Duke's library for 90 years until Pope Clement VIII transferred it to another palace in the city of Modena. During a rebellion in 1859 the map disappeared, only to be discovered nine years later being used as a folding screen inside the entrance to a sausage factory.

With political agreement now reached on the division of the world between Portugal and Spain, the two Iberian powers found themselves to be in a race to be the first to reach the Indies and the Spice Islands by sailing either east or west around the world.

For the Portuguese, the hope of the riches promised by the Cape of Good Hope and the long awaited discovery of the sea route to India could be delayed no longer.

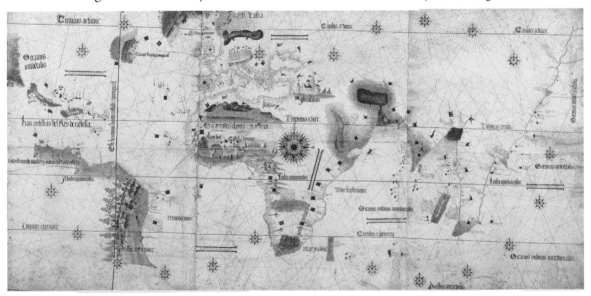

The Cantino Planisphere, 1502 (Biblioteca Estense, Modena)

7   *Vasco da Gama*

This is the land that you have been seeking,
This is India rising before you,
Unless you desire yet more of the world
Your long task is accomplished.
Rejoicing to see he knew the country,
Da Gama contained himself no longer
But knelt on deck, arms raised towards the sky,
And gave his heartfelt thanks to God on high.

—Luiz Vaz de Camões, *The Lusiads*, 1572

In 1491 King John II of Portugal died. In the last hours of his life, and perhaps to ensure his absolution for the murder of his queen's elder brother, he nominated her youngest brother as the successor to the throne instead of his own illegitimate son.

King Manuel, the unexpected heir, inherited both the throne and the great enterprise his predecessors had begun. The new king instructed Bartholomeu Dias to revive the construction of two purpose-built vessels for the voyage to India. These were identical three-masted carracks. Larger than the traditional caravel, they had square-rigged sails and a lateen sail installed to the mizzen. The new ships would be slower and less manoeuvrable but would offer far greater comfort to the crew, and could carry enough arms and food for the projected length of their voyage.

Bartholomeu Dias, the captain who had already experienced the storms of the Southern Ocean and had the confidence to lead an armada on a long voyage into unknown waters, was the most obvious choice as leader. However, King Manuel chose Vasco da Gama to command the expedition instead. Little is known of the 28-year-old before his appointment or even the reasons behind his selection, other than that his family was descended from minor Portuguese aristocracy and had a long history of service to the crown.

DON VASCO DE GAMA.

Portrait of Vasco da Gama, Conrad Westermayer (Australian National Library, nla.pic-an9575065)

This was not just another voyage of exploration down the African coast. Its leader would need to be a diplomat ready to represent his king and have the personal confidence to meet the kings and princes of India on equal terms. He needed to inspire loyalty from all his captains and crew, and to have courage as well as caution, since the fate of the armada would depend on his decisions.

The day before the fleet's departure, King Manuel, together with the nobles, clergy and members of his court, received Vasco da Gama and his captains. The King reminded those assembled how the Venetians had become wealthy and powerful through their monopoly of the spice trade in Europe. He told them it would be ungrateful to his predecessors, including Prince Henry the Navigator, and to God, to fail in this opportunity to make Portugal the most powerful nation in Europe.

After praying at the small chapel of St Mary of Belém, the captains and their crew bade a last farewell to family and friends before departing Lisbon on 8 July 1497. The armada consisted of the two purpose-built carracks—the *Sao Gabriel* and *Sao Raphael* commanded respectively by Vasco and his brother Paullo da Gama—a swift caravel with lateen sails commanded by Nicolao Coelho, and a supply vessel, all manned by 150 crew. Aided by a fair wind that filled their enormous white sails—emblazoned with the crimson cross of the Order of Christ—they set off down the Moroccan coast, past the Canary Islands and on to the Cape Verde Islands. There they rested for a week before heading south-west in a semicircular ocean voyage that took advantage of the counterclockwise rotation of the oceanic currents in the South Atlantic. They had entered unknown waters and were taking a daring course, far different from that taken by previous expeditions which had hugged the African coastline. For three months they remained out of sight of land, a remarkable achievement considering Columbus had faced the prospect of mutiny after only one month in the open ocean. Slowly turning south then east, the expedition made landfall at Saint Helena Bay only 150 kilometres north of the Cape of Good Hope.

Eight days later the armada rounded the Cape and entered what was for them uncharted waters. Of course the Indian Ocean was already known, having been navigated for centuries by the peoples of Austronesia, by Greeks and Romans, Arabs and Persians, Indians and Chinese. There was nothing for the Portuguese to discover; their mission was to trade and to conquer.

The official painting of the voyage of discovery shows the armada sailing up the coast of East Africa led by the *Sao Raphael* and the burning of the supply boat after all its stores had been consumed.

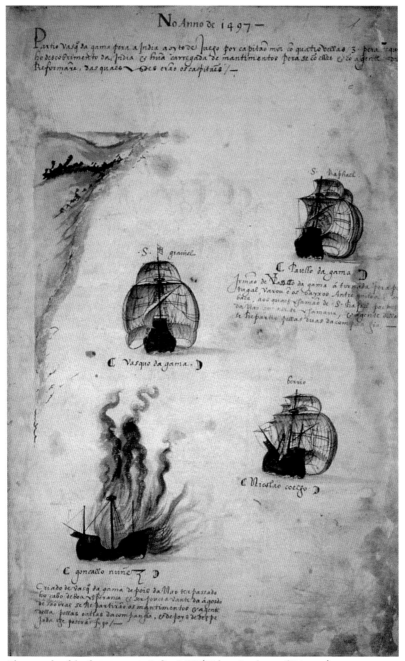

The armada of the first voyage to India, 1497 (Lisbon Academy of Sciences)

Heading north, the fleet stopped in Mombasa and then Malindi on the East African coast. The Muslim traders in the port cities and the Portuguese were suspicious of each other and only in Malindi, which had a strong native ruler, did Vasco da Gama feel he could safely rest and resupply his crew.

With the assistance of the local ruler, da Gama was able to hire the services of an Arab pilot known as Malemo Cana. When he showed him an astrolabe of wood the pilot expressed no surprise, saying that Arab navigators used similar instruments made of brass. The pilot had his own quadrant, which he used to measure the altitude of the sun and the pole star, and da Gama was even more impressed when Cana showed him an Arab chart of the whole coast of India drawn with meridians and parallels.

The local knowledge and navigation skills of the Arab pilot were crucial to the expedition's successful voyage across the Indian Ocean. The armada anchored off Calicut on the south-eastern coast of India on 24 May 1498. A Portuguese prisoner, or delgradado, brought specifically for the purpose was ordered to go ashore and carry out a reconnaissance of the city. Such prisoners might earn their freedom by conducting such a dangerous mission, assuming of course they survived the experience. Taken to the commercial part of the city, the unknown prisoner found to his surprise, two Arabs from Tunis who spoke Castilian and Genoese. The encounter is said to have produced the following conversation:

> The devil take you, who brought you here?
>   They asked him what we were looking for so far from home.
>   And he answered we come in search of Christians and spices.
>   They said why did the King of Castile and the King of France and the Lord of Venice not send anyone here?
>   And he answered the King of Portugal did not wish to let them send anyone here.
>   And they told him: the King did well.

After four days of further contacts by other crew members, Vasco da Gama was invited to meet the Zamorin, the Hindu ruler of the city, at his court. Da Gama selected twelve of his most senior and trusted men for his delegation and they went ashore to meet their escort in full military uniform, complete with decorations, and carrying trumpets and flags befitting their mission. On their journey, the Portuguese were shown a Hindu temple built like a monastery. Believing that the Hindu religion was a form of heretical Christianity, they mistook an image inside the 'church' to be that of the Virgin Mary:

> Somebody said the name of Holy Mary, leading us to believe it was her image. And since it seemed to be so, Vasco da Gama knelt down and prayed and us with him. And João de Sá, who was doubtful as to whether this was a Christian church because of the ugliness of the pictures which were painted on the walls, said as he knelt down: if this is the devil, I worship the true God. And Vasco da Gama who heard him, smiled at him.

The delegation did not arrive at the Zamorin's palace until late afternoon. There, the court officials received them with great dignity and the Portuguese visitors were ushered through a very large courtyard and four more doors before they reached the reception area. When Vasco da Gama met the Zamorin, he greeted him in the Indian manner—by putting his hands together and raising them upwards. Da Gama told the Zamorin that he had been sent as an ambassador of the King of Portugal. The Portuguese had spent the past 60 years searching for a route to India, he said, because they knew that in these lands there were Christian kings like themselves. He told the Zamorin that, yes, they came seeking Christians and spices and they wanted to be brothers and friends.

There is a painting in the Maritime Museum in Lisbon showing Vasco da Gama standing in an exaggerated pose addressing the Zamorin at his court. The Zamorin is sitting on a golden throne surrounded by his courtiers, naked to the waist, wearing a turban and adorned with gold and jewellery.

After their audience, da Gama and his delegation made their way through the night and a sudden tropical downpour to their assigned quarters. The following day, two court officials visited the delegation wishing to see the gifts to be presented to the Zamorin at their next meeting. This did not go well, as the gifts were the same as the Portuguese used for trading in Africa. They included twelve pieces of cloth, four scarlet hoods, six hats, four strings of coral, a case containing six hand-wash basins, a case of sugar, two casks of oil and two casks of honey. The court officials began to laugh at the offering laid out before them, saying it was not fit to give to the Zamorin and that even the poorest merchant gave him more than this. Da Gama responded by saying that he was an ambassador not a merchant and that when the King of Portugal sent him back to Calicut he would bring many valuable gifts. News spread of the inadequate gifts brought by the Portuguese, and during the following day they had to suffer the indignity of local merchants coming to their quarters to mock their meagre offerings.

This lack of appropriate gifts and suitable goods for trade was strange and gives credence to the belief that the report by the Portuguese spy Pero da Covilhão of his visit to Calicut never reached Lisbon or was lost after the death of King John II.

Vasco da Gama and the Zamorin had already agreed on a second meeting, but da Gama was kept waiting outside the reception area for hours before being granted an audience. All he had to present to the Zamorin were letters from King Manuel, one written in Portuguese and one written in Arabic. Unfortunately da Gama's translator then admitted that he could not read Arabic and he had to give the letter to one of the Gujarati Muslims in the court, trusting that he would faithfully read its message to the Zamorin.

A close alliance had existed for at least four centuries between the Hindu rulers and the Muslim merchants of Calicut. These merchants became more hostile as they realized that a new trade route would be against their long-established interests and were actively conspiring against the Portuguese. After further misunderstandings and difficulties with the Zamorin and the Muslim merchants, followed by a bout of mutual hostage-taking, the Portuguese were in fear of their lives. As a result of his skilful diplomacy, Vasco da Gama was able to leave Calicut with all his crew, a small but precious cargo of spices, and a letter from the Zamorin to King Manuel which forthrightly declared:

> Vasco da Gama, a gentleman of your house, came to my land, which pleased me greatly. In my land there is much cinnamon, and much clove, and ginger, and pepper and many precious stones. And what I want from your land is gold, and silver, and coral and scarlet cloth.

On 5 October 1498, the three Portuguese ships left Calicut for Portugal. It was a long journey home, made more difficult by the delay in the onset of the monsoonal winds and an outbreak of scurvy amongst the crew. Scurvy is an affliction caused by a diet lacking fresh fruit or vegetables and the vitamin C that comes with them. The initial symptoms are the swelling of hands and feet, and bleeding of the gums. As the disease progresses, the victim's teeth fall out, then there is haemorrhage, organ failure and death.

After three months' sailing, the armada reached the coast of East Africa and was able to resupply with fresh food and water at Malindi. Vasco da Gama wrote of the Arab traders of Malindi offering oranges to his afflicted sailors and of their miraculous recovery. Although the Arabs seemed to understand the cure for this vitamin deficiency, it was almost 300 years and thousands of deaths later before the British Navy prescribed a daily ration of lemon or lime juice for its sailors.

After leaving Malindi, Vasco da Gama had less than 100 surviving crew members to man three ships, and after transferring supplies and equipment he ordered the *Sao Raphael* to be burned. On 20 March 1499, the remaining two vessels rounded the Cape of Good Hope and set a course towards Lisbon. Northbound and running under full sail the crew embraced each other with joy, before kneeling to give praise to the Lord and asking for a safe journey home.

Lisbon greeted the return of the armada with enormous excitement on 14 September 1499. The sea route to India was now open. Despite the loss of almost half the crew, the voyage had been a success and the small but precious cargo of spices repaid the expenses of the voyage six times over.

After the return of the expedition, all said that King Manuel had chosen its commander wisely. The success of the expedition owed everything to the bravery and diplomatic skill of Vasco da Gama, especially when it came to dealing with the treachery of the Moors.

King Manuel granted Vasco da Gama the title of Admiral of the Sea of India, with the full honours, benefits, freedoms, powers, stipends, rights and collection of rents that accrue to an admiral of the realm. In a letter to the Catholic monarchs in Rome, the King triumphantly announced:

We sent Vasco da Gama, our noble servant and his brother Paullo da Gama with him, on a quest of discovery. They set off with ships to cross the seas and were gone for two years. They entered and sailed the sea there to find great cities, buildings, riches, and large settlements. There they found an extensive trade in spices and precious stones from Mecca to Cairo via sailing ships. Our discoverers actually saw them and consider them a large well equipped fleet. From Cairo the trade spreads itself out all over the world and we have the following products of it: cinnamon, cloves, ginger, nutmeg, pepper and other spices. We also have the wood and leaves of the same. We also have many fine stones such as rubies, among others.

We have sent news as we know Your Majesties will receive it with the greatest of pleasure and contentment.

For the next voyage to India, the King decided to send a large armada capable of showing Portuguese military supremacy, as well as the proper diplomatic gifts and trade goods the first voyage had surprisingly lacked.

8   Pedro Alvares Cabral

On you, the fearful Moor has his eyes
Fixed, knowing his fate prefigured;
At a glimpse of you, the unbroken
Indian offers his neck to the yoke.

—Luis Vaz de Camões, *The Lusiads*, 1572

After the return of Vasco da Gama from Calicut, King Manuel assumed the grandiose title of Lord of Guinea and of the Conquest, Navigation and Commerce of Ethiopia, Arabia, Persia and India, and ordered that a Portuguese armada four times the size of the da Gama expedition be readied to sail to India.

The King selected Pedro Alvares Cabral to command the second Portuguese armada. Cabral was from an aristocratic family, his mother a descendant of the first King of Portugal and his father a governor. We know little about him or the reasons for his selection as commander and there is no record of him having ever been to sea prior to this voyage. He was certainly less experienced than some of the captains of his armada, such as Bartholomeu Dias or Nicolao Coelho, and events will show that he did not have the diplomatic skills of Vasco da Gama.

The armada consisted of thirteen ships—eight carracks, three caravels, a support ship and an armed galleon—all crewed by 1300 men. There was also an element of private commercial interest in this second voyage: a Portuguese noble had financed one of the ships and Italian merchants another.

Ready to leave Lisbon on 8 March 1500, the ships were decked out with many coloured flags. Lining the docks were friends and family dressed for a fete, and musicians with bagpipes, fifes, drums and horns entertained the crowds. The King gave his last instructions to Cabral and presented him with a banner bearing the royal coat of arms. The armada took the usual route to the Cape Verde islands and then sailed south and west taking advantage of the same South Atlantic currents used by the da Gama expedition.

Sailing farther west, they unexpectedly encountered the coast of South America, where they landed on the central coast of Brazil near Porto Seguro. Cabral claimed this new land for Portugal, not knowing he had discovered an entire continent. He had his priest raise a cross while naming it the Island of the Vera Cruz, or the True Cross. The Portuguese described the natives there as dark with long hair, and entirely naked. They were also fascinated by the fact that the natives slept in hammocks.

Cabral immediately sent a vessel back to Portugal to inform King Manuel of the new land they had discovered. The ship carried samples of produce and timber from Brazil as well as several natives and their handicrafts. Master John, the astronomer assigned to the armada, also sent his report back to Lisbon. It contained the first European description of the Southern Cross, and explained his method of using its stars to locate the South Pole.

Because of the way Brazil bulges out into the South Atlantic, it lay in the Portuguese half of the world as defined by the Treaty of Tordesillas. This explains why the Brazilians speak Portuguese and the rest of South America speaks Spanish. The map known as the the 1502 Cantino Planisphere shows the Portuguese flag firmly planted in their new 'possession' of Brazil, as well as in India where the Portuguese were determined to establish a permanent presence.

Leaving Brazil and sailing across the South Atlantic towards the Cape of Good Hope, the armada encountered a terrible storm that sank four of its ships, including the one commanded by Bartolomeu Dias. Tragically, he and his crewmen were drowned off the cape he had named the Cape of Storms. The official painting of the vessels of the armada shows some of the ships as so heavily loaded they are barely above the waterline. The four ships lost off the Cape are shown sinking with the terse comment, 'Lost in a storm'.

The province of Gujarat lies on the Gulf of Cambay on the coast of north-western India. The region became Islamicized in 1297 when it was invaded by the forces of the Sultan of Delhi. Gujarati merchants were known as men who understood merchandise, who were steeped in the sound and harmony of it, and quick and diligent in their trade. It was said Cambay stretched out two arms, her right arm towards Aden and her left arm towards Calicut and Malacca. The region was a centre for cotton growing and the Gujaratis held the secrets necessary to prepare colourful dyes such as indigo blue and madder red. Great quantities of Gujurati cottons with their rich designs and brilliant colours were loaded at Cambay, and were one of the favoured trading items along the Spice Route.

The rulers of the great trading ports like Aden, Hormuz, Cambay, Calicut and Malacca encouraged open trade. They made large profits from taxes and welcomed all nationalities. 'The land for the King and the sea for the merchants' was the unwritten law that had developed over centuries along the shores of the Spice Route. The Arabs, the Indian Muslims, the Chinese and the Indonesians competed

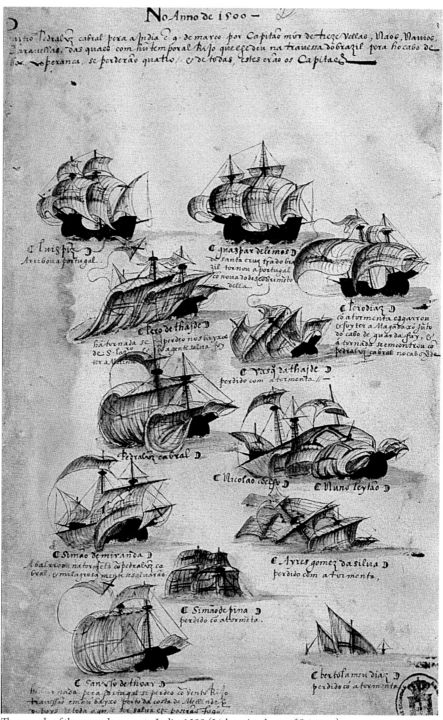

The armada of the second voyage to India, 1500 (Lisbon Academy of Sciences)

openly for their share of the spice trade and the idea that any nation could claim sovereignty over the sea was entirely alien. The Arab and Gujurati traders had achieved their domination of the seaborne trade in the Indian Ocean quite peacefully. The largest of their trading vessels contained no artillery and even the wealthy trading ports had only light defences and possessed no ocean-going warships. An open and tolerant trading system had existed for thousands of years along the Spice Route.

The written orders that Pedro Alvares Cabral had received from King Manuel gave him the authority to wage war on any Arab or Gujurati ships he encountered at sea and confiscate their cargoes. However, to maintain good relations with the Zamorin, he was instructed not to attack any such ships in Calicut.

On 13 September 1500, the seven remaining vessels of the Portuguese armada anchored off Calicut. They must have been an imposing sight since all the ships were heavily armed and were more than twice the size of the other ships in the harbour. Cabral sent ashore a delegation that included an Arab trader and four Indian fishermen who had been captured by Vasco da Gama and taken to Lisbon. The delegation reached agreement with court officials for the Zamorin to meet Cabral at an especially prepared house on the shore after an exchange of hostages to ensure there was no treachery. Cabral and his delegation went ashore dressed in full military uniform with all their medallions and honours, but none could compare to the riches of the Zamorin as described by one of their party:

> The Zamorin was nude above the waist, and had around him a cloth of fine white cotton, which was wound around him many times and worked in gold. He had on his head a cap of brocade made like a long and very high helmet, and he had his ears pierced. In them he had large pieces of gold with rubies of great price and likewise diamonds, and two very large pearls, one round and the other pear-shaped, larger than a large filbert. And on his arms he had bracelets of gold from the elbow down, full of rich stones with jewels and pearls of great value. Likewise on the fingers of his hands he had many rings full of jewels with rubies, emeralds and diamonds.

Cabral brought a lavish array of gifts for the Zamorin, hoping to erase the memory of the miserable offerings brought by Vasco da Gama. These included a silver basin embossed with gilded figures, two silver maces with silver chains for the mace bearers, two large cushions of brocade, two large cushions of crimson velvet, a large carpet, two fine tapestries, two pieces of scarlet cloth, a length of crimson satin and a piece of crimson taffeta. These gifts must have impressed the Zamorin, for he received Cabral hospitably and granted the Portuguese the use of a building or 'factory' near the shore, where they could commence trading for spices.

Cabral also presented the Zamorin with a letter from King Manuel. However, it included some unusual demands. The Portuguese still wanted to believe that the Hindu religion was a heretical form of Christianity, and that the Zamorin, as a 'Christian', should favour the Portuguese over the Muslim traders. They demanded precedence for themselves in the spice market over the long-established Arab and Gujarati merchants who lived in the city, and Cabral told the Zamorin that, to comply with his duty as a 'Christian' king, he should be prepared to expel all Muslims from his Kingdom.

This was an outrageous demand and the Zamorin rightly asked why he should expel the more than 4000 Muslim households, whose families had lived in Calicut for centuries and from whom his kingdom received much profit. However, in the letter from King Manuel there was clear threat:

> And if it should happen that owing to ill-will and minds obstructive of good, which are never lacking, we find in you the contrary of this … Our fixed purpose is to follow the will of God rather than that of men, and not fail through any contrarities to prosecute this affair and continue our navigation, trade and intercourse in those lands which the Lord God wishes to be newly served by our hands.

Reading this text, it seems obvious that despite the lavish gifts given to the Zamorin, the Portuguese were in Calicut not just to trade, but were also ready to use their superior force of arms to capture the spice trade from the Muslims. The Portuguese started trading for spices but after three months had filled only two of their seven ships. Accusing the Muslim merchants of withholding merchandise, they again demanded the Zamorin give them precedence in the marketplace, stating that they would not allow any other ships to leave the harbour until theirs were first filled with spice.

The north-east monsoon now started to blow and for the Arab merchants conditions were perfect for the westward crossing of the Indian Ocean to Aden. A large 'Mecca' ship owned by Arab traders and fully laden with spices prepared to leave the harbour, but in an open act of piracy seen by all of Calicut the Portuguese seized the ship and its cargo.

Rioting broke out in the city. During the night mobs attacked the Portuguese factory, killing 53 Portuguese and capturing 17 others as hostages. At dawn, Cabral ordered his guns to open fire. The Portuguese bombardment continued for two days, destroying large parts of the city, forcing the Zamorin to make a humiliating escape from his palace, and sealing the fate of those unfortunate Portuguese held hostage ashore. The Portuguese seized ten other Arab or Gujarati merchant ships in the harbour, confiscating their cargoes and slaughtering most of their crew.

The contemporary Portuguese historian João de Barros felt compelled to justify these acts and wrote:

> It is true that there does exist a common right to all to navigate the seas, and in Europe we acknowledge the right which others hold against us, but that right does not extend beyond Europe, and therefore the

Portuguese by the strengths of their fleets are justified in compelling all Moors to take out safe-conducts under the pain of confiscation and death. The Moors and Gentiles are outside the law of Jesus Christ, which is the true law, which everyone has to keep under pain of damnation to eternal hell fire. If then the soul be so condemned, what right has the body to the privileges of our laws?

After this death and destruction, Cabral sailed his ships south along the coast to the port of Cochin. The Rajah of Cochin, having probably heard the news of the fate of Calicut, treated the Portuguese obsequiously and quickly filled their ships with spices in exchange for gold. Fully laden, the seven remaining ships of the armada departed for Lisbon. The wreck of another ship off Madagascar on the voyage home meant that of the thirteen vessels that left for India only six returned to Lisbon on 21 July 1501.

In spite of the loss of so many ships and crew, King Manuel was delighted. The size and value of the cargoes was proof that the new trade route to India was practicable and profitable. In fact, even before the Cabral fleet returned to Lisbon, King Manual had dispatched another fleet to bring back as much spice as possible from India. Cabral had also succeeded in bringing back from Cochin two brothers named Matthias and Joseph, who were able to communicate to Europe the existence of a native Christian Church amongst the Hindus and Muslims of South India.

The Venetians were in shock over the potential loss of their monopoly over the European spice trade and their spies were all over Lisbon, trying to get information and maps of the new trade route. There is a letter from Angelo Trevisan di Bernadino, the secretary to the Venetian Ambassador in Spain, to his superiors in Venice advising them of his attempts to obtain information about the voyage:

> We are daily expecting our doctor from Lisbon, who has left our magnificent ambassador Pisani there: and who at my request has written a short account of Cabral's voyage from Calicut, of which I will make a copy for Your Magnificence. It is impossible to procure a map of that voyage because the king has placed a death penalty on anyone who gives it out.

Three months later, his spies had done their work and obtained a copy of a map of the voyage, as Di Bernadino was able to write:

> If we return to Venice alive, Your Magnificence will see maps both as far as Calicut and beyond there ... I promise you that everything has come to order; but this Your Magnificence may not care to divulge. One thing is certain, that you will learn upon our arrival as many particulars as though you had been as far as Calicut and farther.

The Venetians felt the effect of the Portuguese seizure of the Muslim trading ships in the Indian Ocean almost immediately, for in 1502 there was not enough pepper in Alexandria to load their ships. They first reduced the number of galleys in their merchant fleets and then, instead of sending a trading fleet to Alexandria every year, they sent only one fleet every other year. As Girolamo Pruili, a Venetian banker and diarist, recorded:

> Therefore, now that this new route has been found by Portugal, this King of Portugal will bring all the spices to Lisbon and there is no doubt that the Hungarians, the Flemish and the French, and all the people from across the mountains that once came to Venice to buy spices with their money will now turn to Lisbon because it is nearer to their countries and easier to reach; also because they will be able to buy at a cheaper price, which is most important of all.

King Manuel became known throughout Europe as Manuel the Fortunate and began to live in the luxury and style of a Roman Emperor. New buildings and monuments were erected in Lisbon reflecting the city's new-found wealth and the architectural influences of both Africa and India. The ruling class decorated their homes with oriental carpets, bedspreads of colourful Indian cotton and cushions of silk. Spices such as pepper, cinnamon, cloves, nutmeg and mace were on every dining table. A view of the city of Lisbon shows the vessels loading and unloading their oriental goods in front of the Praça do Comércio, and the royal coat of arms of the Kingdom of Portugal.

At the site of the small chapel of St Mary of Belém, where Vasco da Gama and his men had prayed before their departure for India, the King built the magnificent Mosteiro de Jerónimos. The Mosteiro is a monument to the first Portuguese voyages to India. It is the finest example of the exuberant and exotic Manueline style of Indian influenced

The City of Lisbon, Braun and Hogenberg, *Civitates Orbis Terrarum*, 1572 (Beinecke Rare Book and Manuscript Library, Yale University)

Portuguese architecture and holds the remains of King Manuel, Vasco da Gama and the poet Luis Vaz de Camões.

King Manuel decided that, to live up to his self-proclaimed title of Lord of Guinea and of the Conquest, Navigation and Commerce of Ethiopia, Arabia, Persia and India, the next armada to sail to India should be even larger, capable of both ensuring Portuguese military supremacy at sea and establishing a land base in India.

9 Alfonso de Albuquerque

Whoever is lord of Malacca has his hand on the throat of Venice.
As far as from Malacca, and from Malacca to China, and from China to the Moluccas, and from the Moluccas to Java, and from Java to Malacca and Sumatra, all is in our power.

—Tomé Pires, *Suma Oriental*, 1514

In 1505, an armada consisting of 22 fighting ships and 2500 hand-picked sailors and soldiers sailed from Portugal. Most of the financing for this armada came from German merchants, such as the House of Fuggers, who were ready to provide all the copper, gold and silver needed to finance the spice trade from their German mines. King Manuel appointed Francisco de Almeida as commander and the first viceroy of Portuguese India, with orders to seize Muslim shipping and impose a Portuguese monopoly over the Spice Route by blockading the mouth of the Red Sea to stop any spices reaching Alexandria and Venice.

In response, the Egyptian Mamluks, with the support of the Ottoman Turks and their Venetian mercantile allies, assembled a fleet of vessels at Suez on the shores of the Red Sea. The Egyptian fleet, which consisted of six warships, six galleys and over 1000 men under the command of Amir Hussein, crossed the Indian Ocean to the Gujarati port of Diu in 1508, where it was joined by local ships supplied by Malik Ayyaz the Governor of Diu. The combined Egyptian–Turkish–Gujarati fleet successfully carried out a surprise attack, destroying a large part of the Portuguese armada at Chaul.

The two fleets met a year later off the island of Diu, which lies at the entrance to the Gulf of Cambay, for what would be a decisive battle. With the Muslim fleet having lost the element of surprise, the outcome of the attack mounted by Francisco de Almeida with his superior ships and artillery was really never in doubt, especially after Malik Ayyaz secretly allied himself with the Portuguese and never fired a shot against their vessels. The outcome of the battle was that the Portuguese retained their naval superiority in the Indian Ocean, and Malik Ayyaz retained control of the port of Diu and his share of its taxes.

Alfonso de Albuquerque came from a family related to King Manuel and his father held an important position in the royal court. He arrived at Cochin in 1508 bearing a

Battle between Turkish and Portuguese ships (Turkish Naval Museum)

commission from King Manuel naming him the next Viceroy of India. Jealously guarding his own new-found power, Francisco de Almeida refused to recognize Albuquerque's commission and had him arrested and clapped in irons. Only after the arrival of the next fleet from Portugal, commanded by Grand Marshall Fernando Coutinho, was Alberqueque released and installed as Viceroy in 1509.

Having established their hegemony over the seas, the Portuguese still needed to establish a permanent land base in India. One fleet under the command of Fernando Coutinho and another under the command of Alfonso de Albuquerque appeared off Calicut in 1509 carrying a large expeditionary force. After a lengthy bombardment of the city, the Portuguese troops landed. Forcing their way towards the Zamorin's palace, the invaders were cut to pieces in fierce hand-to-hand combat with the Zamorin's Palace Guard. The Grand Marshall and 70 of his soldiers lost their lives; Albuquerque received wounds to his neck and left arm and was carried unconscious to his ship. Thus ended the first Portuguese attempt to challenge the power of an Indian ruler on land.

The Portuguese needed a new strategy and the Royal Council chose the island of Goa to be the main bastion of the King's newly declared Estado da India. Goa had been part of the Hindu empire of Vijayanagar until its capture only 40 years earlier by the Muslim Bahimi Sultanate. A strategic location, it was almost entirely encompassed by the mainland and offered safe anchorage from the roughest monsoon weather.

Portuguese attack on Goa 1509, Braun and Hogenberg, Civitates Orbis Terrarum, 1572 (Beinecke Rare Book and Manuscript Library, Yale University)

Led by Alfonso de Albuquerque, the Portuguese attacked Goa in 1509, briefly occupying the city until forced to withdraw in the face of a fierce counterattack by Muslim forces. The Portuguese needed an ally, and the Hindu empire of Vijayanagar was quick to realize that, by supporting the Portuguese and regaining an outlet to the sea, they could more readily obtain horses, arms and equipment needed for their campaigns against the Muslim Moghul emperors to the north.

After six months the Portuguese attacked Goa again, this time allied with Timmoja, who was either an admiral of the Vijayanagar navy or a pirate, depending on which version of history you read. A bloody battle ensued, and with the city at his mercy Albuquerque showed a fondness for atrocities as he sacked and plundered the town. A lithograph of the attack on Goa shows the fortress, the defensive marine barriers the Sultan had erected to protect the island, and the Portuguese ships bombarding the city.

Albuquerque and his soldiers went about rebuilding the fortress and establishing a municipality. He appointed persons of both high birth and merit to fill important offices of the state, and laid the foundations of the city that was to become the capital of the Portuguese empire in the East. The friendly relations between the Hindu empire of Vijayanagar and the Portuguese authorities in Goa, united in their enmity against Islam, enabled the Portuguese to retain their occupation of Goa with little or no military presence for hundreds of years. In fact, Goa remained a Portuguese colony for 450 years, until annexed by India in 1961.

For the Portuguese, a further prize lay to the east. This was the port of Malacca, on the Malay Peninsula. Because of its geographic location, Malacca had become the main trading port of the region, frequented by ships from India, Persia, Arabia and Egypt in the west, from China and Japan in the east, and by traders from Sumatra, Java and the Moluccas. To become the Lords of Malacca would allow the Portuguese to control the trade between Lisbon, India, China and the Spice Islands.

The first Portuguese ships reached Malacca in 1509. The contemporary Portuguese chronicler Tomé Pires wrote:

> When Diego Lopes de Sequeira arrived before the port of Malacca, there were at that time … according to what is truly stated … a thousand Gujarati merchants in Malacca, among whom there were a great many rich ones with a great deal of capital, and some who were representatives of others; and with the Parsee [Persians], Bengalese and Arabs there were more than four thousand men here, including rich merchants and some who were factors for others.

The chief Portuguese factor, Ruy de Araujo, led a delegation of nine Portuguese ashore to formally meet the Sultan of Malacca. Araujo presented the Sultan with gifts consisting of a length of crimson-dyed cloth, three pieces of printed linen, four pieces of red velvet, a length of coloured satin, a large mirror framed in gold, a sword with a gold-plated hilt, a dagger, a lance, and six flasks of French perfume. The Sultan was well pleased with the gifts and gave orders for the Portuguese to be taken to a building near the harbour where they could store their goods and begin trading.

The Chinese and the Javanese merchants were ready to trade with the Portuguese, who had cloth and goods of high quality. But for the Arabs and the Gujarati Indians it was a different story. News of the Portuguese atrocities committed against their Muslim brothers in Calicut, Goa and on the high seas had preceded the arrival of the Diego Lopes de Sequeira in Malacca. The leader of the Gujurati merchants warned the Sultan and his advisers of the danger and began to foment opposition against the Portuguese. The Sultan's court was split between those who favoured peaceful trade with the Portuguese until their intentions became clear and those who favoured a pre-emptive strike against them.

In the end a plot was hatched to attack the Portuguese when they were busy ashore receiving a shipment of cloves from some Javanese traders. A group of Malays boarded the Portuguese flagship under the pretence of challenging de Sequeira to a game of chess. Their leader stood behind him watching the chess game, but had his kris ready to stab him in the back at a predetermined signal. Above, on the topsail, the Portuguese lookout was keeping an eye on the Malays surrounding de Sequeira when he heard a shout from the town and saw Portuguese sailors being attacked and others running to their boats on the shoreline. The lookout yelled a warning, 'Treachery, treachery! They are killing our men ashore.' Upsetting the chess board, the Portuguese tried to seize the Malays who dived overboard and swam to their boats. De Sequeira ordered his crew to take to their boats and rescue those ashore. Ferdinand Magellan was able to rescue his friend Francisco Serrão and three or four other seamen who were under attack as they fled from the beach in a small boat.

After they regrouped, the Portuguese learned that 60 of their men were either dead or seriously wounded and that another twenty, including Ruy de Araujo, had been captured and were being held hostage ashore. Next, to his great dismay, de Sequeira saw a fleet of vessels emerge from behind Cape Rachado. He made the sudden decision to return to Goa before his fleet became trapped in the harbour.

Alfonso de Albuquerque needed time to muster a fighting force able to take Malacca by storm, and in 1511 he arrived off the city with a fleet of fifteen vessels and a force of 700 Portuguese, including Ferdinand Magellan, Antonio de Abreu and Francisco Serrão as his captains, and 300 Malabari soldiers. A single volley from the fleet's cannon was enough for Sultan Ahmad Shah to release the Portuguese prisoners. Albuquerque then demanded the Sultan surrender the city. The Sultan refused to answer his demands, as he had 4000 men at arms able to defend the city but needed time to rally all his forces. A probing assault by the Portuguese on the main bridge across the Malacca River led to fierce fighting but the Portuguese were unable to hold any ground. After a six-week siege, the Portuguese prepared for an all-out assault on the city. The attack took place on the day of the Festival of Saint James, the patron saint of both the Portuguese army and of the religious order of which Albuquerque was a commander. Although the objective was control of the trading port, the religious fervour behind the Portuguese attack is evident in the address Alfonso de Albuquerque gave to his men before the battle:

> It is a great service we shall perform to Our Lord in casting the Moors out of this country, and quenching the fire of this sect of Mohamed so that it may never burst out again hereafter; and I am so sanguine as to hope for this from our undertaking, that if we can only achieve the task before us, it will result in the Moors resigning India altogether to our rule, for the greater part of them live upon the trade of this country and are becoming great and rich, and lords of extensive treasures … and I hold it as very certain that if we take this trade of Malacca away out of their hands, Cairo and Mecca are entirely ruined, and to Venice no spiceries be conveyed except that which her merchants go and buy in Portugal.

The Portuguese divided their forces to attack from both from land and sea, arming with cannon a large junk that they floated towards the bridge to attack from close range. Routed by heavy cannon fire and fierce hand-to-hand combat, the Malay fighters retreated. In the end the Sultan fled and the city surrendered to the Portuguese.

Alfonso de Albuquerque installed Rui de Brito as governor and a powerful Hindu merchant, Nina Chatu, as prime minister. The new governor allowed the Indonesian, Hindu, Chinese and Japanese merchants to continue to live in Malacca but expelled the Arab and Gujarati traders.

Having conquered Goa and Malacca, Albuquerque had completed the first stage of the Portuguese plan to build a commercial empire in the Indian Ocean, based on their naval superiority and control of the major ports of the region. He now turned his attention to the capture of the strategic port of Aden, at the entrance to the Red Sea and the gateway for the spice trade with Mecca, Cairo and Alexandria.

In 1513, Albuquerque lay siege to Aden and mounted probing attacks on the city.

A painting of the attack on Aden shows the city surrounded by mountains and protected along the seafront by a massive fortress wall. Thirteen Portuguese war galleons are at anchor, and smaller boats ferry soldiers ashore, where they are attempting to scale the fortress wall. Despite repeated attempts to conquer the fort, the heat, lack of water and lack of timber to build ladders forced the Portuguese to withdraw.

The Portuguese attempt to capture Aden, Lendas da India (Lisbon Academy of Sciences)

Alfonso de Albuquerque's grand scheme was that after the capture of Aden he could use the Ethiopian port of Massawa on the Red Sea as a staging base for an invasion of Arabia. His dream was for Portuguese forces, aided by the supposed Christian armies of Prester John, to capture Mecca and ransom the Muslim Holy City in exchange for Christian control of Jerusalem and the Holy Land.

Next, Albuquerque prepared his forces for the capture of the port of Hormuz at the entrance to the Persian Gulf. In 1515, after an extended siege, the ruling Sultan ordered the closure of the gates to his palace and the opening of the fortress gates, effectively surrendering to the Portuguese.

Returning to Goa, Albuquerque was met at sea by a fleet arriving from Portugal and learnt that he was to be replaced as viceroy by one of his arch rivals, someone he had previously sent back to Portugal in chains. He wrote a letter to King Manuel defending his conduct and voiced his bitterness by stating that he was in ill favour with the King for love of his men, and with his men for love of the King. Already suffering from ill-health due to the rigours of battle and his advancing years, Albuquerque felt betrayed by the King he had so faithfully served, and he died at sea on 16 December 1515.

He had done more than any other Portuguese commander to enhance the prestige of his king and country, combining resolute determination with great personal bravery and ruthless cruelty towards his enemies, the Moors.

Albuquerque understood that the success of the Portuguese Empire of India depended upon a land base that he established at Goa and the control of the key ports of Malacca, Hormuz and Aden. Within a period of five active years, he had completed this grandiose plan except for the capture of Aden. The Portuguese never succeeded in taking Aden and had to resort to an annual blockade of the entrance to the Red Sea in an attempt to stop spices from reaching Alexandria, Gaza and then Venice.

Trade in spices became a monopoly of the Portuguese crown or its nominees. Asian or Arab ships needed to buy a Portuguese licence or cartaz to be able to operate, or be subject to seizure.

Now established in Goa, the Portuguese had not forgotten that part of their mission as envisaged by the Pope and Prince Henry the Navigator was to find their Christian allies in India and discover the lands of the fabled priest-king Prester John and his Christian armies.

The Portuguese found the South Indian 'Thomas Christians', who traced their faith back to the Apostle Thomas. This is based on the apocryphal Acts of St Thomas, a Gnostic tract written in the third century at Edessa, in Southern Turkey, a centre of early Christianity. According to this tract, when the Apostles allocated themselves different parts of the world to spread the gospel, India fell to Thomas, but he was reluctant to travel, saying that his health was not good and he spoke only Hebrew, whereupon Jesus appeared and sold him as a slave to an Indian merchant.

The Thomas Christians of southern India consider themselves to be the descendents of the first people converted by St Thomas. They are also called Syrian Christians because they acknowledge the authority of the patriarch of Antioch. They also call themselves Nasranis, meaning the people who followed 'The Messiah, the Nazarene', and they preserved the rituals of the early Jewish Christians and their texts written in Aramaic. Their symbol is the Syrian Cross, which is a Christian Cross mounted on a Jewish Menora, and their ritual services are held on the Jewish Sabbath.

Marco Polo wrote of his visit to the purported tomb of St Thomas, in south-east India during his return from China in 1294:

The body of St Thomas lies in the province of Maabar [near Madras] in a little town. There are few inhabitants, and merchants do not visit this place; for there is nothing of merchandise that could be got from it, and it is a very out-of-the-way spot. But it is a great place of pilgrimage for Christians and for Saracens [Muslims]. For I assure you that the Saracens of this country have great faith in him and declare that he was a Saracen and a great prophet and call him avarium, that is to say holy man.

After the establishment of a Roman Catholic diocese in Goa, the Thomas Christians Church came under great pressure to convert to Latin rite, since the Catholic Church considered them heretics. During the Goa Inquisition, Archbishop Menez ordered the persecution of all those priests who opposed conversion, the separation of all the married priests from their wives, and the burning of all the texts of the Syrian Christian Church, including their Bible, which is known today as the Lost Aramaic Bible.

In 1520, a Portuguese mission led by Rodrigo de Lima landed in Massawa on the Red Sea. Their route led them to the ancient Ethiopian capital of Axum, where they observed in awe the thousand-year-old stone churches and palaces that had been built in Ethiopia's greatest era. Travelling further inland, they were eventually allowed to meet the Emperor, Lebna Dengal, at his impoverished and nomadic court. There were no vast Christian armies and Albuquerque's dream of capturing Mecca had died with him.

The Portuguese mission was able to locate Pero de Covilhão, who had been refused permission to leave Ethiopia for almost 30 years. Now an old man, he was found living on a large estate with numerous wives. The Portuguese mission was also prevented from leaving Ethiopia, but after six years was able to make its way back to Massawa and return to Goa, although without Pero de Covilhão, who had decided he was too old and frail to make the journey back to Portugal.

The Portuguese Empire of India created by Alfonso de Albuquerque flourished and there was no better example of its prosperity than the city of Goa. Travellers were full of admiration for the magnificence of its buildings and the luxury of its people: 'Golden Goa', in their estimates, surpassed even Lisbon itself. A description by the French traveller Francois Pyrard in 1620 paints a fascinating picture of the city:

> It is about a hundred and ten years since the Portuguese made themselves masters of this island of Goa, and I have often wondered at the rapidity with which the Portuguese have been able to erect stately edifices, so many churches, convents, palaces, fortresses, and other buildings, after the European fashion; at the internal order, regulations and government which they have established, and at the power they have attained, everything being managed as in Lisbon itself. This city is the metropolis of the whole of the Portuguese dominions in India, and as such it commands considerable power, wealth, and celebrity. The Viceroy has his residency there, and keeps his court in the style of the King himself … Thus, whoever has been in Goa may say that he has seen the choicest rarities of India, for it is the most famous and celebrated city, on account of its commercial intercourse with people of all nationalities of the East, who bring there the products of their respective countries, articles of merchandise, necessaries of life, and other commodities in great abundance, because every year more than a thousand ships touch there laden with cargo.

After the capture of Goa, Malacca and Hormuz, the Portuguese not only had their hands on the throat of Venice, but were also now in a position to send an expedition to locate the fabled Spice Islands, the source of the cloves, nutmegs and mace that would bring them even more power and profit.

10   *Francisco Serrão*

After the capture of Malacca the first priority of the Portuguese was to load their admiral's flagship with the spoils of war. Alfonso de Albuquerque collected more than 60 tons of booty from the Sultan's Palace, and Malay workers were now busy loading his flagship, the *Flor do Mar*, under the supervision of their new masters. The palace had been stripped of all its gold—gold bars, golden statues, gold coins, gilded furniture and even the gilded jewel-encrusted howdah the Sultan used to sit atop the Royal Elephant. Next to be carried up the gangplank were the crown jewels consisting of diamonds, rubies, emeralds and sapphires stowed in 200 golden chests. The last of the booty to board the *Flor do Mar* was the troupe of Malay dancing girls who were being sent to entertain King Manuel's court in Lisbon.

The treasure was never destined to leave the Malay world. Fate intervened only two days after the admiral and his flagship departed Malacca when the four vessels of the fleet ran into a storm off the north coast of Sumatra. Forced off course, the *Flor do Mar* foundered on a reef and, pounded by storm-driven waves, started breaking up. Albuquerque and his officers abandoned the sinking ship and rowed off in a longboat with whatever treasure they could carry, leaving the rest of the passengers and crew to their fate. After the storm had blown over, Albuquerque was rescued by one of the remaining vessels of the fleet but it is written that only three of those remaining on the *Flor do Mar* survived the storm to reach shore alive.

A sultan's treasure was left on the sea floor, treasure that has become both legendary and elusive. Both sixteenth-century and modern treasure hunters are said to have plundered the wreck site without leaving any record of where it is and what valuables might have been recovered.

The next priority of the Portuguese was to reach the Spice Islands. Even though cloves, nutmeg and mace had been traded through Asia to Europe for thousands of years, the location of the Spice Islands was still shrouded in mystery. Around 1000 an Arab writer named Ibrahim ibn Wasif Shah speculated on their location and described a unique form of trading:

> Also somewhere near India is the island containing the Valley of the Cloves. No merchants or sailors have ever been to the valley or have seen the kind of trees that produce the cloves. Its fruit they say is sold by genies; the sailors arrive at the island, place their items of merchandise on the shore, and return to the ship. The next morning they find beside each item a quantity of cloves.

The Moroccan-born geographer Al-Idrisi, writing around 1150, traces cloves to the island of Sumatra. Marco Polo, on his return voyage from China in 1293, spent many months in Sumatra and wrote that cloves came from Java. The Venetian traveller Nicolo de Conti journeyed through India to Sumatra and Java, and on reaching Java in 1430 learnt that the Spice Islands were still further away and that the spices grew on separate islands, although he confused the names:

> At fifteen days from beyond these islands [Java], two others are found to the eastwards; the one is called Sandai, in which nutmeg and maces grow; the other is named Bandan; this is the only island in which cloves grow, which are exported hence to the Java islands.

Ludovico de Varthema, an adventurer/trader known as a Gentleman of the City of Bologna, journeyed by land across Asia and then travelled by junk into the South China Sea and beyond. He claimed to have visited both Banda and Ternate around 1505 and gives a reasonably accurate description of the spice trees. But his description of the islanders reads like fantasy and one has to conclude that he never reached the Spice Islands.

Only a few months after the capture of Malacca, three Portuguese ships under the command of Antonio de Abreu sailed eastwards towards the Spice Islands. The small fleet comprised the flagship *Santa Caterina*, the *Sabaia* captained by Francisco Serrão, and an unnamed caravel captained by Simão Alfonso Bisagudo. They were a crew of 120 including 60 Malays and Javanese, their Malay pilot Nahkoda Ishmael, who was familiar with the trading route to the Spice Islands, and Francisco Rodrigues, the Portuguese pilot who chronicled their journey. The expedition had been given explicit orders from Alfonso de Albuquerque to honour local customs and law as this was to be a mission of exploration and trade, not conquest and plunder.

The Portuguese captains and crew had recently fought in the battle that led to the capture of Malacca, and their commander Antonio de Abreu was still recovering from facial wounds he received in combat. History records very little about Francisco Serrão prior to his participation in the conquest of Malacca, other than he was related to Ferdinand Magellan and they grew up together as pageboys in the royal court of Portugal.

Taking advantage of the monsoonal winds, the small fleet travelled south-east through the narrow straits between Sumatra and the island of Bangka before entering the Java Sea. Sailing along the north coast of Java, the local pilots would have used the numerous volcanoes rising above the green, terraced rice fields as their landmarks before stopping to resupply at the port of Gresik in East Java.

The chart by Francisco Rodrigues shows the location of a reef off the east coast of Madura Island where the *Sabaia* ran aground, cutting a huge gash in her hull. Working quickly, Francisco Serrão and his crew managed to transfer some of their equipment and supplies to the other two vessels before the *Sabaia* sank to the bottom of the Java Sea.

The two remaining ships continued eastwards past the islands of Bali, Lombok and Sumbawa with their towering volcanoes, to a cape they named Cabo de Flores, or the Cape of Flowers, after the vivid red flamboyant trees that grow in profusion along this peninsula on the eastern end of the island now called Flores.

From Flores they sailed north, setting their course by a bright beacon on the horizon, as described by Francisco Rodrigues:

> Antonio de Abreu and those who went with them set their course toward the north of the small island called Gunung Api because from its highest point streams of fire run continuously to the sea, which is a wonderful thing to behold.

Gunung Api, literally Fire Mountain, still exists as an isolated volcano rising out of the middle of the Banda Sea and is not to be confused with the similarly named volcano in the Banda Islands. The two vessels continued north to the island of Buru, where they encountered the onset of the monsoonal winds from the north and were unable to make any progress towards Ternate. The vessels turned east, sailing along the south coast of Ceram until forced to shelter for a month at the easternmost point of the island. Still unable to reach the Clove Islands because of adverse prevailing winds, the tiny fleet turned south towards the Nutmeg Islands.

The nutmeg tree is indigenous only to the tiny islands of Banda, Lontar, Ai and Run, all of which are mere specks in the Banda Sea. The largest is Lontar, a remnant rim of an older volcano that erupted catastrophically sometime in the past. In the centre of the old crater the almost perfectly symmetrical cone of an active new volcano rises out of the sea to a height of 656 metres. Anchored in its lee, the Portuguese could see the slopes covered with the evergreen nutmeg trees they had come so far to find. The nutmeg is a fleshy apricot-like fruit and the aromatic spice comes from the grated nut, as well as from the bright red outer covering of the seed, known as mace. Nutmeg was not without purported medical properties as it was said to cure 'stinking breath, clear the eyes, comfort the stomach, liver and spleen, and digest meat'.

The arrival of Antonio de Abreu and his two ships at Banda in 1512 was the culmination of a fifteen-hundred-year quest by Europeans to reach the fabled Spice Islands. This quest began with the early Greek traders in the Arabian Sea, followed by the Romans in the Indian Ocean, the Portuguese voyages down the west coast of Africa inspired by Prince Henry the Navigator, and the westward voyage of Christopher Columbus across the Atlantic. There is no record of how Antonio de Abreu and his captains and crew celebrated this historic event, or if they ever made any fine speeches on their arrival in Banda.

The Portuguese found the Bandanese friendly and eager to trade for the goods they had brought from Malacca. They bought a local junk to replace the vessel lost on the outward journey and loaded their ships with nutmeg, mace and some cloves traded from North Maluku. Enjoying the hospitality of the islanders, they stayed a month in Banda waiting for favourable winds to aid their return journey.

Fully laden, the fleet ran into a storm in the middle of the Banda Sea. The junk captained by Francisco Serrão was separated from the other vessels and started breaking up in the heavy seas. Serrão and his crew of Portuguese and Malay sailors saved their lives by running the vessel onto a small islet in the Lucipara Shoals. According to legend, the Portuguese then ambushed some local fishermen as they came ashore to plunder their vessel and forced them to take the shipwrecked crew north to the island of Ambon.

The Portuguese had kept their swords, armour and muskets and were able to impress their Ambonese hosts with their use of modern weaponry. News of their military prowess quickly spread throughout the islands. Curious to meet these fair-skinned foreigners, Sultan Bolief of Ternate sent his brother to persuade the shipwrecked Portuguese to return with him to Ternate. They travelled north in large outrigger canoes known as kora-kora, each manned by up to 100 rower-warriors and flying colourful flags and banners. The crew rowed to the steady beat of drums and cymbals as they made their way up the Patinti Strait with the mainland of Halmahera on one side and the chain of volcanic islands rising out of the sea on the other.

The twin islands of Ternate and Tidore lie at the northern end of this chain, covered in the clove trees that are native to the islands, Francisco Serrão and his comrades could smell the sweet fragrance of clove even before they reached their final destination. When the fair-skinned strangers landed on the island, the Sultan of Ternate embraced every man. Beaming with pleasure and admiration, he lifted his hands to heaven. The contemporary Spanish historian Bartolomé de Argensola quotes him as saying:

These my people, are the warriors you have so longed for on account of my prophecy. Honour them, and let us all vie in entertaining them, since the grandeur of our country depends on their arms.

Francisco Serrão could not have believed his good fortune. After failing to reach Ternate because of the adverse prevailing winds and being shipwrecked for a second time, providence had delivered him to this tropical paradise rich in the valuable spices they sought.

Antonio de Abreau had no idea of the fate of Serrão. His two vessels continued on their return journey, reaching Malacca one year after they had left on this first expedition to the Spice Islands. There, Francisco Rodrigues completed his record of the expedition, including charts and drawings of the islands they visited, and these were discovered as recently as 1937 in the Bibliothèque de l'Assemblèe Nationale de France. He must have had access to Chinese or Malay maps showing a larger part of the world, since his maps include parts of the islands of Sumatra, Borneo and Java, which the expedition did not visit. If they are ever located, these charts might solve the mystery of the extent of the voyages of the Chinese Treasure Fleets. Alfonso de Albuquerque refers to these voyages in a letter he wrote to King Manuel:

> Your Highness can truly see where the Chinese and the Gores [Taiwanese] come from, and the course your ships must take to the Clove Islands, and where the gold mines lie, and the islands of Java and Banda, of nutmeg and maces, and the land of the King of Siam, and also the end of the navigation of the Chinese, the direction it takes and how they do not navigate further.

Francisco Serrão found his place in this tropical paradise: the Sultan adopted him as his personal counsellor and he became a prominent figure of the royal court. He dressed for state occasions in his military uniform, making a striking contrast with the silk-robed and turbaned dress of the Sultan and his courtiers. He adapted to the slow rhythm of life on Ternate, to the changes in the monsoonal seasons, and the cycle of cultivation and harvest of the clove trees. He is believed to have taken one of the island princesses as a wife, thus consolidating his position in the island hierarchy. This news reached Alfonso de Albuquerque, who wrote from Hormuz that Serrão was alive and in possession of the Clove Islands, which he was governing for the Sultan.

The first ruler of Ternate to adopt an Islamic name was Sultan Zainal Abadin (1480–1500). His instructors were probably trader missionaries who brought their Sunni Islam to the Moluccas, and Serrão observed that it was only the Sultan, his family and his immediate followers who had become Muslims. After these Arab traders reached the Spice Islands in their search for cloves and nutmeg, Islam also reached the end of its long journey eastwards and today the islands of Maluku are the remotest part of the Islamic world, far from Mohammed's birthplace on the Arabian Peninsula.

A Portuguese fleet under the command of Antonio de Miranda de Azevedo reached

Banda in 1513, but it was not until 1515 that two vessels under the command of Alvaro Coelho reached Ternate. They returned to Malacca laden with cloves, as well as some of the Serrão crew and letters from Francisco Serrão to Alphonso de Albquerque, Rui de Brito the Governor of Malacca, and Ferdinand Magellan.

In a letter to the Portuguese King, Sultan Bolief wrote that he would entrust him with his land and all in it if the Portuguese would build a fortress on Ternate and provide him with arms. The Sultan had been quick to see how he could use the firearms and military prowess of the Portuguese to strengthen his own power in the region.

Having gained a position of influence on the island, Francisco Serrão refused orders from his superiors to return to Malacca. The Portuguese commanders were no longer sure where his true loyalties lay. Some thought he had pretensions of becoming a White Rajah, but as long as he was working in their common interests it was better to leave him alone.

In 1518, the Portuguese reached an agreement with Sultan Bolief to establish a permanent trading post on Ternate, to supply him with arms and build a fortress on the island in exchange for what the Portuguese expected would be a monopoly on the clove trade. So it was that almost 100 years from the days and dreams of Prince Henry the Navigator and their first forays down the west coast of Africa, the Portuguese had not only reached the Spice Islands but were about to establish a permanent presence there.

The Portuguese now had some control over the trade in cloves, nutmeg and mace, all the way from their source in the Spice Islands to Lisbon. However, their control of the Indian Ocean was incomplete and ships from ports such as Aceh in North Sumatra continued to run the Portuguese blockade and carry spices directly to Aden and the Red Sea. For most of the sixteenth century the Portuguese accounted for about 75 percent of the spices brought to Europe and, contrary to all predictions, the spice trade through Venice via the traditional routes through the Red Sea or the Persian Gulf accounted for the other 25 percent. The Portuguese never undercut prices in Europe, as feared by the Venetians, because King Manuel needed to recover the increasing costs of his Empire of India, based in Goa.

It is interesting to speculate on the actual value of cloves and for this we have some information from an early resident of Malacca, Tomé Pires. In his book *Suma Oriental* he states that trade goods purchased in Malacca for one cruzado could be traded in Ternate for one bahar (approx 800 kg) of cloves, which was then worth 10 cruzados in Malacca. Since the price of cloves went up ten times between Ternate and Malacca, and if we assume the price went up another ten times between Malacca and Goa, and another ten times between Goa and Lisbon, then one kilogram of cloves worth $1 in Ternate could be worth $10 in Malacca, $100 in Goa and $1000 in Lisbon, an increase of 1000 percent.

In Malacca, Ferdinand Magellan received letters from his comrade Francisco Serrão describing his life on Ternate, the position of influence he had obtained with the Sultan and the riches that would accrue to him through the clove trade. No doubt he asked his lifelong friend and comrade to join him in the new life he had established in the fabled Spice Islands.

11   Ferdinand Magellan

Magellan was perfectly certain to find the Strait because he had seen it on a nautical chart made by one Martin Behaim, a great pilot and cosmographer, in the treasury of the King of Portugal, and depicted just as he had found it.

And, because the said Strait was within the boundaries of the sovereigns of Spain, he therefore had to move and offer his services to the King of Spain to discover a new route to the said islands of Molucca and the rest.

—Antonio Pigafetta, *Magellan's Voyage*, 1525

Ferdinand Magellan was born in 1480 into a Portuguese noble family. He received his education at the court of King John II and, like many young nobles, could have looked forward to a military command or diplomatic post. Instead, he began his career as a soldier and adventurer by joining the 1505 armada to India under the command of Francisco de Almeida. He was a captain in the first expedition to Malacca, led by Diego Lopez de Sequeria, and then in the second expedition commanded by Admiral Alfonso de Albuquerque, fighting in the battle that led to the Portuguese capture of Malacca.

Ordered to return to Lisbon, Magellan was denied any chance of joining Francisco Serrão in Ternate and learned the Portuguese viceroy now considered his friend a renegade, since he had refused orders to return to Malacca.

From Lisbon he was sent as part of an expeditionary force to Morocco, but returned from there embittered after being wounded and facing trumped-up charges of corruption related to his position as quartermaster. Magellan felt humiliated and was at the lowest point of his career. Hoping to redeem himself, he sought an audience with King Manuel, but his strident demands for compensation and recognition of his lifelong service to the crown made a bad situation even worse and the meeting ended with Magellan being told that the King no longer valued his services.

It is a measure of Magellan's determination that he made the decision to go into exile and bring his knowledge, experience and ambition to reach the Spice Islands to the rival court of Spain. He arrived in Seville in October 1517, bringing valuable information for the Spanish; this included his letters from Francisco Serrão describing Ternate and the Moluccas, as well as charts of the Java and Banda Seas he had obtained from the de Abreu expedition. However, what really caught the attention of the Spanish was a globe constructed by the Portuguese cartographers Pedro and Jorge Reinel, which showed that the Spice Islands could lie within Spain's half of the world as determined by the Treaty of Tordesillas. The Portuguese considered all this information a state secret, the penalty for disclosure was execution, but Magellan had made his decision and there was no turning back.

Magellan needed a sponsor in Spain, and soon after arriving in Seville he met a Portuguese expatriate named Diogo Barbosa. A long-time resident of Spain, Barbosa was now a Knight Commander of the Order of Santiago, and within a year Magellan had married his daughter, Beatriz. With the backing of the Barbosa family he was now able to meet with officials of the powerful Casa de Contratación, or House of Trade. With their support secured, Magellan arrived in the Spanish capital in January 1518 to the meet with the King's ministers and to propose his audacious voyage to King Carlos.

Magellan laid out his maps and the globe to show his proposed voyage before the King. He showed him the letters from Francisco Serraō describing the Spice Islands and their location. He even introduced the King to his personal Malay slave Enrique, whom he had acquired in Malacca and who would act as interpreter when they reached the Moluccas. Just as Christopher Columbus had convinced King Ferdinand before him, Ferdinand Magellan convinced King Carlos that there was an alternative route to the Indies by sailing west around the world, and that the riches of the Spice Islands rightfully belonged to Spain. Of course, he was telling the King exactly what he wanted to hear, for if the voyage were successful the Spanish would be able to seize the trade in spices from the Portuguese and the Venetians.

The influential German trading group known as the House of Fugger had financed the early Portuguese voyages to India but withdrew from Lisbon in protest at the imposition of the crown monopoly. Since then the group's commercial representative in Seville had encouraged Spain to challenge the Portuguese spice monopoly by following Columbus's route westward to the Spice Islands.

King Carlos was not only enthusiastic about what Magellan showed him, but already had the financial backing of the House of Fugger to put his plan into action. Events moved quickly. It took only two months of deliberation for the King to award Magellan's commission in March 1518. Magellan must have found it hard to believe his good fortune, for the King appointed him captain-general of the expedition as well as granting him one-twentieth of the profits and the right of governorship of any new lands he might discover.

Five ships were found, but they were small and needed extensive refitting to make them suitable for such a voyage. They would be provisioned for two years and manned by 237 officers and crew. Magellan called on the seafaring experience of some of his fellow compatriots as two of the five captains and 37 of the crew were Portuguese.

At the last minute Antonio Pigafetta, a young Italian from a noble family of Vicenza and part of a papal embassy to the court of King Carlos, joined the fleet. After hearing of the expedition he obtained permission from the King as well as his master to volunteer for the voyage, a fortunate occurrence because Pigafetta's journal is one of the few surviving documents telling of the world's greatest voyage of maritime exploration.

When news of Magellan's commission reached Portugal, alarm bells started ringing. The ambassador to Spain tried to convince Magellan to return to Portugal and relinquish his plans to sail for the Spanish. Magellan suspected, probably correctly, that if he returned to Portugal his fate would be gaol, trial for treason and a swift execution.

After more than a year of preparation and numerous delays, the Armada de Molucca was finally ready to depart and received the following letter of command from King Carlos:

> In as much as I know for certain, according to the information which I have obtained from persons who have seen it by experience, that there are spices in the islands of Maluco; and chiefly, you are going to seek them with this said fleet, and my will is that you should straightway follow the voyage to the said islands … I command you all and each one of you that in the navigation of the said voyage you follow the opinion and determination of the said Ferdinand de Magallams, in order that first and foremost, before any other part, you should go to the said islands of Maluco, without any shortcoming in this, because thus it is fitting for our service.

Just before their departure, Juan de Cartagena was appointed captain of the *San Antonio* and inspector-general of the armada. Having neither rank nor experience, Cartagena owed his position to being a relative of the powerful Bishop Fonseca, who controlled the Casa de Contratación (allegedly one of his illegitimate sons).

There is a portrait of Magellan, probably painted in Seville before his departure for the Moluccas, showing him looking serious but relaxed. Magellan was apparently rather short and walked with a limp as a result of a battle injury. An unimposing figure, he lacked any aura of authority, which may have been one of the reasons for his ensuing difficulties with the Spanish captains.

Pigafetta wrote in his journal of the address Magellan gave to his captains and crew before their departure from Seville:

> The captain-general, a wise and virtuous man and mindful of his honour, would not begin his voyage without first issuing some good and honourable regulations, as it is the good custom to make for those who go to sea. But he did not wholly declare the voyage which he wished to make, lest the people from astonishment and fear refuse to accompany him on so long a voyage as he had in mind to undertake, in view of the great and violent storms of the Ocean Sea wither he would go. And for another reason also. For the masters and captains of the other ships of his company loved him not. I do not know the reason, unless it be that, the captain-general was Portuguese, and they were Spaniards or Castilian which people have long born ill-will and malevolence toward one another.

Five ships, the *Trinidad, Victoria, San Antonio, Concepción* and *Santiago*, all painted black and under the command of Ferdinand Magellan, left the Castilian port of San Lucar de Barrameda on 10 August 1519 heading into the South Atlantic. Their orders were to find a western route to the Spice Islands, a route that Columbus had ventured to find almost 30 years earlier.

Understanding of the geography of the world had changed since that time, for after the discovery of the Americas, the Spanish explorer Vasco Balboa had crossed the Isthmus of Panama in 1513 and seen the great expanse of the Pacific Ocean laid out before him. Furthermore, in 1515 a Spanish expedition commanded by Juan Diaz de Solis had explored the South American coast, reaching as far south as the entrance to the Rio de la Plata between Uruguay and Argentina, and returned believing this could be the entrance of a western passage to the Pacific Ocean.

Pigafetta kept his journal from the moment Magellan's expedition left Seville. It evolved from a routine diary of life at sea to a graphic chronicle of the fate of the expedition. He had the wisdom to see the major flaw in the expedition, one that might ultimately determine its fate. This was the contempt the Spanish had for the Portuguese and their unwillingness to submit to Magellan as their commander.

Two interesting events occurred during the Atlantic crossing. The master of the *Victoria* was caught in the act of sodomizing a cabin boy. This was probably not such an unusual event amongst sailors confined for months together at sea, but since they were caught in flagrante delicto, this mortal sin could not be ignored. Under Spanish law the only punishment was death, and Magellan ruled that Antonio Salamón be hanged and his body committed to the Atlantic Ocean. Next, Juan de Cartagena the newly appointed captain of the *San Antonio,* chose to ignore orders issued by Magellan. As captain-general of the expedition, Magellan quickly exerted his authority by arresting Cartagena and having him manacled and imprisoned aboard the captain's own ship. But this would not be the end of the problem.

The fleet arrived at the mouth of the Rio de Janeiro in Brazil in December 1519. Although the region had been claimed by Portugal, there were no signs of a Portuguese presence and Magellan felt secure enough to drop anchor, reprovision his ships and let the crew enjoy the welcoming pleasures of the Indian women.

Continuing down the coast, the expedition explored the estuary of the Rio de la Plata before it turned to fresh water, thus ruling out any possibility of it being a channel westwards to the Pacific. By March 1520, the armada had reached 49 degrees south and was already facing a battering from storms and heavy seas. It was now in uncharted waters and Magellan sailed south only by day so as not to miss the passage to the west that he was convinced existed. The days were getting shorter, the temperatures colder and the storms more ferocious. To continue would put the whole expedition at risk, and Magellan decided it would be prudent to winter in a sheltered bay he named Port St Julian.

The armada would need to conserve its limited stores of food and wine over the winter. For the captains and crew already hostile to Magellan, enduring a long cold winter on half rations was the last straw. Pigafetta's journal reads:

> Now in this harbour much dissatisfaction and mistrust grew up against Magellan. Immediately after we had dropped anchor, he gave orders for dwellings to be erected on the shore; he also ordered a cut in rations, to ensure that our food supplies would last the winter. The captains and the crews objected to both these orders, and the dissatisfied demanded to return home.

What followed was a Spanish-led mutiny. The captain of the *Concepción*, Gaspar de Quesada, and some of his men boarded the *San Antonio,* taking command of the vessel and releasing Juan de Cartagena, who had been imprisoned by Magellan for insubordination. The mutiny soon spread to the *Victoria,* whose captain, Luis de Mendoza, resented Magellan. But the *Santiago* under the command of a Spaniard named Juan Serrano remained neutral.

That left only his own flagship, the *Trinidad*, loyal to Magellan and the situation seemed desperate. With his usual determination, Magellan acted swiftly, sending two longboats to the *Victoria.* The first one, led by his master-at-arms, Gonzalo Gomez de Espinosa, was filled with men who might be considered sympathetic to the mutineers and carried a letter from Magellan to Mendoza. A second longboat, sent to follow them, was filled with Magellan's most trusted men, those who were ready to die for their captain-general. Luis de Mendoza allowed the first party to board the ship and the events that followed are described by Gines de Mafra, a seaman on board the *Trinidad*, in his diary:

> Mendoza, a daring man when it came to evil deeds but too rash to take advice, told them to come aboard and give him the letter, which he set about reading in a careless manner, and not as befits a man involved in such serious business. Mendoza responded to the letter with mockery and laughter, crumpled the orders into a ball and tossed it overboard. Espinosa then grabbed Mendoza by the beard and stabbed him in the throat.

The crew of the second longboat stormed the ship and, by raising Magellan's colours to *Victoria*'s mast, announced to Gaspar de Quesada and the other mutineers that the advantage had turned against them.

The *Concepción* and the *San Antonio* remained at the far end of the harbour while the *Trinidad*, the *Victoria* and the *Santiago* blockaded the entrance. The mutineers would have to fight their way out. Magellan doubled the watch and readied the three vessels for combat. Waiting until nightfall, he sent some seamen to cut the anchor moorings of the *Concepción*, knowing that on the ebb tide she would drift towards the entrance of the harbour and his waiting ships. As the *Concepción* drifted towards them, Magellan's men boarded the vessel and, meeting very little resistance, were able to arrest Gaspar de

Quesada and his henchmen. The *San Antonio* and Juan de Cartagena were now isolated and had no choice but to surrender.

Magellan survived the mutiny, reinforced his authority, and his justice was swift and terrible. The body of Luis de Mendoza was drawn and quartered on the deck of the Trinidad in front of all the captains and crew. Gaspar de Quesada was to be beheaded and his servant and co-conspirator, Luis de Molina, was given a brutal choice, either execute his master or die along with him. Begging his master's forgiveness, Molina cut off Quesada's head in front of the assembled crew.

A more difficult choice awaited Juan de Cartagena, the former captain of the *San Antonio* and inspector-general of the fleet, who had been appointed to the armada because of his blood ties to the powerful Bishop Fonseca. Magellan had to devise a different fate, and it was a fate probably far worse than a swift execution. Juan de Cartagena, together with a disloyal priest named Pero Sanchez, were abandoned in the remote wilderness of Port St Julian and never heard of again. The remaining 40 mutineers including Juan Sebastian Elcano were all sentenced to death, but these were much-needed hands and their sentences were commuted to hard labour, including working the pumps and cleaning out the putrid bilges.

In August 1520, after more than five months in the confines of Port St Julian, four ships of the Armada de Molucca resumed their voyage south, since the *Santiago* had been shipwrecked while exploring down the coast. After only three days sailing they reached a small inlet leading to a series of westward trending bays.

The Strait of Magellan as it is now called, is a series of interlinking waterways extending for 660 kilometres between the Atlantic and the Pacific Oceans. In places it is only two kilometres wide. The frigid waters of the strait are surrounded by bleak, windswept prairies in the east, and its deep fjords are lined by dark forests of Antarctic beech in the west. Glaciers spawned off the southern Andes flow into the strait, creating walls of solid ice that rise above its waters. The Strait of Magellan separates Patagonia from Tierra del Fuego, and sailing through the narrow waterway against the prevailing westerly winds and without room for tacking can be extremely difficult. The alternative is an even more hazardous journey around Cape Horn, where the waters of the Atlantic and Pacific Oceans clash, creating mountainous waves, and ships come face to face with the ferocious winds of the Roaring Forties. The map drawn by Antonio Pigafetta is oriented with south to the top of the page and he names it the Patagonia Strait.

Finding the correct passage through this uncharted maze of waterways was a challenge, and Pigafetta wrote in his journal:

> After going and setting course to the fifty-second degree toward the said Antarctic Pole we found by miracle a strait … Which strait is in length one hundred and ten leagues, and in width somewhat less than half a league. And it falls into another sea called the Pacific Sea. And it is surrounded by very great

and high mountains covered with snow. In this place, it was not possible to anchor, because no bottom was found. Wherefore it was necessary to put cables ashore of twenty-five or thirty cubits in length. This strait was a circular place surrounded by mountains, and to most of those in the ships, it seemed that there was no way out from it to enter the said Pacific Sea … The captain sent forward two of his ships, one named the *San Antonio* and the other the *Concepcion*, to seek and discover the outlet of the said strait … we thought indeed that they had perished, first because of the great storm, and then we had not seen them for two days. And while in suspense, we saw the two ships approaching under full sail and flying their banners, coming towards us. When near us, they suddenly discharged their ordnance at which we very joyously greeted them in the same way. And then we all together, thanking God and the Virgin Mary, went forward.

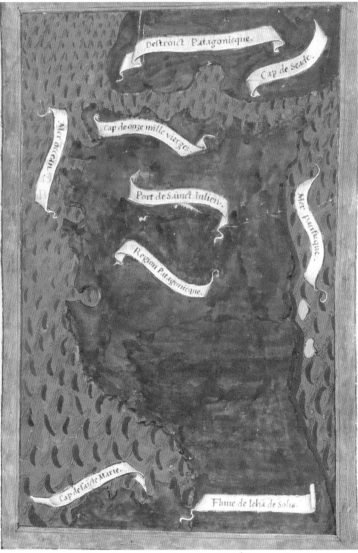

Map of the Strait of Magellan, Antonio Pigafetta, 1525 (Beinecke Rare Book and Manuscript Library, Yale University)

The pilot of the *San Antonio*, Estavao Gomez, believed that since the armada had confirmed the existence of the strait, it should return to Spain to assemble a new fleet and be better prepared to face the unknown crossing of the Pacific Ocean. Magellan ordered the *San Antonio*, captained by Alvaro de Mesquita, to reconnoitre another outlet to the south and to rejoin them again on the north side of Broad Lake. The *San Antonio* never returned and Magellan had to conclude that, under the cover of darkness, its captain, pilot and crew had set sail for Spain.

Basing their calculations on the Reinel globe, the Martin Behaim globe, Ptolemy's estimation of the circumference of the earth and the estimation of the breadth of the Asian continent from the travels of Marco Polo, Magellan and his pilots felt sure that they were now within striking distance of the Spice Islands. The armada, now reduced to three vessels and 200 men, decided to proceed, not knowing the enormous breadth of the Pacific Ocean and how much misery and suffering lay ahead.

Taking a north-westerly course, the armada crossed the equator by February 1521. Magellan was utterly confounded, as he had expected to reach the Moluccas by this time. Even worse was the fact that the further west they sailed the more likely it was that the islands lay in Portuguese territory. At some point Magellan flung his charts into the sea, crying in despair that the Moluccas were not to be found in their appointed place.

During their course across the Pacific the armada passed only two uninhabited islands, missing every one of the island groups where they could have reprovisioned, and both ships and crew were now barely functional. Suffering from thirst and hunger, they had lost 29 men to scurvy, which Pigafetta describes as the worst of misfortunes. The gums of some of the men swelled over their upper and lower teeth so they could not eat. It was three months and twenty days before they finally sighted the island of Guam, where the fruit and vegetables they obtained began to restore the crew to health. In April 1521, the Armada de Molucca entered the port of Cebu in the Philippines and, after an exchange of emissaries, Magellan went ashore with his entourage to meet Humabon, the King of Cebu. Dressed in regal splendour, with a large gold necklace and two gold earrings, Humabon received his foreign guests and invited them to a meal that included turtle eggs and palm wine. Afterwards the captains were invited to the king's hut for an evening of entertainment. As they entered, four young girls were playing music on metal gongs. Pigafetta describes the scene:

> Those girls were very beautiful and almost as white as our girls and as large. They were naked except for palm cloth hanging from the waist and reaching to the knees. Some were quite naked and had large holes in their ears with a small piece of wood in the hole … They had long black hair, and wear a short cloth about the head, and are always barefoot. The prince had three quite naked girls dance for us.

Pigafetta puts his own emphasis on the 'quite naked girls' by mentioning them three times in his account and leaves little doubt about the outcome of the evening, or the similar celebrations of mutual goodwill that were taking place elsewhere between the sailors and the island beauties. Later he confided to his journal that he and the other crew members had been intimate with the women of Cebu and could not resist describing the bizarre sexual customs of the island, including the use of the 'palang':

> The males large and small, have their penis pierced from one side to the other near the head, with a gold or tin bolt as large as a goose quill. In both ends of the same bolt, some have what resembles a spur, with points upon the ends; others are like the head of a cart nail. I very often asked many, both old and young, to see their penis, because I could not credit it. In the middle of the bolt is a hole, through which they urinate. The bolt and the spurs always hold firm.

Pigafetta explains how the palang enhanced the sexual experience for men and women, prolonging lovemaking for hours as the couple are locked in an embrace of passion, unable to make any sudden movements or withdraw the penis.

After a number of weeks in Cebu, it became clear that Magellan had plans to make the island the central base for the Spanish in the Philippines. He now had the advantage of an interpreter: as Enrique his slave and manservant was able to communicate in Malay, the traditional trading language used throughout the archipelago. Magellan arranged for King Humabon and several thousand of his people to be converted to Christianity. Exhorting the King to burn all his idols, he set up a Christian cross in the centre of the village that everyone should worship daily with clasped hands held up to heaven. Now that he had a reliable ally—and a newly baptized Christian one at that—Magellan sent word to the local chiefs that they should pay tribute to Humabon and submit to his rule, which meant Spanish rule.

Magellan's letter of command from King Carlos clearly stated that he should go directly to the Moluccas without any deviating. He had already shown the natives examples of the spices he was seeking: he already knew these were not grown locally and that he would have to travel on to the Moluccas. Yet here he was, within striking distance of the expedition's destination, undertaking mass religious conversions and getting involved in local politics.

Perhaps after crossing the immense Pacific Ocean, Magellan and his pilots were convinced that the Moluccas lay within the Portuguese half of the world and that there would be little advantage in pressing on to the Spice Islands. Perhaps he was already struck by gold fever, as according to Pigafetta's description of Cebu:

> In the island of that king who came to the ship are mines of gold, which is found by digging from the earth large pieces as large as walnuts and eggs. And all the vessels he uses are likewise of gold, as are also some parts of his house, which was well fitted in the fashion of the country. And he was the most

The *Victoria* crossing the Pacific Ocean, Abraham Ortelius, 1592 (National Library of Australia, nla.map-nk1528)

handsome person whom we saw among these peoples. He had very black hair to his shoulders, with a silk cloth on his head, and two large gold rings hanging from his ears. He wore a cotton cloth, embroided with silk, which covered him from his waist to his knees. At his side he had a dagger, with a long handle and all of gold.

Magellan probably planned to establish his governorship of Cebu and his right to one twentieth of the ensuing profits according to the royal charter. Whatever Magellan's plan, it ran into a problem when Lapulapu, a chief on the island of Mactan, refused to pay tribute and submit to Humabon's rule, daring the Spanish to attack.

Magellan had no reason to believe that his superior arms would not prevail in the ensuing battle, but his officers warned him they had already suffered many casualties in crossing the Pacific and this was an unnecessary sideshow with no strategic purpose.

On that fateful day, Magellan was forced to lead a small party of 49 of his most faithful followers against Lapulapu. Eleven decided to stay and guard their small boats while the remaining 38 men waded ashore to make battle with over 1000 armed warriors. The ships of the Armada de Molucca remained at anchor in deep water, too far away to provide the artillery support that might have frightened off the native warriors. Pigafetta describes the events of 27 April 1521:

> When the day came, we leapt into the water, being forty-nine men, and so we went for a distance of two crossbow flights before we could reach the harbour, and the boats could not come further inshore because of the stones and rocks that were in the water. The other eleven men guarded the boats. Having thus reached land, we attacked them. These people had formed three divisions, of more than one thousand and fifty persons. And immediately they perceived us, they came about with loud voices and cries, two divisions on our flanks, and one around and before us … they fired at us so many arrows, and lances of bamboo tipped with iron, and pointed stakes hardened by fire, and stones, that we could hardly defend ourselves … Then they came so furiously against us that they sent a poisoned arrow through the captain's leg … On this they all at once rushed upon him with lances of iron and bamboo and with these javelins, so that they slew our mirror, our light, our comfort and our true guide.

Magellan and eight others were killed in the battle and their bodies floated unrecovered in the sea while his armada stood by and watched. Magellan's vision and determination against all odds to find a western route to the Spice Islands came to this sorry end in Mactan harbour, and Pigafetta wrote an epitaph for his captain-general:

> So noble a captain … he was more constant than anyone else in adversity. He endured hunger better than all the others, and better than any man in the world did he understand sea charts and navigation.

Two men emerged as the new leaders of the expedition, Duarte Barbosa, Magellan's brother-in-law, and Juan Serrano, the Castilian captain of the *Santiago* who had remained neutral during the mutiny at Port St Julian.

Magellan had written his will before leaving Seville, specifying that from the day of his death his slave Enrique would be free and relieved of every obligation and subjection. Suffering from battle wounds and bereft at the loss of his master and protector, Enrique remained in his bunk, declaring he was a free man and refusing to act as an emissary and interpreter as ordered by Barbosa and Serrano. In reply, they insisted that even with his master dead, he remained a slave and would be whipped if he did not obey their orders.

With his Spanish allies now preparing to leave Cebu, Humabon found himself at the mercy of the other island chiefs, especially the newly emboldened Lapulapu. Plotting against the expedition was the only way for him to demonstrate his loyalty to his fellow chiefs and save his own kingdom. He invited the Spanish to a farewell banquet and, possibly with the collusion of Enrique, had them all massacred. Thus did the Spanish lose a further 27 of their most prominent crew members, including both their new leaders. Enrique was never heard from again.

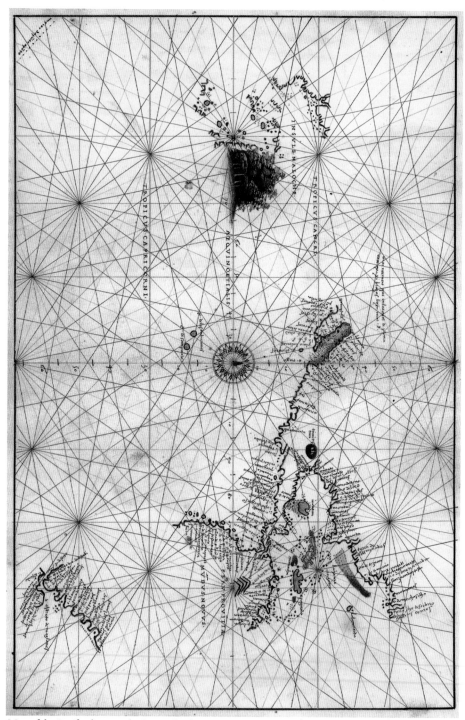

Map of the Pacific showing the Spice Islands, Battista Agnese, 1544 (Library of Congress)

Ignoring the desperate cries of their dying comrades, those remaining on board the vessels of the armada lost no time in departing Cebu. João Lopez Carvalho assumed command and, with only enough men to crew two vessels, he scuttled and burnt the *Concepción*. Without Magellan's determined leadership, the armada then spent eight months wandering the Sulu Sea, sailing as far south and east as Brunei, and committing acts of piracy against Chinese junks before reaching their destination.

The *Victoria* and *Trinidad* arrived in the Moluccas just before sunset on 8 November 1521. Casting anchor off the island of Tidore, the two remaining vessels of the Armada de Molucca discharged their artillery in celebration, for their 27-month-voyage had brought them halfway around the world before finally reaching the Spice Islands.

The 1544 map by Battista Agnese shows what was known of the Americas, including the Strait of Magellan, and an empty Pacific Ocean except for two small islands. It is highlighted by a lavish display of green, representing the clove trees of the Spice Islands.

12   *Juan Sebastian Elcano*

That your most illustrious Lordship may know the islands where the cloves grow; there are five of them, namely Ternate, Tidore, Motir, Machian and Bacan.

Ternate is the first and principal one.

And when its king was alive he was the master of nearly all the others.

Tidore was the island where we were, which has its king as we have said.

All that province where the cloves grow is named Molucca.

—Antonio Pigafetta, from his report to King Carlos of Spain, 1522

Rising directly out of the sea before the armada lay the volcanic island of Tidore. As the setting sun coloured the sky, the sailors could see before them forests of clove trees covering the slopes of the volcano and smell the scent of exotic spices that filled the air.

The next day the armada had a royal visitor. The description by Antonio Pigafetta clearly demonstrates the wealth the Sultan of Tidore had derived from the clove trade:

Next day the King came to the ships in a prahu, and went around them. We met him in a boat to show him honour, and he made us enter his prahu and sit near him. He was sitting under a silk umbrella, which sheltered him. In front of him was his son with the royal sceptre, there was also two men with gold vases to give him water for his hands, and two others with gilt caskets full of betel. The King gave us a welcome, and said that from a long time back he had dreamed that some ships were coming to Molucca from distant countries and that to assure himself with respect to this he had examined the moon, and that he had seen that they were really coming, and that they indeed were our ships.

The captains knelt and kissed the Sultan's hand. They had him seated in a chair of red velvet and clad him in a robe of turquoise-yellow silk. Other gifts included scarlet cloth, crimson satin, yellow damask and fine white linen, as well as six crystal glasses and other goods. Sultan Almanzor told the captains that he and his people desired to be true friends and loyal vassals of the King of Spain, and he had dreamt of ships coming from distant and strange parts to the Moluccas. The Sultan was obviously eager to receive Spanish support to counter the Portuguese pledge to supply Ternate with arms and build a fortress.

While the Armada de Molucca had reached its destination, Magellan had been killed before he could accomplish his dream of reaching the Spice Islands to meet his friend Francisco Serrão. Pigafetta describes their relationship:

> Francisco Serrão was a great friend and relative of our good and loyal dead captain-general, and was the cause for moving him to make this enterprise and voyage, because he had several times, when our captain was at Malacca, written to tell him he was there. Since Dom Manuel, then King of Portugal, refused to increase the pensions and pay of our said captain-general by more than one testoon a month in spite of all his feats and merits, he came to Spain where he received from his Sacred Majesty all that he would ask.

The next evening, a gaunt-looking figure clad in native dress paddled a dugout canoe towards their vessels. The Spanish would not have recognized him as a compatriot until he hailed them in Portuguese. This was Pedro de Lorosa, the last of the shipwrecked Portuguese sailors who had reached Ternate with Francisco Serrão eleven years earlier and who was now the only Portuguese remaining on the island. He told the Spanish that Francisco Serrão had died eight months earlier and he suspected his death was murder. Anxious to communicate in his native tongue, he talked until early the next morning, telling tales of his adventures in the Spice Islands. He told how Francisco Serrão had brokered a peace between Ternate and Tidore that required the Sultan of Tidore to grant one of his daughters as a wife to the Sultan of Ternate and to give up almost all the children of his chief men as hostages. This agreement caused continuing resentment on Tidore, and Pedro de Lorosa believed the island chiefs conspired to lure Francisco Serrão to Tidore to buy cloves and then had him poisoned.

This was a harsh introduction to the intense rivalry between the twin islands. Remembering the treachery that led to the recent deaths of their comrades on Cebu, the Spanish vowed to be very careful in their dealings with the Sultan and his people. Not wishing to delay their stay on the island, the Spanish indicated they were anxious to begin trading. Pigafetta wrote:

> On Tuesday the 12th of November, the king caused a house to be constructed in one day to take our merchandise, and we carried almost all of it thither. And to guard it we left three of our men. Then forthwith we began to trade in this manner. For two cubits of fairly good cloth, we were given a bahar of cloves … For fifteen cubits or pieces of not very good cloth, one bahar. For fifteen axes, one bahar. For thirty-five glasses, one bahar. And the king had all of that. For seventeen cathils of cinnabar, one bahar. For seventeen cathils of quicksilver, one bahar. For twenty-five pieces of linen, one bahar. For twenty-four of finer quality, one bahar. For one hundred and fifty knives, one bahar. For fifty pair of scissors, one bahar. For forty caps, one bahar. For ten ells of Gujarat cloth, one bahar. For a quintal of bronze, one bahar. All the mirrors were broken, but the king wished to have all the small good ones. Many of these goods were from the aforesaid junks that we had taken, and our urgent desire to return to Spain made us trade our goods more cheaply than we should otherwise have done.

The measurements are Asian in origin. One bahar is about 800 kilograms, one quintal is around 45 kilograms, and one cathil or cati is around 1 kilogram. One cubit is equivalent to a metre of cloth and an ell around 1.5 metres of cloth.

The Spanish traded for cloves until they had nothing left to exchange. The scent of the precious cargo loaded onto their ships permeated the air and, to the sailors' delight, masked the usual shipboard smells of bilge water, sweat and rotting food.

Forever the cultural observer, Antonio Pigafetta noted that the Sultan and many of the islanders were Muslims and that the Sultan had 200 wives and 26 children. Pigafetta was now the interpreter for the expedition. A gifted linguist, he learnt much Malay from Enrique and compiled a Malay dictionary of 450 words, which he published together with his journal of the voyage. Pigafetta also had time to explore Tidore and observe the forests of clove trees:

> On that Sunday I went ashore to see how the cloves grow. The tree is tall and as thick across as a man. Its branches in the centre spread out widely, but at the top they grow into a kind of peak. The leaf is that of a laurel, and the bark the colour of brown tan. The cloves come at the tip of the branches, ten or twenty together … When the cloves sprout, they are white; when ripe, red; and when dried black. They gather them twice a year, once at Christmas and again on the feast of St John Baptist … Nowhere in the world do good cloves grow except on five mountains on these five islands, but that some are found in the island of Giailolo, and in an island called Mare, which is a small island between Tidore and Mutir, but they are no good. We saw almost every day a cloud descend and encircle first one of these mountains and then the other, whereby the cloves become more perfect. Each one of these people has trees, and watches over them in his place without cultivating them

Pigafetta sketched a clove tree, which is included together with a map of the Moluccan Islands in his illustrated manuscript entitled *Magellan's Voyage*, published in 1525.

The Spanish now set about reprovisioning the armada for its voyage home. Local boats full of chickens, goats, coconuts, rice and a variety of fruit and vegetables came out to the ships every day. The Spanish exchanged some of their artillery, along with four barrels of gunpowder, for 80 butts of water for each ship. The armada would have to avoid all Portuguese shipping and Portuguese-controlled ports, and would probably be unable to resupply during the voyage home.

After a month on the island, the ships and their precious cargo were ready to leave for Spain, with João Lopez Carvalho in command of the *Trinidad* and Juan Sebastian Elcano in command of the *Victoria*. As the vessels moved out of the harbour the *Trinidad* began taking on water, and the armada's flagship was on the verge of sinking. Without the determined leadership of Magellan, his flagship had fallen into a state of disrepair through sheer neglect and would need extensive repairs. Sultan Almanzor was distraught and cried, 'Who will go to Spain to give the King news of me?' To which they replied that the *Victoria* would continue its voyage in order not to lose the wind.

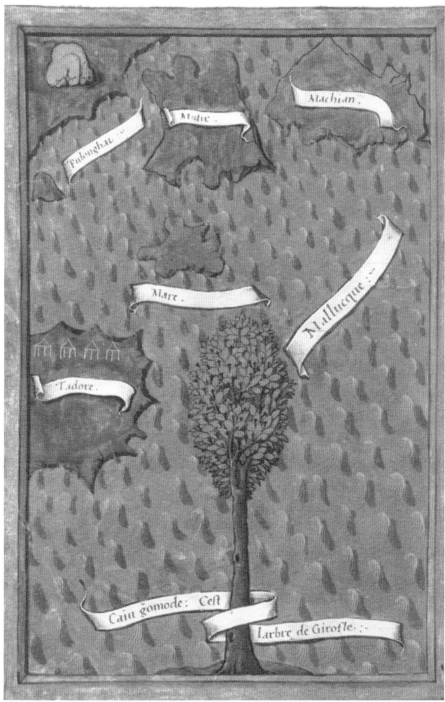

Map of the Moluccas with a clove tree, Antonio Pigafetta, 1525 (Beinecke Rare Book and Manuscript Library, Yale University)

The northerly monsoon had started to blow and the two captains decided that the *Victoria* should immediately depart westwards for the Cape of Good Hope and that, after repairs, the *Trinidad* would sail eastwards across the Pacific. Crew members were free to choose which vessel and captain they thought most likely to survive the hazards of the journey and deliver them safely back to Seville. Sixty of the crew decided to sail immediately aboard the *Victoria*; the remaining 54 decided to wait for the repairs to the *Trinidad* before sailing east.

The two ships would now be alone on the high seas with no support in case of shipwreck, encounters with Portuguese vessels or just the failure of their worm-ridden hulls. The decision by the two captains to return to Spain separately and in opposite directions meant their chances of returning to Seville had gone from small to almost nothing. The *Victoria* sailed from Tidore on 21 December 1521; the remaining crew accompanied the ship a little way in small boats and then bade a tearful farewell as if this was their last parting.

Juan Sebastian Elcano, the captain of the *Victoria*, was born in a coastal town in the Basque country of northern Spain. Accustomed since childhood to life at sea, he later took part in Spanish naval campaigns off Algeria and Italy before taking up trading ventures around the Mediterranean. These were not always successful and, finding himself in financial difficulties, he was forced to surrender his ship to Genoese bankers in repayment of a debt. There may have been other owners of the ship or other debtors, for Elcano faced arrest on his return to Spain and legend has it that he obtained a pardon and release from gaol only by agreeing to join Magellan and the Armada de Molucca.

The *Victoria* first sailed south-west to the island of Timor, where it took on more supplies and traded for sandalwood. It was here that a seaman and a cabin boy deserted ship, preferring an uncertain life in Timor to what would probably be a certain death at sea.

Seeking to avoid Portuguese ships, Elcano set a southerly course across the broad expanse of the Indian Ocean, taking the *Victoria* to almost 40 degrees south where he discovered a 900 metre high lump of volcanic rock, now known as Amsterdam Island. Only halfway towards the Cape of Good Hope and battered by the winds and swells of the Roaring Forties, they hoped to find a secure anchorage at the island to make necessary repairs to their dangerously leaking ship. After days of tacking against the wind, they finally had to abandon their attempt to reach the lee of the island.

Although the epic European voyages of this period have been called the Voyages of Discovery, during the voyage of the Armada de Molucca all the land they 'discovered' was already occupied by indigenous inhabitants. Even the frigid wilds of Tierra del Fuego were populated. So this tiny uninhabited pinnacle of rock in the South Indian Ocean is probably the only land the armada truly discovered.

Rounding the Cape of Good Hope against the prevailing winds was incredibly difficult. A fierce storm brought down the *Victoria*'s foremast and it took the Spanish seven weeks of constant struggle with gigantic waves that threatened to sink their leaking, worm-ridden vessel. Pigafetta describes the ordeal:

> In order to round the Cape of Good Hope we went as far south as forty-two degrees towards the Antarctic Pole. We remained near this Cape for seven weeks with sails furled because of the west and northwest wind on our bow, and in a very great storm … And it is the greatest and most perilous cape in the world. Some of our men, both sick and healthy, wished to go to a place of the Portuguese called Mozambique, because the ship was taking in too much water, and also for the great cold, and still more because we had nothing else to eat except rice and water, since for want of salt the meat that we had was rotten and putrefied. But some others, more mindful of their honour than of their own life, determined to go to Spain alive or dead. At length by God's help, on the sixth of May we passed this Cape at a distance of five leagues from it, and had we not approached so close to it we should never have been able to pass it.

Back in the Atlantic, the *Victoria* sailed a north-westerly course for two months, until in June 1522 she crossed the equator. Within this time 21 of the crew had died of scurvy. With nothing left to eat and the weak and exhausted crew dying around him, Elcano took the risk of putting the *Victoria* into the port of Santiago in the Cape Verde Islands. Because this was Portuguese territory, the Spaniards had to invent a story about being a storm-battered Spanish cargo ship seeking refuge.

Elcano sent some of the crew ashore in a longboat to obtain desperately needed food and water. They learnt the date was Thursday, 10 July 1522. This was puzzling to Pigafetta, as he had scrupulously kept track of the days during their voyage. He wrote:

> We charged our men in the boat that when they were ashore they should ask what day it was. They were answered that to the Portuguese it was Thursday, we were much amazed, since to us it was Wednesday, and we knew not how we had fallen into error, especially since the pilot Alvo and I had both written in our log and diary each day without any intermission.

The explanation is the earth is spinning west to east completing a rotation every day, and since the *Victoria* had been sailing from east to west against this motion, the Spaniards had lost 24 hours in their journey around the world. We now have an International Date Line in the mid-Pacific to allow international travellers to compensate for this effect.

The Spanish only had cloves to trade for food, and the Portuguese authorities soon became suspicious of the true nature of their voyage. While making a second trip ashore in the longboat, thirteen of the crew were detained by the Portuguese. Fearing he and the rest of his men would soon be arrested, Elcano hurriedly weighed anchor and set sail for Spain with only 21 crew left on board.

The last two months of their journey must have been a nightmare, for the *Victoria* was little more than a floating wreck and her crew the living dead. The survivors were forced to man the pumps 24 hours a day to keep the vessel afloat, working the sails to keep her on course drained any remaining energy, and three more men died of hunger and fatigue. It is impossible to describe how the survivors must have felt as they approached Seville, for all would have despaired many times during their voyage around the world of ever sighting their homeland again.

History has described their return to Spain as triumphant, but the condition of the *Victoria* and her wretched crew must have been a pitiful sight. Pigafetta wrote:

> On Saturday the sixth of September, 1522, we entered the Bay of San Lucar, and we were only eighteen men, the most part sick, of the sixty remaining who had left Molucca, some of whom died of hunger, others deserted at the island of Timor, and others had been put to death for their crimes. From the time that we departed from that Bay until the present day we had sailed fourteen thousand four hundred and sixty leagues, and completed the circuit of the world from east to west. On Monday the eighth of September we cast anchor near the Mole of Seville, and there we discharged all the artillery. And on Tuesday we all went, in our shirts and barefoot, and each with a torch in his hand, to visit the shrine of Santa Maria de la Victoria and that of Santa Maria de Antigua.

Detail showing the *Victoria* being guided by an angel, Abraham Ortelius, 1592 (National Library of Australia)

Detail from the map by Ortelius shows the *Victoria* being guided across the Pacific Ocean by an angel. The Latin text reads:

> I was first to circle the world by means of sails,
> Carrying you, Magellan, leader, through the new strait.
>   Therefore am I justly called Victoria [Victory].
> With sails as wings, and glory my prize, I fought the sea.

Of the five ships and 237 men of the Armada de Molucca that had departed from San Lucar de Barrameda three years earlier, the *Victoria* and its eighteen survivors had achieved the greatest voyage in maritime history—the first circumnavigation of the world. These thin and ragged sailors had measured the true dimensions of our planet and turned the concept of a spherical earth by the Greek astronomers such as Eratosthenes and Ptolemy into a hard-won reality. The skill of their captain, Juan Sebastian Elcano, had brought them home, but they would have wished that Magellan were still with them, for without his vision and determination the *Victoria* would never have found the Strait of Magellan or crossed the Pacific. Only a few pages of Pigafetta's journal describe their return journey. Sick from hunger and fatigue, his only priority was survival. He is strangely silent about Juan Sebastian Elcano and we learn nothing about his role as captain during this crucial part of their epic voyage.

Importantly for both King Carlos and the financiers of the armada, the *Victoria* had returned with a full cargo of cloves, nutmeg and sandalwood. The cloves weighed in at 25 tonnes and were of first-grade quality. Valuable proof of the new trade route they had discovered, these were quickly sold in the spice markets of Europe making enough money to cover several times the cost of the entire venture. The captain of the Victoria, Juan Sebastian Elcano, penned his report to King Carlos:

> Most high and illustrious Majesty: Your high Majesty will learn how we eighteen men only have returned with one of the five ships which Your Majesty sent to discover the Spicery with Captain Ferdinand Magellan, to whom we glory; and so that Your Majesty may have news of the principle things which we have passed through. First we reached 54 degrees south of the Equator where we found a Strait which passed through Your Majesties mainland to the sea of India, which Strait is 100 leagues and from which we debouched; and in the time of three months and twenty days, encountering highly favourable winds, and finding no land save two small uninhabited islands; afterward we reached an archipelago of many islands quite abundant in gold. We lost by his death the said Captain Ferdinand Magellan, with many others, and unable to sail for want of people, very few having survived, we dismantled one of the ships and with the other two sailed from island to island, seeking how to arrive, with God's grace, at the isles of Maluco, which we did eight months after the death of the said Captain, and there we loaded two ships with spicery … On our return, we resolved either to die, or honourably serve Your Majesty by informing him of the said discovery, to depart with one ship only, and she in such bad state … The treaties of peace and amity of all the kings and lords of the said islands, signed by their own hands we bring to Your Majesty, for they desire to serve you and obey you as their king and natural sovereign.

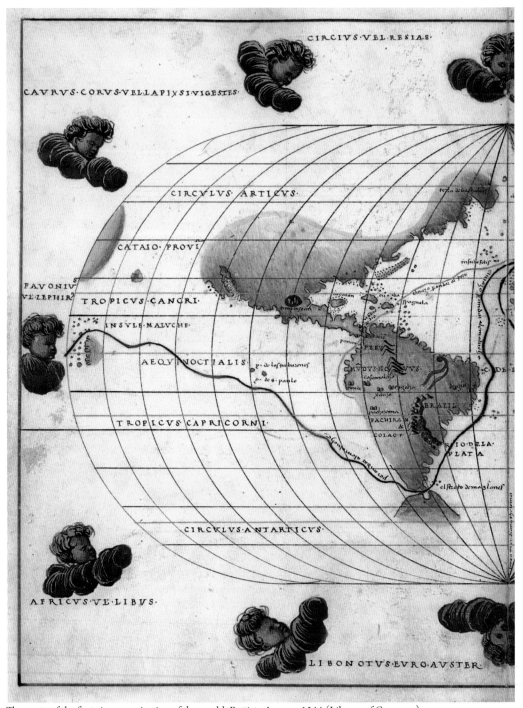

The route of the first circumnavigation of the world, Battista Agnese, 1544 (Library of Congress)

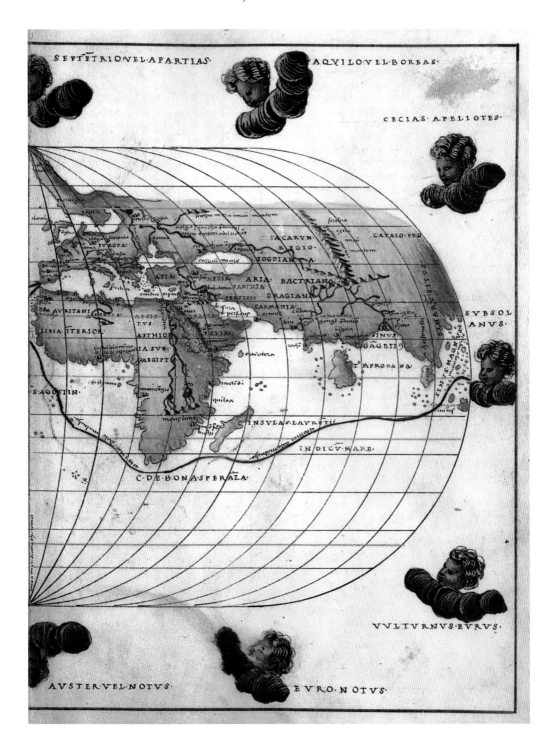

Juan Sebastian Elcano, the gaoled bankrupt and former mutineer, was now exalted as a returning hero. Invited to court, he was rewarded by the King with an annual pension of 500 ducats and granted a coat of arms displaying two crossed cinnamon sticks, three nutmegs and twelve clove buds. But his triumph was to fade into history and today there are many who think that Magellan was the first commander to circumnavigate the world.

Pigafetta travelled to the court separately, declaring that he had a gift for the King that was neither gold nor silver but something that such a sovereign would esteem more highly. And with that he presented King Carlos with a copy of his journal. He then returned to Vicenza in Italy, where he started work on a formal narrative of the voyage based on his journals. He completed his manuscript, entitled *Magellan's Voyage*, in 1525.

Maps were prepared of the voyage and a world similar to the one we know today emerged for the first time. A particularly striking map is that produced by Battista Agnese in Venice around 1544, showing the route of the first circumnavigation of the world. It is interesting that he had no access to Portuguese maps of India and still deferred to Ptolemy for the depiction of India and Sri Lanka. A close look at the map shows the route of the Spanish galleons bringing gold and silver from Peru to the Isthmus of Panama for transhipment to Spain, and the location of Mexico City still surrounded by a vast lake.

13   Ternate and Tidore

Over the Eastern Oceans cast your eyes,
To see where the islands numberless are spread,
Tidore, Ternate, view mountains whence arise,
Flames undulating round the burning head:
Trees of hot clove thou shall behold, likewise,
With blood of Portugal e'en purchased.

—Luis Vas de Camões, *The Lusiads*, 1572

Sultan Almanzor had promised the Spanish enough workmen and shipwrights to refit the *Trinidad* for her return voyage, and after three months work she was now seaworthy. During this time, João Lopez Carvalho had died and the *Trinidad* was now ready to make the Pacific crossing under the command of Gonzalo Gómez de Espinosa. There must have been a Portuguese arrest warrant waiting in Malacca for Pedro Alfonso de Lorosa, since after eleven years of living on Ternate he decided to join the Spanish on their journey back across the Pacific.

Laden with cloves, the *Trinidad* sailed north to the Philippines before turning to make the first eastward crossing of the Pacific. Facing constant headwinds, the crew struggled northwards hoping to pick up some winds to fill their sails for the crossing. After five months at sea the *Trinidad* had made little progress and had already lost more than half her crew to scurvy. Then during a five-day storm, her mainmast was broken in half and the vessel severely damaged. There was no choice but to turn back to the Moluccas. The *Trinidad* limped southward, and after making landfall at Benaconora, in the Southern Philippines, her depleted crewmen were too weak to sail any further.

Shortly after the Spanish had departed from Tidore, a fleet of seven Portuguese vessels dropped anchor off Ternate. On board was the first Portuguese governor of the Moluccas, Antonio de Brito, with orders to build a fort and establish a permanent Portuguese presence on the island. He arrested the four Spaniards who had been left behind on Tidore to operate a trading post, and Sultan Almanzor quickly changed his allegiance back to the Portuguese.

A message from the crew of the *Trinidad* begging for help and supplies reached Tidore and Antonio de Brito. There was no mercy. A fully armed Portuguese caravel stormed Benaconora, arresting Espinosa and his surviving crew and taking possession of the *Trinidad*, including Magellan's logbooks. Pedro Alfonso de Lorosa was executed for whatever sins he had committed, but the Portuguese spared the lives of the Spanish, using them as forced labour to help build the fort. In a touch of irony, much of the timber used to construct the fort and the cannon to protect it came from the *Trinidad*, the flagship of the Armada de Molucca and a symbol of Spanish sea power.

The Portuguese finished building the fort in February 1523. In the opening ceremony Antonio de Brito declared Sultan Bolief to be the greatest servant of his Highness the King of Portugal, and that he would become the 'Lord of all the Isles'.

Under successive Portuguese governors, the fort, which became known as Fort Gamalama, grew to include a walled town, with facilities for the storage of cloves and other goods, as well as residences for the governor, soldiers, sailors, merchants, artisans, wives and children. The fort and its town provided a secure Portuguese enclave within an alien and often hostile land and became a symbol of Portuguese control of the Spice Islands.

Antonio de Brito had orders from his king to enforce a crown monopoly on the clove trade, a policy that was not only immoral but also impractical. All the Portuguese on the island, including the governor and his officials, were busy trading in cloves for their own personal profit. The Sultan and the islanders were equally busy ignoring the Portuguese monopoly and trading cloves with traditional Javanese traders. These traditional traders were essential to life on the island, since they brought rice and other necessities of daily life on Ternate that the Portuguese were not interested in providing.

The Moluccans had previously harvested cloves by breaking the clove-bearing stems and carrying them in baskets to waiting ships. The Portuguese introduced new methods—handpicking the clove buds, drying them until they turned black in the sun, and then bagging and storing them in readiness for the next Portuguese ship.

Every year the Royal Clove Ship departed Goa in April, arriving in Ternate after the clove harvest had finished in October. Following the loading of cloves in Ternate and nutmeg in Banda, the ship sheltered in the Bay of Ambon, waiting for the trade winds to change in favour of the return voyage. Leaving Ambon in May, the vessel returned to Goa in time to rendezvous with the spice ships leaving for Portugal.

An idea of the size of the cargo of these Lisbon-bound spice ships was given when the English captured a Portuguese vessel, the *Madre de Deus*, off the Azores in 1592. An inventory of the cargo showed she carried 425 tonnes of pepper, 45 tonnes of cloves, 35 tonnes of cinnamon, 3 tonnes of mace, 3 tonnes of nutmeg, 25 tonnes of cochineal and

2.5 tonnes of benjamin (an aromatic resin), as well as ebony, ivory, pearls and precious jewels. The cargo value of this single ship was estimated at half a million pounds, almost half of England's treasury at the time.

At first the islands might have seemed to be a peaceful and idyllic tropical paradise, fanned by a gentle sea breeze scented by exotic spices, with a compliant population that could easily be controlled by a powerful colonial master. However, the Portuguese quickly found themselves embroiled in the rivalry and intrigues from within the Sultan's court and between the twin islands of Ternate and Tidore.

After the death of Sultan Bolief, his brother Prince Darwis ruled as regent on behalf of the two young heirs to the throne. The Queen Mother, Niay Tsjili, a princess of Tidore and opposed to Prince Darwis, aimed to unite the islands of Ternate and Tidore under the rule of one of her sons. Antonio de Brito became caught up in the conspiracies of these two formidable antagonists and in the end found himself isolated in the fort, surrounded by not only hostile Ternateans but also by mutinous Portuguese. He had little choice but to petition Goa for his recall and replacement.

The new governor, Garcias Hendrik, decided to bring peace to the islands by offering Portuguese protection to Sultan Almanzor of Tidore in return for his surrendering the cannon provided by the Spanish and giving one of his daughters in marriage to Prince Darwis. It might have seemed like a good idea at the time, but there was duplicity on all sides. Unfortunately, Sultan Almanzor fell sick and died while being attended by a Portuguese physician. Of course the poor physician was accused of poisoning the Sultan and the new governor's attempts at peacemaking ended in disaster.

Back in Europe, the return of the *Victoria* to Spain had caused a diplomatic storm. King John III of Portugal lodged a protest with King Carlos claiming that the Spanish had encroached on his territory as defined by the Treaty of Tordesillas. In response, King Carlos cleverly offered to submit the dispute to arbitration. The Portuguese made a strategic mistake by agreeing to this process, since it implied that Spain might have a claim to the Spice Islands.

Both sides gathered experts to support their claim. However, by the time the two sides sat down to negotiate, Pedro Reinel and his son Jorge, who had provided maps to Magellan, were firmly back in the Portuguese camp. On the other hand, another Portuguese mapmaker, Diego Riveiro, who had made the maps for the Armada de Molucca, stayed on the Spanish side. Pietro Martire d'Anghiera, Secretary to the King of Spain, described the Spanish delegation:

> Nunno Garcia, and Diego Rivero, being all expert pilots and clever in the making of sea charts, should be present, and bring forth their globes and maps with other instruments necessary to declare the location of the Islands of the Moluccas about which was all the contention and strife.

Their first meeting was held on a bridge spanning the Portuguese–Spanish border. Both sides were represented by nine members, as well as their mapmakers and cosmographers. Neither the Portuguese nor the Spanish were able to accurately measure longitude, so neither could determine the position of the Moluccas with any degree of accuracy. Each side had its cosmographers make persuasive arguments with charts and globes, but there was no resolution to their differences and the talks ended in a stalemate. In fact, another 200 years were to pass before the invention of the shipboard chronometer by the English watchmaker John Harrison allowed for the accurate measurement of longitude.

The Spanish decided to take advantage of the stalemate by sending an armada across the Pacific to capture the Spice Islands by force. Their first armada left in 1525 under the command of Frei Garcia de Loayasa, with Juan Sebastian Elcano as his second-in-command. Of the seven vessels only four were able to battle their way through the Strait

The Strait of Magellan, Jodocus Hondius, 1635 (Princeton University Library)

of Magellan, and the rest were either smashed to pieces or retreated to the Atlantic. A map by Jodocus Hondius shows the Strait in some detail and explains the difficulty in traversing such a narrow waterway against the prevailing winds.

A huge gale then scattered the armada across the Pacific and the vessels were never to see each other again. Only the flagship, *Santa Maria*, continued on the mission to seize the Moluccas for the Spanish King. In mid-Pacific Frei Garcia de Loayasa died of scurvy and Juan Sebastian Elcano assumed command, but tragically the former captain of the *Victoria* and hero of the world's first circumnavigation also died of scurvy.

Finally the *Santa Maria* reached the Moluccas and anchored off Tidore, its rigging reduced to mere rudiments, the ship barnacled and worm-eaten, its crew exhausted and starving. The Portuguese immediately engaged the Spanish ship in combat, and after firing off its cannon the *Santa Maria* proceeded to sink out of sheer decrepitude, the crew swimming ashore to be welcomed by the Sultan of Tidore. Assured of the arrival of more Spanish vessels, the Sultan switched his allegiance back to the Spanish and they set about building Fort Mariaco on the west coast of the island.

The next Spanish armada left from Acapulco on the Pacific coast of Mexico in 1527, shortening the length of the voyage and avoiding the hazards of the Strait of Magellan. The three ships, commanded by Alvaro de Saavedra Ceron, also ran into a Pacific storm which sank two of the ships, leaving only the flagship *Florida* to reach the Moluccas to reinforce the Spanish fort on Tidore. Realizing that still more reinforcements were needed, the captain of the *Florida* twice attempted to sail back across the Pacific, but was thwarted by the prevailing easterly winds and had to return to Tidore.

Only the narrow strait between the two islands separated the Portuguese on Ternate from the Spanish on Tidore, and both sides were determined to rule the Moluccas with the support of their local allies. They both knew this struggle would decide not only who would control the clove and nutmeg trade from the Spice Islands, but also the fate of the Portuguese and Spanish empires in the Far East.

Eventually, King Carlos came to realize that because of the difficulties of crossing the Pacific, his claim to the Spice Islands was commercially impractical, and heavily indebted to the Habsburg bankers who had financed his wars with France, he decided to give up his claim in return for compensation from the Portuguese. In 1529 the two crowns signed the Treaty of Saragossa, which ceded the Spice Islands to the Portuguese. By the use of clever diplomacy, together with his cunning cosmographers, King Carlos had turned a dubious claim to the Spice Islands into 350,000 solid gold ducats. He even had a clause inserted into the treaty allowing him to reclaim his rights if new geographical evidence on the location of the Spice Islands emerged in his favour.

The two crowns agreed that the line of demarcation should lie 17 degrees east of the Moluccas, placing them within Portugal's hemisphere of influence. Legalese has not changed in almost 500 years and the text reads as follows:

In order that it may be known where the said line falls, a model map shall at once be made on which the said line shall be drawn in the manner aforesaid, and it will thus be agreed to as a declaration of the point and place through which the line passes. This map shall be signed by the said Charles V, Lord Emperor and King of Castile, and by the said Lord King of Portugal, and sealed with their seals. In the same manner, and in accordance with the said model map, the said line shall be drawn on all the navigation charts whereby the subjects and natives of the kingdoms shall navigate.

The news of the Treaty of Saragossa had to be rushed to the Moluccas to stop any more killing between the two Iberian rivals. Too late, for in 1527 a fleet commanded by Jorge Menesez reinforced the Portuguese, and in early 1528 a force of 100 Portuguese and 1000 fighters from Ternate crossed the narrow channel between the two islands, capturing the royal town of Mariaco and besieging the Spanish fort. The Sultan of Tidore had to accept the terms of the peace, which meant submission again to the Portuguese and his old enemies from Ternate. The Spanish captain agreed to surrender the fort in return for safe conduct for his men to Jailolo on Halamahera, where they remained for several years until news of the Treaty of Saragossa finally reached them and the Spice Islands fell completely under Portuguese domination. A perspective drawing of the Spice Islands shows the forts built by the Portuguese and the Spanish.

Of those Spanish from the Armada de Molucca remaining in the Spice Islands, it has

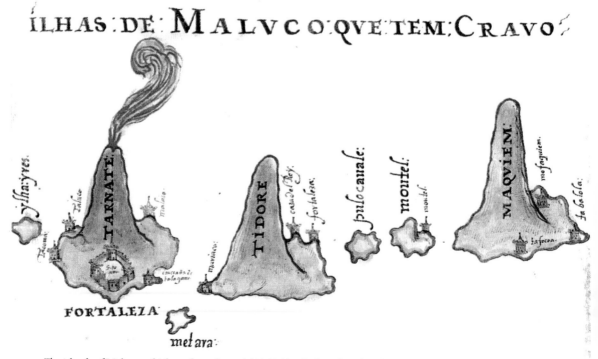

The islands of Molucca which produce cloves, 1615, Erédia Codex of S. Julião da Barra

been documented that Gonzalo Gómez de Espinosa, Gines de Mafra and at least two others from the crew of the *Trinidad* did eventually make their way back to Spain.

Today we know that North Maluku lies between 127 and 128 degrees east, well within the Portuguese hemisphere of influence as originally defined by the Treaty of Tordesillas. The final comment is from the Spanish historian Bartolomé de Argensola, who wrote in 1609 of the diplomatic controversy over the Moluccas:

> The most bloody Theatre of continual Tragedies was Ternate and all the Moluccas. There both Nations of Castile and Portugal decided their Quarrel by the Sword, whilst their Kings in Europe only contended by Dint of Cunning, and Cosmography.

After the Treaty of Saragossa, the Spanish decided to base their Pacific trade in the Philippines. In 1564, the Spanish admiral Miguel Lopez de Lagazpi sailed from Acapulco and occupied Cebu. In 1571 he captured the city of Manila. From this time, the Spanish used Manila as their base but they still had to learn how best to use the trade winds to return across the Pacific Ocean.

An Augustinian friar, Brother Andrés de Urdaneta, had first crossed the Pacific at the age of seventeen with the ill-fated Loayasa/Elcano expedition. During this voyage, he had risen from the position of Elcano's pageboy to become an officer. In subsequent years, Urdaneta had formed a theory that the winds and currents in the northern Pacific circulated in a clockwise direction, whilst in the southern hemisphere they circulated in an anticlockwise direction. This made it impossible to sail across the Pacific in the equatorial regions, against the winds that blew incessantly from the east.

The Spanish King asked Urdaneta, now 52 and in poor health, to help organize a new expedition to the Philippines. On the return voyage from Manila he attempted to prove his theory by sailing as far north as possible before turning eastwards across the Pacific. The powerful winds of the North Pacific allowed him to reach the coast of California in three months. From there they sailed south to Acapulco, where the Augustine friar was hailed as a hero.

Soon a galleon was sailing annually from Manila to Acapulco with a cargo of spices traded from the Moluccas as well as Chinese silks, porcelains and lacquer ware. The Spanish transported these cargoes, together with gold and silver from Peru, across the Isthmus of Panama to the Caribbean ports, where they were loaded onto the treasure fleets bound for Spain.

One hundred years after the first voyage of Christopher Columbus towards the Indies, the annual voyage of the Manila galleons was the fulfilment of his dream of sailing west to bring the riches of the Indies to Spain. A flourishing trade developed and the Manila galleons returned across the Pacific loaded with Spanish silver dollars minted in Peru. Worth eight reales and known as 'pieces of eight', they became the preferred trade currency throughout the Orient and the Indies.

The route of the Manila galleons was the final connection in a trading network that now encircled the world and was the beginning of the modern global economy. Along the Indian Ocean and Pacific Ocean trade routes, silver and gold flowed to the Indies and the Orient, while spices, silks, porcelain, lacquerware and other exotic oriental trade goods flowed back to Europe.

14   *The Sultans*

Evil and strife are endemic to the Moluccas, for the clove though a creation of God is
actually an apple of discord and responsible for more affliction than gold.

—João de Barros, early Portuguese historian, 1537

After the signing of the Treaty of Saragossa in 1529, the Portuguese could now concentrate
on the development of the spice trade, rather than fighting their Spanish rivals.

The Royal Clove Ship continued its annual visits, following the trade winds between
Goa and the Moluccas, and the volume of trade increased. Nearly all the provisions for
the fort in Ternate came with the vessels from Goa, and there was no more important
a word in their reports to the viceroy than mantimentos, that is, provisions—of both
supplies and armaments. The superiority of Portuguese weapons made it difficult for any
enemy to take the fort by military force, but blockade and starvation were a real threat,
especially if the trading ships bringing provisions from Goa or Malacca failed to arrive.

At the far end of the Portuguese seaborne empire, Fort Gamalama was thousands of
miles and months, if not years, from the authority of the King in Portugal, his viceroy in
Goa or the Portuguese governor in Malacca. The personnel assigned to the settlement
were also a problem, as Ternate had become a dumping ground for the criminal and
the unwanted. The seventh Portuguese governor, Antonio Galvao, was blunt in his
description:

From all quarters of the winds murderers come to India, and from there they are degraded to Malacca,
and for monstrous cases they are transferred further on to Malucco, which is the hotbed of all the evils of
the world, whereas it could be turned into a place good for souls, lives and trade.

The difficulty of enforcing the royal trading monopoly, demanded by the Portuguese
crown and the viceroy in Goa, still existed. All the Portuguese, from the governor down

to his servants, expected to supplement their income from personal trade in cloves. They arrived for their term of residence with sea chests crammed with personal trade goods and left with caches of cloves they had acquired in competition with the crown.

This private trade provided constant opportunity for internal rivalry, abuse of authority and embezzlement. The recall of one Portuguese governor for misuse of his authority only led to his replacement by another governor equally capable of the same misdeeds.

The Portuguese governors could also not avoid becoming embroiled in the politics of the dynastic succession of the Sultans of Ternate and the continuing rivalry between the Sultans of Ternate and Tidore. The Portuguese were unaware of the deep-rooted dualism in the relationship between the twin islands and the two sultanates, and that the Moluccans believed rivalry, war and antagonism between the sultanates were necessary for the survival and prosperity of the region.

Prince Darwis, ruling as regent after the death of his brother, Sultan Bolief, conspired with the Portuguese to confine Bohejat and Dajalo, the two young princes and heirs to the throne, inside Fort Gamalama supposedly for their protection. The Portuguese believed that by thus confining the youthful princes and controlling their education, they would be more amenable to Portuguese influence and guidance when one of them became sultan. For Prince Darwis, since Islamic law forbade his ascendency to the throne, it was simply a means of consolidating his power as regent.

Later, under pressure from the local population, both Prince Darwis and the Queen Mother demanded the release from Portuguese custody of the two princes. An impasse continued until Bohejat, the eldest son and heir apparent to the throne, died of poison. The Queen Mother accused Prince Darwis of being responsible; he in turn blamed it on the Portuguese; the Portuguese said it was a Tidorean conspiracy; and to complete the circle of allegations the Tidoreans blamed it on Prince Darwis. The people of Ternate identified the regent as the probable villain and his popularity slipped in favour of his brother, Prince Bayaco.

Prince Darwis now sought to restore his popularity and assert his power by leading a region-wide insurrection against his former ally—the Portuguese. Thoroughly sick of his scheming, the Portuguese lured him into the fort for peace talks, then had him arrested, convicted of treason and promptly executed. To demonstrate the finality of this event, they threw his severed head and quartered body over the ramparts for all the population to see.

The island erupted in violent demonstrations against the Portuguese and the fort came under siege. With the Portuguese community confined to Fort Gamalama and forced to live on subsistence rations, it was time to replace the governor and make a fresh start.

The new governor promised the Queen Mother that under certain conditions he would release Prince Dajalo from the fort and have him installed as Sultan. The Queen Mother could not agree to these conditions, accusing the governor of interfering in her son's rightful succession to the throne and lamenting that this was a cruel reward for her husband allowing the Portuguese to build a fort on their island. With some mutinous Portuguese, she hatched a plot to release Prince Dajalo, who was now old enough to succeed his father. As soon as he was liberated from the fort the Council of Regents installed him as sultan.

A new era could begin. Unfortunately this only lasted as long as the Queen Mother, who was the power behind her son, remained alive. After her death another contender for the throne arose. A young prince named Tabridji, supported by the Portuguese and other Ternatean factions, took up arms against Sultan Dajalo, forcing him to flee to Tidore. Tabridji became Sultan in 1523 but failed to be as compliant to Portuguese demands as they had hoped. His reign came to an end when he was arrested for treason and, in a new strategy, the Portuguese shipped him off to exile in Goa.

When word reached the viceroy in Goa of the continued turbulent situation in the Moluccas, he appointed Antonio Galvão to be the next and the seventh Portuguese governor. Galvão had a reputation of honesty and competence, and he became known in history as 'Good Governor Galvão'—largely through the publication of his own memoirs.

Arriving in 1536, he found Fort Gamalama in ruins, the morale of the Portuguese community low and the local population dispersed in the hills. On the adjacent island of Tidore, Sultan Dajalo was now in command of thousands of men ready to invade Ternate, destroy the fort and humiliate the Portuguese.

After futile peace overtures, Galvão had to act quickly before the morale of the Portuguese defending the fort deteriorated even further. He anchored his small fleet off Tidore and probed its defences with cannon during the day. Secretly landing his men at night, he prepared to attack Fort Mariaco at dawn. Writing in his 1544 manuscript, *A Treatise on the Moluccas*, Antonio Galvão describes the events of that day:

> They had not yet reached the fortress when Dajolo, bold as he was, and supported by his men, came rushing upon them, just as he was there in the vanguard, without waiting any longer for the other Kings nor their troops, and approaching he said 'Here we are' … It came to fighting with swords, this being the weapon that we use most. As soon as he had been severely wounded, and most of his people too, and some of them had been killed, they turned their backs. All of us together entered the fortress, while the other Kings came to its rescue from the other side. Antonio Galvão, once inside ordered assembly sounded and had his men line up. Having passed them in review, he found them all in high spirits and well content and without injury, for which he thanked God.

The Portuguese succeeded in taking the fortifications and, unbeknown to them, Sultan Dajalo later died of his wounds. The campaign continued for several more days, but after the loss of the charismatic sultan the Tidoreans sent a mission to meet Governor Galvão and make peace:

Meanwhile the message arrived that the King was approaching with all his brothers. Antonio Galvão went out with all his civil and military officials, to receive them outside the city. The King walked in the middle and Kaitjil Rade in front; and all were dressed in white on account of Dajalo and the cousin of the king of Jailolo, wherewith they made known that they were in mourning for having been defeated.

Antonio Galvão started rebuilding Fort Gamalama as well as the town and the harbour. He opened schools and performed other good works which gained him his reputation as 'Good Governor Galvão'. Unfortunately for him, the appearance of Portuguese traders from Goa carrying documents authorizing them to buy cloves privately undermined all the work he had done to establish his authority and enforce the crown monopoly. This led to his alienation from many of his own men, who scrambled to join the private traders and profit from the cloves they had collected. Galvão wrote in his memoir:

> Jorge Mascarenhas arrived with the prohibition of buying clove, but not for himself nor for those arriving with him, though generally the regulations of the King forbade it to everyone ... Therefore some shouted that they were going to set fire to the ship since they were not willing to accept what was imposed on them by regulations coming from India, and they demanded that he himself should be the first to observe the law ... And thereupon Mascarenhas retired to his ship and fortified himself with other ships lying there ... They laid out a gangway to the shore to pick up anyone who wanted to sail with them ... And the first to ally themselves with Jorge Mascarenhas and to open up this path were men who had previously violated their bail or had broken out of prison. With matches kindled and muskets loaded, all who were able to do so took refuge there, saying that they had not come here to guard the fort but to do business, and that since Antonio Galvão wanted the regulations of the King to be observed, he should see to defending it against the Moors himself.

Governor Galvão's position became untenable, and a new governor arrived with orders to replace him. Like almost all of his predecessors Galvão departed Ternate in disgrace, but at least not in chains, and returned to Lisbon to write his memoirs.

The Portuguese had to find a more compliant leader than Sultan Tabridji or his predecessors, and their choice was a son of Sultan Bolief by a non-royal mother. Sultan Hairun came to power in 1540 and rapidly acquired the skill and cunning needed to appear compliant to both his own people and the Portuguese. He had to seem to be a loyal vassal of the King of Portugal as well as a strong defender of the Islamic faith and of the rights of his people. His rule as sultan also coincided with the most turbulent period in the history of the Spice Islands, caused by the active preaching and conversions by Jesuit missionaries.

There was little ethnic, racial, religious or political unity in the Moluccas and the appearance of the Portuguese and the Spanish, as well as Islam and Christianity, only added to the conflict already endemic in the region.

The celebrated Francis Xavier was born in 1506 at Castle Xavier in the area of Navarre in north-eastern Spain, into an aristocratic family. He was studying in Paris when he joined a group of followers of Ignatius Loyola and together with him founded the Society of Jesus. With the Catholic Church weakened by corruption and the forces of the Reformation, Loyola and his Society of Jesus provided the Church with a new heroic brotherhood ready to convert people in new lands to the Catholic faith. Loyola personally selected Francis Xavier to head the first Jesuit missions in Asia, and he sailed to India in 1541, undertaking missions in Goa and then Malacca, until he felt a calling to expand Christianity in the Moluccas at the expense of Islam.

Arriving in Ternate in 1546, he introduced a routine of simple catechism instruction to the native wives and children of the Portuguese, as they knew hardly anything about Christianity. Francis Xavier realized that it was the ritual of the Church, with its ceremonies, candlelight and music, rather than its religious doctrine that appealed to local people. Combining Catholic ritual with the native love of music was an effective way of conveying the Christian message.

Xavier even sought to convert Sultan Hairun to Christianity. They had established a relationship of mutual respect, and Hairun requested the missionary to enlighten him regarding the differences between the two faiths. The Sultan remained unconverted and Francis Xavier wryly commented:

> If he fails to become a Christian it is not because of any devotion to Mohammed, but because he is in thrall to carnal sins. The only thing Moorish about him is that he was circumcised as a child, and then as a man took unto himself a hundred principal wives and many other less important ones.

Francis Xavier heard of Christian villages in the remote Moro area off the north-east coast of Halmahera where the natives practised ritual headhunting and cannibalism. After the murder of the clerics who had baptized them, the new converts in this area had been left abandoned and without religious instruction. Replying to those friends who argued it was too dangerous to go there, Francis Xavier said he was ready to sacrifice his temporal life and offer himself to danger and death in whatever shape it may come. The first priest to visit the Moro Christians in seven years, he strengthened the converts in their faith and baptized their children, walking the jungle paths between villages in the heat of the day—since nobody dared venture out at night. He stayed in these Christian villages for three months and on his return to Ternate wrote:

> I am giving you this account so that you may know the abundant spiritual consolations that are to be found on these islands. For all the toils and dangers that are willingly encountered here for the love and service of God our Lord alone, are treasures abounding in great spiritual consolations, so much so in fact, that here on these islands a man might well lose the sight of his bodily eyes within a few years, from

the abundance of his consoling tears ... It would be better they be called 'Islands of Hope in God' rather than 'Islands of Moro'.

Having established his missions in the Moluccas, Francis Xavier wrote to Goa asking for more Jesuit missionaries to continue his good works in the area. He then returned to Malacca and was to spend another seven years in the Orient, taking up missions in Aceh, Japan and China before dying of fever in 1552 on the island of Sancian, in the Bay of Canton. Canonized in 1622 at the same time as Ignatius Loyola, he is the patron saint of missionaries and his remains are kept in a silver casket within the Basilica of Bom Jesus in Goa. The Kobe City Museum has a painting made by a Japanese artist around 1623 that depicts Francis Xavier preaching in Japan.

The greatest coup by the Jesuit missionaries in the Moluccas was the conversion to Christianity of the Sultan of Bacan, together with members of his court and community. The priests erected a great cross on the shores of Bacan, and the Sultan and 800 of his people were baptized in a mass conversion. There were also setbacks, and the fury of Muslim jihads following Christian conversions were such that the Jesuits often lost more bodies than they gained souls.

Languishing in exile, Sultan Tabridji came under the influence of one Jordão de Freitas. He also had a remarkable spiritual conversion and in 1544 was baptized as Dom Manuel Tabridji in the Catholic Cathedral in Goa. Whatever the reason for his conversion, his

Portrait of Francis Xavier, c. 1623 (Kobe City Museum)

status immediately changed from liability to asset. He received a pardon from the viceroy and immediately declared that Ternate was to be a Christian kingdom and a subject of the King of Portugal.

In 1545, the Jesuits accused Sultan Hairun of directly supporting jihad against them and appealed to the Portuguese King for his arrest. Wishing to have a smooth transition of power, the viceroy in Goa arranged for the return of the previously arrested and now rehabilitated Dom Manuel Tabridji as the first Christian King of Ternate. In 1545, Tabridji together with Jordão de Freitas who was to be the new Portuguese Governor of Ternate, departed Goa. Their plan went horribly wrong when, on the return voyage, Tabridji died in Malacca, in what some have described as mysterious circumstances.

Not wishing to have another dynastic crisis on their hands, and choosing pragmatism and profit over missionary zeal, the Portuguese authorities allowed Sultan Hairun to remain on the throne. However, he continued to enrage both the Portuguese officials with his persistent violations of their self-declared clove monopoly and the Jesuits with his support of the Muslim communities against the proselytizing of the Christian missionaries. Finally, when the Portuguese arrested Sultan Hairun, the Ternateans rose up in protest and Fort Gamalama was again under siege. This lasted until some of the starving Portuguese in the blockaded fort began to sympathize with Hairun and decided to mutiny, locking up the Portuguese governor in his own prison and releasing Sultan Hairun from custody.

The Jesuits once again complained to the King, and in 1565 the Portuguese sent a fleet of a dozen ships with 1000 men to reinforce their now tenuous control over Ternate. Sultan Hairun, on receiving the ships, demanded to know if it was true that they carried orders for his arrest. After consultations, the Portuguese decided it was best to make a show of confidence in the Sultan and keep him in power. However, conditions continued to deteriorate and Portuguese rule in Ternate became untenable because of a bitter feud between Sultan Hairun and the new Portuguese governor, Captain Mesquita.

The final act occurred in 1570 when Captain Mesquita, having lured the Sultan into the fort for peace talks, had him separated from his retinue and murdered.

The Sultan's eldest son, Prince Baabullah, led the ensuing siege of the Portuguese fort, and Captain Mesquita escaped on the next boat to Malacca. Forced to live on subsistence rations and their lives again under constant threat, the Portuguese opened negotiations. Sultan Baabullah promised to lift the siege if they agreed to return Captain Mesquita to Ternate to face trial for murder and his certain death.

The Portuguese finally submitted to this demand, but the ship taking Captain Mesquita back to Ternate ran into a storm and was forced to take shelter in the Javanese port of Demak, where supporters of Sultan Baabullah seized it and slaughtered Captain Mesquita and all the Portuguese on board. This vessel also carried supplies to relieve the siege of Fort Gamalama, and its capture made the situation for the Portuguese holed up in the fort even more perilous.

Reduced to a desperate state and with no hope of food or reinforcements from Goa or Malacca, the remaining occupants of Fort Gamalama had to negotiate with Sultan Baabullah for their survival. After being guaranteed safe passage to Malacca, they filed out of the fortress, led by a priest holding a white flag, and left the island they had tenuously controlled for over 60 years. A memorial erected at the site of Fort Gamalama depicts the events from 1570 to 1575 and has images of the stabbing of Sultan Hairun, the siege of the fort, and the Portuguese leaving the island on 31 December 1575.

Sultan Baabullah became a national hero for his defeat of the Portuguese and had

Memorial at Fort Gamalama (Ian Burnet)

Fort Gamalama rebuilt as a royal palace for himself. He was interested in the restoration of the clove trade to merchants of all nationalities and derived the bulk of his revenues from a 10 percent export duty. Trading links were restored with Arab, Gujarati, Achenese and Javanese traders, which filled the royal coffers and renewed the influence of Islam both in the court and in society at large.

To strengthen his power base, the Sultan shrewdly developed and maintained alliances with the other Islamic powers along the spice trading routes outside of Portuguese control, such as Demak in Java, Macassar in Sulawesi, and Aceh in North Sumatra.

The fiercely independent Acehnese had developed an alternative trading route that avoided the Portuguese-controlled Strait of Malacca. This followed the traditional route along the north coast of Java, then turned south-west through the Sunda Strait and up the west coast of Sumatra to Aceh, at the northern tip of the island. From there Gujarati or Arab ships carried spices directly across the Indian Ocean, running the Portuguese blockade of Aden and the Red Sea ports.

When James Lancaster of the English East India Company visited Aceh in 1601, he described sixteen foreign ships in the harbour—from Gujarat, Bengal, Calicut and Java. This renewed trade was so successful that by 1600 the port of Alexandria supplied Venice with almost as much pepper, cloves and other spices as before the voyage of Vasco da Gama to India, 100 years earlier.

The expulsion of the Portuguese and the Jesuit missionaries removed a source of instability from the region. Ternate soon became the most prosperous trading centre in all of Indonesia in what was to be the Golden Age of the Ternatean Sultanate. We have a good description of Sultan Baabullah and his court by an unexpected foreign visitor to Ternate—the famous English privateer Captain Francis Drake.

15   Francis Drake

And therefore that valiant enterprise, accompanied with happy success, which that right rare and thrice worthy Captain Francis Drake achieved, in first turning up a furrow about the whole world, doth not only overmatch the ancient Argonauts, but also outreacheth in many respects, that noble mariner Magellanus and by far surpasseth his crowned victory.

—Francis Drake II, *The World Encompassed*, 1628

Francis Drake was born in Devon in 1540 and at an early age moved with his family to the River Medway in Kent, where the king's ships lay at anchor and the royal dockyard at Chatham was under construction. There, he grew up surrounded by ships and sailors and at only thirteen years of age found himself apprenticed to a ship's captain. With a natural love of the sea, the eager young Drake learned all the seafaring and navigational skills that his master could teach him as they traded goods up and down the English coast and across to France and Holland. When the old captain died, he left his ship to his young apprentice. At only 20 years of age, Drake found himself the master of his own vessel.

Three years later Drake decided to sell his ship and join William and John Hawkins on a slaving expedition, bringing 450 male and female slaves from the coast of Guinea to be sold to the Spanish sugar plantations in the West Indies. Drake was related to the Hawkins family, who were already the richest and most famous merchant-adventurers of the day. This was the beginning of his adventures in the Caribbean.

In the following years Drake and his crewmen conducted a series of pirate attacks on the ships bringing gold, silver, oriental goods and spices to Spain. Unofficially sanctioned by Queen Elizabeth, they were known as privateers. Drake's adventures culminated in an audacious raid on a Spanish mule-train in Panama in 1572.

Drake had learned that trains of pack mules carried vast quantities of Peruvian silver and gold across the narrow Isthmus of Panama for transhipment to Spain. Allied with a group of escaped Negro slaves and some French corsairs from Le Havre, the privateers ambushed a train of 50 mules carrying treasure along the jungle paths towards the coast.

There is no mention of silks and spices, but after burying fifteen tons of silver bars Drake and his men staggered back to their boats with as many gold bars and silver reales as they could possibly carry. It was a fabulous sum, said to be worth one fifth of the Queen's annual revenues, and Drake became not only an extremely wealthy man but also the most famous English privateer in Europe and all of the Spanish Main.

In November 1577, Drake departed Plymouth with a fleet of five ships and 164 men under mysterious circumstances. He had recruited the seamen for a voyage to Alexandria in Egypt, but most of them believed their real destination was the Caribbean for another lucrative raid on Spanish treasure ships. The fleet sailed to the coast of West Africa, where Drake captured some Portuguese ships to supplement his supplies and kidnapped a Portuguese navigator to guide him across the Atlantic. Before departing West Africa, Drake gathered his captains and crew and revealed they were on a voyage to discover new lands in the Southern Ocean, including Terra Australis. For now, Drake's plan to sail through the Strait of Magellan and raid the unsuspecting and unprotected Spanish treasure ships in the Pacific Ocean remained a closely held secret.

A portrait of Francis Drake shows a man of supreme confidence, a bon vivant who dined off the finest silver and delighted in regaling the ten 'gentlemen adventurers' who had joined his flagship with stories about his exploits on the Spanish Main. A natural leader, he demanded complete loyalty from his men but was also a braggart and easily antagonized by anyone who dared oppose him.

By June 1578, the fleet had crossed the Atlantic and reached Port St Julian on the South American coast, where Magellan had wintered in 1520. Here Drake's fleet spent two months during the worst of the winter, and like Magellan he had a mutineer to execute. A certain Mr Thomas Doughty, the most senior of the gentleman adventurers, had sought to undermine Drake's command during the Atlantic crossing. Antagonizing Drake was never wise and he read out the charges:

Portrait of Sir Francis Drake, Jacobus Houbraken, 1740
(National Library of Australia, nla.pic-an9348475)

Thomas Doughty, you have sought by divers means, inasmuch as you may to discredit me, to the great hindrance and overthrow of this voyage … the which if you can clear yourself of, you and I shall be very good friends, whereto the contrary you have deserved death.

A court of the fleet's officers found Doughty guilty of mutiny and Drake offered him three choices: execution, abandonment at Port St Julian, or remaining in chains until his trial in England. Francis Fletcher, chaplain of the fleet and chronicler of the Drake voyage, wrote that Thomas Doughty did not show any hesitation:

He professed with all his heart that he did embrace the first branch of the General's proffer, desiring only his favour, that they might receive the Holy Communion once again together before his death.

The next morning the condemned man and his judge took communion together. Thomas Doughty and Francis Drake knelt before the chaplain and received the sacrament while Doughty declared before God his innocence of the charges laid against him. The gentleman adventurer and the captain-general then dined together in Drake's cabin, a last supper before they were rowed ashore to where the crew were assembled in a square around the executioner's block. According to the chaplain, Thomas Doughty placed himself in the hands of the provost-marshal and then:

Without any dallying or delaying the time, he came forthe and kneeled downe, preparing at once his neck for the axe and his spirit for heaven.

The enforced confinement and inactivity at Port St Julian allowed plenty of time for discontent to fester among the captains and crew. Especially amongst the men who had believed they were sailing for the Spanish Main and a fortune in gold and silver. After the execution of Thomas Doughty, no one would speak openly, but Drake sensed that the mood was for turning back. As the weather improved and the fleet made ready to depart its winter haven, he addressed the assembled crew:

We are, all of us, far from our own country, our families and friends. We are in the midst of enemies and we are few in numbers. Every man here is precious … Yet some of you seem determined to die, for you plot mutiny and spread discord and you know well what I must do to such men as that. God's life! I say there must be an end to plots and grumblings.

He went on to offer the vessel *Marigold* to those who wanted to return to England, but with the threat that if in future he found any of them on the high seas he would sink their vessel from underneath them. None of the malcontents was willing to step forward. Thus did Drake reinforce his command over the expedition.

The fleet scuttled one vessel on the voyage south and another had become unseaworthy, so only three vessels departed their winter anchorage, the flagship *Golden Hind*, the *Elizabeth* and the *Marigold*. Sailing south, they entered the Strait of Magellan. Francis Fletcher eloquently describes their passage:

> The land on both sides is very high and mountainous, having on the north and the west side the continent of America, and on the south and east part nothing but islands, among which lie innumerable frets or passages into the South Sea. The mountains arise with such tops and spires into the air, and of so rare a height, as they may well be accounted amongst the wonders of the world; environed, as it were, with many regions of congealed clouds and frozen meteors.

On 6 September 1578 the fleet cleared the strait only to encounter a fierce Pacific storm that raged for seven weeks, driving their vessels further and further south. As the ships of the fleet struggled to stay afloat, they heard through the roar of the storm desperate cries from the *Marigold* as she sank with the loss of the entire crew. The *Elizabeth* was separated from the flagship, her fate unknown. After the storm abated, Drake and his crew on the *Golden Hind* headed north to a pre-arranged meeting point off the coast of Chile.

Unbeknown to Drake and the crew of the *Golden Hind*, the *Elizabeth* had survived the storm and taken shelter in the Strait of Magellan. There Captain Winter declared to his journal that it was his intention to rejoin the *Golden Hind*, but the master and crew of his vessel would go no further, arguing forcefully that they had been hired by Drake for Alexandria and if this was Alexandria they would rather be hanged in England.

Reaching Valparaiso, in Chile, Drake raided a Spanish ship for its treasure and, more importantly, its wine, bread and bacon. Refreshed and resupplied, the English marauders started their four-month reign of terror along the Pacific coast. In a raid on the port of Arica, Drake plundered two more Spanish vessels. Off the vice-regal port of Callao de Lima in Peru he captured a vessel departing the harbour and learnt that a Spanish treasure ship had just left for Panama fully loaded with gold and silver. Unaware of the presence of English pirates in the Pacific and completely unprotected, the treasure ship unusually known as the *Cacafuego* or 'Shitfire' was an easy target for Drake and his crew. They deployed a sea anchor behind the *Golden Hind,* to make it appear to be a fully laden Spanish ship that under full sail was slowly overtaking the *Cacafuego.* The capture of the Spanish vessel was such a huge prize that Drake's men laboured four days in transferring its cargo of 80 pounds of gold, 26 tons of silver and 13 chests of silver reales, as well as precious stones, jewels and a golden crucifix, to their vessel.

Drake had all the plunder and riches his vessel could carry, but he now had to find a way home. Staying well offshore to avoid Spanish shipping, the *Golden Hind* sailed to California, then continued north past the Columbia River as far as the 48th parallel. Drake was searching for the postulated North-East Passage that would allow his return to the Atlantic, but to no avail, and after describing freezing rain and the ship's ropes stiff with cold, he turned back to the warmer clime of southern California. The harbour of New Albion shown on the map of Drake's voyage is thought to be Whale Cove on the coast of Oregon. There the crew took time to rest, take on fresh food and make necessary repairs to the *Golden Hind.*

Drake saw only one course open to him. There was no possibility of retracing his path south and risk being captured by the waiting Spanish. His only choice was to follow Magellan's route across the Pacific to the Spice Islands and then return to England around the Cape of Good Hope. Francis Fletcher wrote in his journal:

> He thought it not good to return by the Straits, for two special causes: the one, lest the Spaniards should there wait and attend for him in great strength, from whose hands, he being left but one ship, he could not possibly escape. The other cause was the dangers of the mouth of the Straits in the South Sea, where the continuous storms blustering, as he found by experience, besides the shoals and the sands upon the coast, he thought it not a good course to adventure that way: he resolved therefore to avoid these hazards, to go forward to the islands of the Moluccas, and hence to sail the course of the Portuguese by the Cape of Good Hope.

Departing California in July 1579, the crew of the Golden Hind set a south-westerly course to the middle latitudes and then turned due west to take advantage of the prevailing winds across the Pacific. They made a relatively easy crossing compared with Magellan's 60 years earlier, and by November 1579 they had reached the Spice Islands:

> These are four high piked islands; their names, Terenate, Tidore, Matchan, Batchan all of them very fruitful and yielding abundance of cloves, whereof we furnished ourselves of as much as we desired at a very cheap rate. At the east of them lies a very great island called Gillola. We directed our course to have gone to Tidore, but in coasting along a little island belonging to the King of Terenate, November 4, his deputy or viceroy with all expedition came off to our ship in a canoe, and without any fear or doubting of our good meaning came presently aboard. Who after some conference with our general, entreated him by any means to run with Terenate, not with Tidore, assuring him that his king would be wondrous glad of his coming, and be ready to do for him what he could, and what our general in reason should require.

Drake decided to trust the Sultan's viceroy and agreed to have the *Golden Hind* towed through a gap in the fringing reef to a protected anchorage in front of Fort Gamalama. During their stay, one of the crew carved a coconut shell with the image of four kora-kora towing the *Golden Hind* into the harbour. The coconut was later mounted in an elaborate silver cup and presented to Francis Drake by Queen Elizabeth.

The following day Sultan Baabullah paid a visit to the *Golden Hind* in his state kora-kora. Cautiously, he did not accept Drake's invitation to come on board but exchanged gifts with him and promised to supply him with food. Fearing treachery, Drake declined to go ashore but sent his emissaries to the palace bearing a velvet cloak for the Sultan. In the town they met four Arabs, two Turks and an Italian—all merchants in Ternate and an indication of the changes in the clove trade after the departure of the Portuguese.

Sultan Baabullah received Drake's emissaries in the Royal Baileu, an open-sided reception hall erected in the courtyard of Fort Gamalama, screened by silk curtains and covered with various oriental carpets and cushions. On their return to the *Golden Hind* the emissaries described their audience with the Sultan:

> The king at last coming from his castle, with eight or ten more grave senators following him, had a very rich canopy borne over him, and was guarded with twelve lances, the points turned downward: our men arose to meet him, and he very graciously did welcome and entertain them. He was of low voice, temperate in speech, of kingly demeanour, and a Moor by nation. His attire was after the fashion of the rest of his country, but far more sumptuous, as his condition and state required: from the waist to the ground was all cloth-of-gold, and that very rich: his legs bare, but on his feet a pair of shoes of cordivant, dyed red: the attire of his head were finely wreathed in divers rings of plaited gold, of an inch or inch and a half in breadth, which made a fair and princely show, somewhat resembling a crown in form: about his neck he had a chain of perfect gold, the links very great and one fold double: on his left hand was a

Sultan Sayfoedin of Tidore (r. 1657–89 (The Bridgeman Art Library Czartoryski Museum, Kracow)

Detail of the gold chain belonging to the Sultan of Ternate (Rijksmuseum, Amsterdam)

diamond, an emerald, a ruby, and a turquoise, four very fair and perfect jewels: on his right hand, in one ring a big and perfect turquoise: and in another ring many diamonds of a smaller size, very artfully set and couched together.

The description of Sultan Baabullah's headdress of rings of plaited gold, one inch to one to one and half inch in breadth, and his chain of gold links is interesting, since there is a portrait of Sultan Sayfoedin of Tidore made around 100 years after this description, showing him wearing a similar golden headdress and gold chain.

Following the successful visit by his emissaries, Drake accepted the invitation to meet Sultan Baabullah. In their meeting, the Sultan proposed an alliance with the English to overthrow the Portuguese, who had returned from Malacca and rebuilt Fort Mariaco on Tidore. Drake promised he would send a major expedition to Ternate within two years, pledging his word as a gentleman to that effect. The two men then sealed the bargain with an exchange of gifts; Drake presented Baabullah with a jewelled ring, a coat of mail and a helmet. Baabullah for his part presented Drake with a ruby ring and a letter pledging his allegiance to Queen Elizabeth.

Drake added six tons of cloves to his already heavy cargo of Spanish gold and silver, and not wishing to further delay his return to England, ordered the *Golden Hind* be readied to leave Ternate. Drake sailed south-west looking for a deserted island with a gently shelving beach where the crew could safely careen the ship and make the necessary repairs in preparation for the long voyage across the Indian Ocean.

Finding a small wooded island off the Celebes (Sulawesi), they made camp and began the laborious task of ferrying all their goods ashore, including the ship's cannon, the six tons of cloves they had just taken on board and the more than 26 tons of silver and gold. The crew then hauled the *Golden Hind* up onto the beach for her hull to be scraped, caulked and given a fresh coat of tar. Drake even organized a work roster so that half the crew could rest on alternate days. Naming it Crab Island, the crew had time to restore their health and enjoy eating the giant land crabs that inhabited the island. They described the crabs as being so big that just one of them could feed four hungry men.

After 28 days on Crab Island and with the *Golden Hind* and its crew now in ship-shape condition, Drake and his crew hoisted sail and resumed their homeward journey.

That afternoon the winds came up, and at eight o'clock, while cruising under full sail, the *Golden Hind* suddenly came to a grinding halt. She had struck a submerged reef and the ship was driven hard aground. Fortunately she was not holed but was held fast by the coral and a strong wind from the starboard. The crew anxiously waited for the tide to lift them off, but the ship remained firmly aground. The situation was perilous. The men could see distant land on the horizon but the ship's boat could carry only ten or twelve men, and the shifting winds and waves might batter their ship against the coral reef at any time, leaving most of the crew to drown.

Drake asked the chaplain, Francis Fletcher, to lead the crew in prayer and to administer the sacrament as they knelt on the deck before him. With the prayers completed, the crew hurried to throw all unnecessary weight overboard, except, that is, for their precious cargo of Spanish gold and silver:

> We lighted our ship upon the rocks of 3 ton of clove, 8 pieces of ordinance, and certain meal and beans; then the wind, as it were in a moment by the special grace of God, changed from the starboard to the larboard of the ship, we hoisted our sails, and the happy gale drove the ship off the rock and into the sea again, to no little comfort from all our hearts, for which we gave God such praise and thanks, as so great a benefit required.

There is an illustration from the book of *Voyages* by Levinus Hulsius published in 1603 showing Drake's crew coming ashore in Ternate to meet the king and his court in the open-sided house or baileu. The next part of the illustration shows the events after the *Golden Hind* ran aground on a shoal off the Celebes and the crew were forced to throw overboard some of its cannon and three tons of cloves.

During their voyage, Fletcher had changed from being a loyal supporter of Drake to one of his severest critics. His conscience was troubled and in his prayers for the crew's

Drake's men coming ashore in Ternate, Levinus Hulsius, *Voyages*, 1603 (Princeton University Library)

salvation he had deeply offended Drake, since he asked them all to repent and ask forgiveness for their sins, including the execution of Thomas Doughty. Drake believed the chaplain had abused his sacred office and sought to rouse the crew against his authority. In a bizarre turn of events, Drake took it upon himself to excommunicate the unfortunate chaplain and had him chained to the foremast, declaring to the assembled crew:

> Francis Fletcher, I do hereby excommunicate thee out of the Church of God, and from all the benefits and graces thereof, and I denounce thee to the devil and all his angels.

The *Golden Hind* eventually reached the port of Cilicap on the south coast of Java, where the crew made repairs to the damaged hull and resupplied with food and water. On 26 March 1580, Drake set a south-westerly course across the Indian Ocean for the Cape of Good Hope and the journey home. The voyage was uneventful except for the usual storms rounding the Cape of Good Hope. The *Golden Hind* entered Plymouth Harbour in September 1580, having taken two years and ten months to make the second circumnavigation of the world.

The nation hailed Drake as a hero. More than half the crew of the *Golden Hind* had

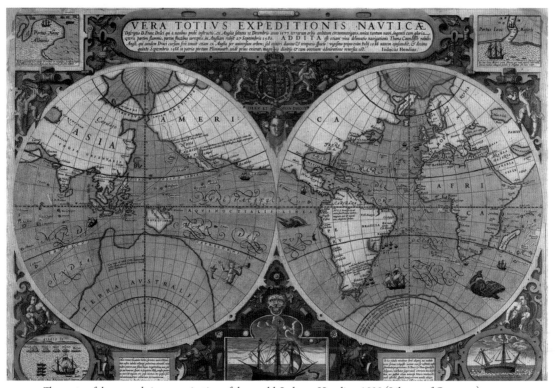

The route of the second circumnavigation of the world, Jodocus Hondius, 1595 (Library of Congress)

survived the journey and Drake's rich booty was secured in the Tower of London. Queen Elizabeth's share of the riches was more than the crown's income for an entire year and the Queen herself boarded the ship on its return to Greenwich, where Drake entertained her with a magnificent banquet. When the feasting was over, Queen Elizabeth summoned Drake to kneel before her and told him, 'Master Drake, the King of Spain has asked for your head, and we have here a weapon with which to remove it'. Taking a gilded sword in her hand, she knighted her pirate, bidding him to rise as Sir Francis Drake.

Sultan Baabullah, the greatest leader in Moluccan history, died in 1583. One version of his death is that written by the Spanish historian Bertolomé de Argensola in 1609:

> He died by the excess of his Love, or rather his inordinate Lust, in the arms of one of his Mistresses. Some say she killed him with Charms, or Poison, which is the Tyrant-Slayer among these Nations, impatient of one Man's long Rule.

Others have written that he was lured onto a vessel, kidnapped by the Portuguese and died on his way to exile in Goa.

Baabullah's son, Said, must have suspected treachery, for he organized a lavish state funeral for his father, inviting all the sultans and their courts from the surrounding islands. A version of this story is that at the end of the ceremonies and after all the mourners had sworn oaths of eternal peace and friendship, Sultan Said signalled to his palace guard and the Sultan of Tidore and his retinue were brutally murdered.

In 1580, the King of Portugal died leaving no direct heirs. Through his mother, the former Princess Isabella of Portugal, King Philip of Spain was able to lay a claim to the Portuguese throne and in 1581 he sent an army into Portugal to enforce his rights. The Iberian rivals were now united, and King Philip saw an opportunity for them to join forces and reconquer Ternate.

In 1585, a Spanish force of 400 men sailed from Manila to join with the Portuguese on Tidore and prepare for an attack on Fort Gamalama. Sultan Said and his troops vigorously defended the fortress, supported by the twenty Turkish gunners he had recruited and an armoury of bombs and grenades at their disposal. The Spanish commander had not expected such a spirited defence and prudently decided to return to Manila for further instructions.

This victory over the Spanish and Portuguese considerably enhanced the prestige of Sultan Said, who was said to have personally joined in the defence of the fortress and shown great courage during the battle. He also re-established the lucrative Asian trade in cloves, and the renewed presence of traders from China, Japan and Cambodia meant further wealth and power for Ternate, making him a worthy successor to his father and grandfather.

16 The Dutch East India Company

It is commonplace and to a certain extent the truth to say that the Dutch East India Company is not just a Company of commerce but also of State.

—Coenraad van Beuningen, Director in the Amsterdam Chamber of the Dutch East India Company, 1685

In 1581, the Protestant Dutch rebelled against their Catholic Spanish masters and formed the United Provinces of the Netherlands. Adept at market-related commercial practices, the merchants of Amsterdam and Antwerp had made their cities the main northern distribution centres for spices imported by the Portuguese.

Following his annexation of Portugal, King Philip of Spain forbade the Lisbon merchants to trade with the Netherlands, hoping to cripple the economy of the rebellious provinces and force an end to their revolt. The effect was the opposite, since the Dutch decided to bypass Lisbon and make their own voyages to the Indies. They were aided in this venture by Jan Huygen van Linschoten, who published his book *Itinerario* in 1596. The introduction to the English translation of his work reads:

Being young and living idelye in my native Countrie, sometimes applying myself to the reading of Histories and some straunge adventurers wherein I tooke no small delight, I found myself so much addicted to see and travaile into straunge countries, thereby to seeke some adventure, that in the end to satisfy myself, I determined … to take the matter upon me, trusting in God that he would further my intent.

The young Van Linschoten left Holland at the age of sixteen and travelled to Spain to stay with his half-brother. Living in Seville, he quickly learnt Spanish and later moved with his brother to Lisbon. In 1583, he sailed from Lisbon to India as secretary to the newly appointed Archbishop of Goa, an important position that gave him access to an enormous amount of privileged information. Van Linschoten never travelled further east than Goa but kept his eyes and ears open for the next five years, assiduously collecting information on every facet of the Indies, the spice trade and the Portuguese Empire of India.

After his return to Holland in 1592, he began writing his famous *Itinerario* or 'Travel account of the voyage of the sailor Jan Huygen van Linschoten to the Portuguese East Indies'. His book revealed a marvellous world to his readers. No one had extensively described the Indies to a wide audience since Marco Polo. He wrote of exotic peoples and places, of different customs and dress, of the treasure and wealth that would come to those willing to risk dangers and privation.

The *Itinerario* even describes some of the many cures attributed to cloves:

> Cloves are much used in meat and medicines … When they are green, they used them with salt and vinegar in Maluco, and some put them in sugar which are very pleasant to be eaten. The water of the green Cloves distilled has a very pleasant smell, and strengthens the heart. Likewise they procure sweating in men that have the Pox. Some lay the poulder of Cloves upon a mans head, that have a pain in it that proceed of cold. They strengthen the Liver, the Maw, and the Hart, they further digestion, they procure evacuation of the Urine, and being put into the eyes, preserve the sight, and four Drammes being drunk with Milk, do procure lust.

Van Linschoten gives a frank account of the Portuguese, their greed and divisiveness and their lack of organization. He undermined the myth of Portuguese invincibility in the region, showing that enterprising competitors could gain a share of the wealth of the Indies. He also published the 'Travel account of the Navigations of the Portuguese', which included vital navigational and cartographic information he had secretly compiled from Portuguese maps and pilots' logbooks during his stay in Goa.

In 1594 the Dutch clergyman and cartographer Petrus Plancius published a map of the East Indies. Engraved on copper plate, it represents a breakthrough in mapmaking, showing a much sharper image than previously achieved, and it remains a masterpiece of cartographic art. Depicted in botanical detail along the base of the map are the valuable commodities grown in the Spice Islands, such as nutmeg, cloves and three different types of sandalwood. A group of Amsterdam merchants commissioned the map as a means of promoting the Company for Far Distant Lands and raising the finance needed to break into the lucrative spice trade.

In 1593, Cornelius Houtman travelled from Holland to Lisbon as an agent for a Dutch trading house. He used this position as a cover to obtain information about the East Indies trade and to confirm what Van Linschoten was writing. On his return to Holland, the Amsterdam merchants who had established the Company for Far Distant Lands appointed him commander of the first Dutch expedition to the East Indies.

The expeditionary fleet of four vessels—the *Amsterdam*, *Mauritius*, *Hollandia* and *Duyfken*—left Amsterdam in 1595, with Houtman carrying proofs of the yet unpublished *Itinerario* and maps from the 'Travel account of the Navigations of the Portuguese'. Van Linschoten advised him to avoid Portuguese ports and the Portuguese-controlled

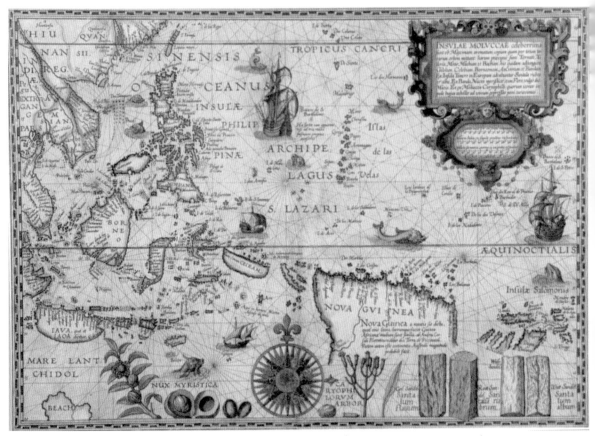

Map of South-East Asia and the Spice Islands, Petrus Plancius, 1594 (Maritime Museum, Rotterdam)

Strait of Malacca by sailing directly across the Indian Ocean to the Sunda Strait between Sumatra and Java, and then to the pepper port of Banten on the north-west coast of Java.

Linschoten believed the Portuguese were not yet trading in Banten, but when the Dutch fleet arrived there in June 1596, a boat carrying six Portuguese merchants came out from the town to greet them. The Portuguese told them five Chinese junks had just sailed north fully loaded with pepper and there was another junk in the harbour trying to buy up all the remaining spices in the port.

The Dutch describe Banten as being shaded by coconut trees, encompassed on both sides by a river, and being almost as large as the old town of Amsterdam. The houses were made of bamboo and stood upon four wooden poles, their rooms hung with silk or cotton curtains. There were no ordered streets and the town was surrounded by foul low-lying water, but the marketplace was full of merchants from Malacca, Bengal, Malabar, Gujarat and the Moluccas, with the Chinese being the most active traders in the town.

The initial Dutch encounter with the native shahbandar of the port and a representative of the Sultan of Banten went well. Houtman presented him with a gift of beautiful crystal glasses, a gilded mirror and some scarlet cloth. In return they were entertained to a banquet and offered a warehouse ashore from which to begin trading. The chronicler of their voyage, Willem Lodewijcks wrote: 'Many Gentlemen, Merchants, Chinese and Arabians came to our warehouse and into our ships offering us pepper, but our factor offered them too little a price'.

The factor was Cornelius Houtman. Arrogant and intemperate, he was a poor choice as commander. When the town's traders were unwilling to sell their spices at the prices he was offering, he seized some junks bringing cloves and nutmeg from the Spice Islands. The Javanese then seized his merchants ashore, holding them hostage until he paid reparations for their release. Frustrated, he took revenge by bombarding the town with cannon fire. No longer welcome in Banten, the Dutch fleet sailed along the north coast of Java looking for another port where they could trade for spices. After they dropped anchor off Tuban, vengeful Javanese boarded one of the Dutch vessels and hacked twelve of its crew to death. Houtman was then involved in a senseless massacre off the island of Madura in East Java where, suspicious of the welcoming motives of a flotilla of small craft circling his ship, he took pre-emptive action and blew them out of the water with a fusillade of cannon fire.

Suffering from scurvy and unable to trade anywhere in Java, the expeditioners were desperate. Then the captain of the flagship *Mauritius* suddenly died and they had to scuttle the *Amsterdam*, which was no longer seaworthy. Cornelius Houtman wanted to sail on to the Moluccas but his captains and crew would go no further, the fleet was in complete disarray and Willem Lodewijcks recorded:

> The 12 January we set sail again, some desiring to sail Eastward, others Westward, but in time we set Westward to sail once again to Banten, wherewith the flagship Mauritius sailed Southeastward, to get about the island of Java, and we followed her.

After reprovisioning in Bali, the three remaining vessels of the fleet departed for their long voyage home. The first Dutch voyage to the Indies had been a disaster, its cargo of spices barely covered its costs and by the time of their return to Amsterdam they had lost two-thirds of the crew to scurvy.

In 1598 the Dutch sent another fleet to the Indies, consisting of eight ships commanded by Jacob van Neck and Wybrand van Wawijk. Trading in Banten, the shrewd Van Neck was able to undo some of the ill will created by Cornelius Houtman by agreeing to pay more than the market rate for spices. A brisk trade followed and within weeks four of his ships were filled with pepper and ready to return to Amsterdam.

A painting by Andries van Eertveldt shows the four ships—the *Holland*, *Mauritius*, *Overijssel* and the small yacht *Friesland*—being welcomed by smaller ships on their triumphant return to Amsterdam in 1599. This second voyage was a legendary success for the Company for Far Distant Lands, yielding a profit of 400 percent for its investors. The ships had returned laden with 300,000 kilograms of pepper, 120,000 kilograms of cloves, as well as nutmeg and mace. Church bells rang out in celebration all over Amsterdam as Jacob van Neck and his crew paraded in triumph through the streets of the city.

Two of the vessels of the second voyage, the *Amsterdam* and the *Utrecht*, commanded by Wybrand van Wawijk continued on to the Spice Islands to trade for cloves. After they cast anchor off Fort Gamalama, Sultan Said came out to greet the ships, although he prudently refused to go aboard.

As a leader of his people, the Sultan was a great warrior and a devout follower of Islam. Van Wawijk described him as a strong man about 36 years of age, with a pleasant disposition and an intense curiosity to learn anything new. He took a special interest in the ship's cannon, which he had the Dutch fire against his own small vessels to observe the effects, and even tried to convince van Wawijk to join him in a raid against the Portuguese fort on Tidore. The Dutch commander cautiously declined.

The next Dutch ships arrived in Ternate in 1601, commanded by Admiral Cornelius van Neck with the *Amsterdam* and the *Gouda*. Sultan Said tried again to convince the Dutch to join him in an attack against Tidore. Van Neck refused, but did agree to demonstrate the power of his cannon with a brief bombardment of Fort Mariaco, now rebuilt by the Portuguese. Unfortunately, this display had to be interrupted when the Dutch Admiral had his right hand smashed by a lucky shot from a defending Portuguese gunner.

After the success of the Amsterdam merchants, their competitors in Rotterdam and Zeeland decided to send their own fleets to the Indies, hoping to gain their share of the hugely profitable spice trade. As strange as it may seem, the merchants from Zeeland appointed Cornelius Houtman to command their fleet. His two ships stopped in Aceh, in North Sumatra, to trade for pepper. It is not clear what caused his problems this time, but Cornelius Houtman was killed and his brother Frederick taken prisoner by the forces of the Sultan of Aceh.

The Amsterdam merchants responded to this competition by sending these instructions to the commanders of their fleets:

> You know as well as we do what losses it would cause us if the Zeeland ships were to arrive before ours are fully loaded. Therefore, buy. Buy everything you can lay your hands on, and load it as quickly as possible. Even if you have no more room for it, keep on buying and bind it to yourselves for future delivery.

An English translation of Van Linschoten's *Itinerario* appeared in London in 1598, and Queen Elizabeth signed the charter of the Company of Merchants Trading to the East Indies in 1601. Later to be known as the English East India Company, this document gave its founding merchants a monopoly over trade to the East Indies for the next fifteen years. Each merchant paid in what he was willing to risk and the total sum was used to buy ships and fill them with cargo to trade in the Indies. At the end of each voyage the ship and its cargo of spices were sold and the profits shared in proportion to each contribution. This financial arrangement, known as 'joint stock', was the forerunner of the modern company, its investors were not lords or 'gentlemen' but ordinary merchants and traders willing to make a speculative investment.

A fleet of five ships left London in 1601, commanded by James Lancaster, with a cargo of iron, lead and English garments. Lancaster carried six letters from Queen Elizabeth for presentation to oriental kings, each identical and with a blank space for the insertion of the name of the appropriate monarch. After capturing a Portuguese galleon off North Sumatra, Lancaster was able to send one of his vessels with a valuable cargo of pepper back to London. The remaining vessels continued on to Banten, where they traded for pepper and other spices.

All five ships of this first English fleet returned to London fully laden, making the voyage hugely profitable for its investors. After this success, the Company of Merchants trading to the East Indies was ready to challenge the Spanish and the Portuguese, arguing:

> Let the Spaniards shewe any juste and lawful reasons … why they shoulde barre her Majestie and all the other Christian princes and states, of the use of the vaste, wyde and infinitely open ocean sea, and of access to the territories and dominions of so many free princes, Kings and potentates in the East.

In a period of only six years, Dutch merchants sent 65 vessels in fourteen separate fleets to the Spice Islands, most of them completing successful voyages and returning with cargoes of spices that brought their owners immense wealth. Curiously, the preferred trade item in the Indies was still Spanish silver dollars, which the Dutch purchased in Europe and packed into chests to form the ballast for their ships sailing to the East Indies.

The government of the United Provinces of the Netherlands realized that to challenge the vice-regal power of the Spanish and the Portuguese in the Indies it needed an agency working in the national interest rather than separate commercial interests. Despite the opposition of the Amsterdam, Rotterdam and Zeeland merchants, the states-general joined them together into the Verenigde Oost-Indische Compagnie (VOC), the Dutch East India Company, in 1602.

A joint stock company open to investment by all and managed by a board of seventeen directors, known as the Gentlemen Seventeen, it proved to be a formidable rival to its English counterpart. Under its charter the company received a monopoly over all Dutch trading activities in the Indies. It could make treaties, establish ports, appoint governors, dispense justice, and even wage war. It maintained its own armed forces, coined its own money and enacted its own laws. Effectively, it was a privately managed for-profit

The six directors of the VOC chamber in Hoorn, Johan de Baen, 1682 (Westfries Museum, Hoorn)

company representing the Dutch government abroad and with the powers of a sovereign state. A painting shows the six directors responsible for the daily management of the Verenigde Oost-Indische Compagnie chamber in Hoorn. Standing behind them is their bookkeeper and on the table is their 'bankbook'.

Following the successful sale of spices from its first voyage, the English East India Company sent a second fleet of four vessels to the Indies, departing in 1604 under the command of Henry Middleton. Arriving in Banten, two of the vessels were loaded with pepper as quickly as possible and returned to London with their valuable cargo. Middleton then sailed to the Spice Islands with the other two vessels to trade for cloves and nutmeg. The *Red Dragon* and the *Ascension* arrived in Ambon in 1605, just in time to witness the arrival of twelve heavily armed Dutch warships, complete with 1500 sailors and soldiers, under the command of Steven van der Haghen.

This was the first fleet to be fully equipped by the newly enacted Dutch East India Company. It was under orders to attack the Portuguese strongholds. The Dutch were now ready to directly challenge the Portuguese and their crown monopoly of the spice trade.

The commander of the Portuguese fortress in Ambon sent an emissary to the Dutch warships saying that if they came in friendship they would be welcome. The Dutch responded by saying they were prepared to capture the fortress by force, unless perchance the Portuguese were willing to hand over the keys. The Portuguese replied that, even though outnumbered, they would defend the fortress and the honour of Portugal to the last man.

The Dutch were triumphant when after a short bombardment the Portuguese commander committed suicide and his men surrendered. Jan Huygen van Linschoten's assessment of the weakness of the Portuguese had proved to be correct and the loss of their fortress in Ambon was the beginning of the decline of the Portuguese Empire of India.

Unable to conduct any trade in Ambon, Henry Middleton decided to sail north to Ternate to trade for cloves while his other vessel sailed south-east to Banda to trade for nutmeg. As the *Red Dragon* came within sight of Ternate, Middleton had the good fortune to rescue Sultan Said from an attack at sea from his Tidorean enemies and take him aboard the *Red Dragon*. Safely delivered to Fort Gamalama, the Sultan professed his eternal gratitude by providing the English with a house in which to live ashore and trade for cloves. Sultan Said entertained Henry Middleton in the richly decorated Royal Baileu and the two talked of the visit of Sir Francis Drake to Ternate almost 30 years earlier and of Drake's promise to Sultan Baabullah to return with forces to support the Sultan against the Portuguese.

Next, the Dutch arrived in Ternate with a fleet of five vessels, fresh from their victory over the Portuguese in Ambon. Captain Sebastiaanszoon told Sultan Said that he had come in response to his repeated requests for Dutch assistance to expel the Portuguese and the Sultan should now join him in an attack on Tidore.

Sultan Said called upon all the Machiavellian skills of his forebears to find a way out of this dilemma. He explained to the Dutch captain that he would be most happy to provide certain logistic support, some men and kora-kora for instance, but he was in no position to send troops. He then explained to Captain Middleton that under Dutch pressure he must close the clove market to the English, but would be most happy to supply them surreptitiously. He then sent a message to his traditional enemy, the Sultan of Tidore, urging him to remain neutral in the conflict, as he himself would only intervene if the Sultan of Tidore did so, or if there were any threat of attack against Ternate. Sultan Said was hoping that the Dutch and the Portuguese would destroy each other and that he and his troops would live to fight another day, in the defence of their island.

Meanwhile, the Dutch, the Portuguese and the English engaged in an exchange of letters and visits, which led to nothing, except that the English would stay neutral in the impending conflict.

Under cover of darkness Captain Sebastiaanszoon landed a strike force of about 150 soldiers on the rocky coast. Climbing an adjacent mount, they set up cannon to fire on the fort from high ground. The English in the *Red Dragon* were able to observe the battle and we have a description of the day's events from Henry Middleton:

> Before it was light, the ships beganne their battery, and they likewise from the mounte. And upon a sodaine the Dutch and the Tarnataens sallied out of their trenches with scaling ladders, and had entered upon the walles before the Portingalls in the fort were aware, and had placed their colours upon on the ramparts; which the Portingalls seeing came with a charge upon them, with shot and fireworks, throwing at them which were so mounted, that they cast down their weapons and leaped downe far faster than they came up, leaving their colours and their equipment behind them; the Portingalls still continuing throwing of fireworks amongst them, whereby divers were hurt and scalded … And the Hollanders and Tarnatans, throwing away their weapons, beganne to take to their heels to runne into the sea. At this very instant when the Portingalls and the Tydorians had the victory in their hands and very ready to charge upon their flying enemies, the fort tooke fire and blewe up even with the ground; so that all the Portingalls which were under the walles of the fort were there buried, and the most part within the fort were blowne up into the ayre.

Just at the moment when the Portuguese had gained the military advantage and the Dutch were in full flight, a fire had spread to the gunpowder magazine and the resulting explosion destroyed the fort, burying the Portuguese within its walls. This was a stunning victory for the Dutch. A lithograph by the artist de Bry, shows in detail the Dutch attack on the Portuguese fortress on Tidore, the explosion of the gunpowder magazine and soldiers fleeing from the burning fortress.

After their victory, Captain Sebastiaanzoon and his fleet returned to reinforce the fortress in Ambon, leaving behind only one merchant and four soldiers on Tidore to defend the considerable gains they had made.

For the English the opportunity provided by Sir Francis Drake to control the trade in the Spice Islands had been lost. Before his departure, Henry Middleton obtained a letter from Sultan Said to King James I, which is now in the British Library:

> Hearing of the good report of your Majestie, by the coming of the great captain Francis Drake, in the time of my father, which was about some 30 yeeres past: by the which captaine, my predecessor did send a ring unto the Queene of England, as a token of remembrance between us: which if the aforesaide Drake had beene living, he could have informed your Majestie of the great love and friendship of either side: he in the behalfe of the Queene: my father for him and his successors. Since which time of the departure of the aforesaid captaine, we have dayly expected his returne … And whereas your Majestie hath sent me a most kinde and friendly letter by your servant Captaine Middleton, that doth not a little rejoice us … And in token of our friendship, which we desire of you majestie, we have sent you a small remembrance

Dutch attack on the Portuguese fortress on Tidore, Levinus Hulsius, Voyages, 1603 (Beinecke Rare Book and Manuscript Library, Yale University)

of a bahar of cloves, our country being poore, and yielding no better commoditie, which we pray your highness to accept in good part.

The loss of the Portuguese fortresses in Ambon and Tidore and the new Dutch alliance with the Sultan of Ternate prompted Pedro de Acuna, the governor-general of the Philippines, to request funding from the Spanish King to mount a new expedition to restore Iberian power to the Moluccas and thwart the Dutch expansion. He gathered a huge fleet consisting of 36 vessels carrying 1423 Spaniards and 344 Tagalogs, as well as 679 men from other parts of the Philippines. Leaving Manila in March 1606, the Spanish established a base on Tidore, where the Sultan promised a fleet of kora-kora with 649 additional men to support the attack against Ternate.

After attacking Fort Gamalama at dawn, this large force overwhelmed the Ternateans and the small Dutch force left to help defend the fort. The Spanish had victory in their grasp by early afternoon, when Sultan Said and members of his court fled in a fleet of kora-kora towards Jailolo. The Sultan sued for peace, agreeing to surrender and acknowledge Spanish sovereignty if he was allowed to return to Ternate, but the Spanish quickly abrogated this agreement, deciding a better outcome would be to remove Sultan Said and his entire court to Manila, to live in exile.

Pedro de Acuna celebrated his capture of Fort Gamalama by staging a triumphal parade through the streets of Manila. He and his officers wore their best military dress but it was the Moluccan exiles who gained all the attention. Dressed in brilliant silks, armed with their ancestral kris, and decorated with jewels and bird-of-paradise feathers, the Moluccan royalty actually seemed to enjoy the spectacle their exile was creating. The contemporary Spanish historian Bartolomé de Argensola described the event:

> Dom Pedro enter'd Manila with the Forces, and ostentations of captive and booty. There wanted not for Triumphal Arches, with such inscriptions as are generally set on them in honour of conquerors. The habit of the prisoners, in rich mantles, turbans, and plumes, was not suitable to their fortune; as making their countenances look more haughty, and representing arrogancy. That King was strong body'd, and his limbs well knit; his neck, and great part of his arms he wore naked; his skin being the colour of a cloud rather inclined to black than tawny. The features of his face were like a European. His eyes large, full and sparkling, to which they add the fierceness of long yebrows, thick beard and whiskers, and lank hair. He always with his campilane or cimiter and criz or dagger; the hilts of them both resembling the heads of snakes gilt.

For the Spanish it was a glorious victory, but for the Ternateans the defeat marked the end of a 30-year period during which its rulers had seized back their island from the Portuguese occupiers and made Ternate one of the richest and most powerful states in the archipelago.

The Dutch responded to the Spanish victory by landing their forces on the other side of the island where they occupied an abandoned Portuguese fort, named Fort Melayo. After rebuilding the fort and reinforcing its garrison, Captain L'Hermite mounted six brass cannon on the battlements and pronounced it battle ready, before sailing with the rest of his fleet to the China coast.

Almost immediately after their departure, a Spanish force stealthily crossed the island to attack Fort Melayo, but was repulsed during furious hand-to-hand combat and retreated to Fort Gamalama. Strangely, this was the last military engagement between the Dutch and the Spanish, and they settled into an uneasy peace, while gathering and storing cloves in their respective forts on opposite sides of this tiny island.

The garrisons must have had a premonition of the future because, following decades of intermittent warfare, Spain and the Netherlands signed a truce in April 1609.

Eventually the Spanish authorities in Manila lost interest in supporting their base in

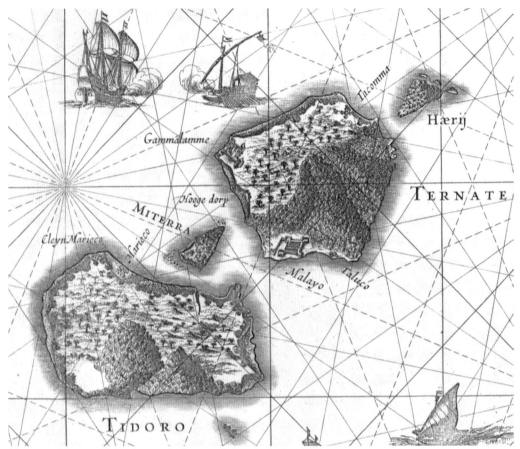

Detail showing Fort Gamalama, Fort Malayo and Fort Marieco, Willem Janszoom Blaeu, 1647 (National Library of Australia, nla.map-rm268)

the Moluccas and decided to abandon the fortress on Ternate. In 1663, Francisco de Attleinso, the last Spanish captain of Fort Gamalama, loaded his men, trade goods and cloves onto twelve junks and sailed for Manila, ending the turbulent 140-year Spanish presence in the Spice Islands that had began with the arrival of the Armada de Molucca in 1521.

Once the Spanish departed, the remainder of the Ternatean court returned from Jailolo and began to build their settlements around the Dutch fort at Malayo, now renamed Fort Oranje. The Ternateans continued their informal alliance with the Dutch, believing them to be only interested in trade and that they would not interfere in local affairs or their religion. This may have been the policy of the early Dutch commanders trying to win local support against a common enemy, but certainly was not be the policy of the future Dutch governor-general, Jan Pieterszoon Coen. This was something the Moluccans came to learn to their lasting regret.

17   Jan Pieterszoon Coen

Your Honors should know by experience that trade in Asia must be driven and
maintained under the protection and favour of Your Honor's own weapons,
and that the weapons must be paid for by the profits from the trade; so that we
cannot carry on trade without war, nor war without trade.

—Jan Pieterszoon Coen, in a letter to the directors of the Dutch East India Company

Jan Pieterszoon Coen was to become a legend. Born in the prosperous Dutch seaport of
Hoorn in 1587, he grew up surrounded by ships loading and unloading their goods and
preparing for their next voyage to the Baltic, the Mediterranean or the East Indies. He
spent his teenage years in Rome as an apprentice bookkeeper with an Italian merchant
house. Returning to the Netherlands, he signed up as a junior merchant with the Dutch
East India Company, departing Amsterdam in 1607 on his first voyage to the East Indies.

Coen was a member of the Dutch fleet that sailed in 1609 to the Banda Islands in
South Maluku with orders to build a fort and consolidate Dutch control over the nutmeg
trade. The tiny islands of Banda are rimmed by coconut trees and covered in evergreen
forest of nutmeg trees and larger kanari trees that protect them from the harsh tropical
sun. Ignoring the objections of the island chiefs, Admiral Verhoeven had his 750 men
start their construction on the site of a previously abandoned Portuguese fort on Banda
Niera. As the walls rose, opposition from the Bandanese increased until the admiral was
forced to arrange a peace meeting with the local chiefs. They lured the admiral into a
deadly ambush and Jan Pieterszoon Coen narrowly escaped death when the Bandanese
surrounded and killed Admiral Verhoeven, along with 42 Dutch soldiers and senior
officials.

Dedicated to the service of the Dutch East India Company, Jan Pieterszoon Coen rose
rapidly through the ranks. In 1613 he was promoted to director-general of East Indies
trade, based in the pepper port of Banten. Five years later and at only 31 years of age,
he became the fourth governor-general of the East Indies. One of his contemporaries
describes this all-powerful position:

As the Governor-General of the Dutch East Indies he had immense authority, which was an arbitrary and independent power in all matters: for there are few or no members of the council, who do not stand in need of his good offices, for example to obtain lucrative employments for their relations or favourites; and if this not be sufficient, to make them obey the nod of the governor, he is not destitute of the means of tormenting them, in every way and under various pretences, of even sending them prisoners to Europe.

Portrait of Jan Pieterszoon Coen, Jacob Waben, 1629 (Westfries Museum, Hoorn)

A portrait of him as governor-general shows a stern and austere man with a long narrow face and deep-set eyes, leaving the lasting impression with the viewer that he was not a man to be crossed.

Coen never hesitated to speak his mind, even to the 'Gentlemen Seventeen' on the board of the Verenigde Oost-Indische Compagnie, whose instructions he often criticized or ignored. They may not have liked him personally, but he continued to produce the results they wanted— the hugely profitable cargoes of pepper, cloves and nutmeg loaded onto the East Indiamen returning to Amsterdam.

The headquarters of the first three governors-general of the East Indies was in Ambon, a location remote from the main sea lanes of the Malacca and Sunda Straits that carried trade around the Orient and the Indies. The Dutch East India Company needed a more central base to build and repair their ships, warehouse their spices and to be their military and administrative headquarters.

Coen sought exclusive trading rights for the company in Banten, but the governing regent had no wish to grant any nation exclusive rights in what was a successful international trading port, and he was justifiably suspicious of Dutch ambitions.

Coen then entered into negotiations with the prince of the neighbouring province of Jayakarta, who was more than happy to use the Dutch to gain his independence from Banten. In 1618, the prince signed an agreement with the VOC allowing the building of warehouses on the east bank of the Ciliwung River where it entered the harbour of Sunda Kelapa.

Unwilling to allow the Dutch a permanent foothold on Java, the English East India Company and the Bantenese separately besieged the Dutch occupants of the fortified warehouses but were never allied. Outnumbered, Coen sailed to Ambon for reinforcements and returned with a large fleet and enough men to build Fort Batavia to protect their warehouses. Once secure in their fort, Jan Pieterszoon Coen and the VOC army turned on the Prince of Jayakarta, razing the adjacent town and routing the Prince and the local inhabitants.

In his history of Java, Stamford Raffles describes the Dutch attack on the palace of the Prince of Jayakarta:

> In a short time, however, when the Dutch had increased in numbers, they fired one of their guns, and the ball discharged from it fell in front of the Prince's palace. The prince inquired why they did so, to which they replied, they were only trying how far the gun would carry, in order that they might be able to assist the prince, should he be attacked by an enemy … The Dutch, at last, fired a gun, the ball of which fell within the palace, on which the Prince conceiving it to be their intention to attack him, immediately considered them as enemies, and collected his people in order to fall upon them without delay. As soon as the Dutch saw the people thus assembled, they fired from their batteries, dealing slaughter all around, and obliged the Prince and his people to retreat out of reach of the shot.

After the razing of Jayakarta, the VOC built the town of Batavia, diverting part of the Ciliwung River to encircle the city with canals that reminded them of their homeland and provided easy movement of goods into and out of the city. Batavia came to oversee a vast trading empire that extended throughout the Far East from India and Sri Lanka to China and Japan.

The Dutch East India Company became a mighty naval, military and trading organization and looked upon the English East India Company as an impertinent intruder into a trade that it intended to develop as a monopoly for itself. In 1619 a treaty allied Protestant England and Holland against Catholic Spain and Portugal, and the directors of the VOC instructed Coen to cooperate with the English in the Indies. Under the treaty, two-thirds of all the spices from the Spice Islands were to go to the Dutch and one-third to the English. Any concession to the English was totally against the nature of Jan Pieterszoon Coen and he wrote to the 'Gentlemen Seventeen' in Amsterdam:

> I admit that the actions of the master are of no concern of the servant … But under correction Your Honours have been too hasty. The English owe you a debt of gratitude, because after they have worked themselves out of the Indies, your Lordships put them right back again … it is incomprehensible that the English should be allowed one third of the cloves, nutmegs and mace, for they cannot lay claim to a single grain of sand in the Moluccas, Amboyna or Banda.

Jan Pieterszoon Coen was always going to take his revenge against the Bandanese for their treachery, having witnessed the murder of Admiral Verhoeven and 42 of his comrades. He requested instructions in writing from the 'Gentlemen Seventeen' in Amsterdam. They ordered him to subjugate the inhabitants of Banda and drive their leaders out of the land.

By 1621 Coen had assembled a fleet of thirteen vessels and an army of over 1500 soldiers in Batavia. Reinforced by additional men and vessels in Ambon, this formidable fighting force finally reached the Banda islands. Everything looked peaceful as they admired the beauty of the islands that lay before them, green emeralds on an azure sea.

Coen was initially cautious, looking for some sort of provocation from the Bandanese. Finally, after provocations on both sides, he unleashed the Banda Massacre, attacking and burning villages all over the island and rounding up men, women and children. Jan Pieterszoon Coen set out to obliterate Bandanese society, with as many as 15,000 islanders slaughtered, enslaved or shipped into exile, and the survivors hiding in the mountains. The Dutch blockaded their mountain hideouts, where most died of hunger. Coen described the obstinacy of these people as so great that they would rather all die together in misery than surrender to his men. With the entire population of the island now virtually eliminated, the VOC established its own colony of Dutch plantation owners and enslaved workers to cultivate the nutmeg trees.

The Dutch had control over all the nutmeg trees grown in the Banda Isles except those on the tiny island of Run, only ten kilometres away from Banda Niera. Run was the last remaining outpost of the English East India Company in the Spice Islands. A tiny band of Englishmen, led by Nathaniel Courthope, had defended the island against the Dutch for six years. Faced by overwhelming force, only after the capture and death of Courthope did the English garrison on Run surrender. After the departure of the English, the native inhabitants of Run were left defenceless. The Dutch killed or enslaved every adult male, and then proceeded to chop down every nutmeg tree on the island, leaving behind a barren, inhospitable and uninhabited rock rising out of the Banda Sea.

Jan Pieterszoon Coen knew that without provocation he could not repeat such brutalities against the islands of Ternate and Tidore. He needed a different strategy to gain a monopoly over the clove trade. This involved the transplantation of clove trees from the Spice Islands of North Maluku to Ambon and its surrounding islands in Central Maluku, which the Dutch now controlled.

On Ambon, the VOC required the obligatory cultivation of clove trees by officially authorized villages. In these villages, each Ambonese head of family had to plant and maintain 100 or more clove trees, and any clove trees that were cultivated without consent were destroyed. The uprooting or burning of clove trees—known as extirpation—became a form of punishment for those villages that dared challenge the Dutch monopoly and trade their excess cloves with native traders from Java or Macassar.

The VOC enforced its monopoly by the hongi-tochten system. The hongi were fleets of kora-kora manned by Dutch soldiers and Ambonese rowers, while tochten meant duty rounds. In the case of trouble in the islands, the Dutch governor of Fort Victoria in Ambon called up the hongi and dispatched it on its tochten. If the troubles were minor, a few Dutch soldiers travelled with the hongi. However, if the troubles were more serious, the hongis would be attached to a military expedition from Batavia.

Even in times of peace, the hongi-tochten fleets were dispatched annually as a show of strength. Consisting of 50 to 100 kora-kora, each manned by 100 men, they created an impressive sight as, with flags and pennants streaming in the wind, they swept along the coast to the sound of drums and cymbals beating out a rhythm for the rowers.

The declining English presence in the Moluccas finally ended after the Amboyna Massacre in 1623. The Dutch commander in Ambon arrested seventeen English traders living in and around Ambon and accused them of plotting to capture the Dutch fortress. No attempt was made to explain how this could be possible without naval support and with only a few swords and muskets between them. Methodical torture of the English traders continued until their tormentors produced a confession, which was all the justification the Dutch needed for the executioner's axe. Pen and paper were thrust into one of the cells and William Griggs was allowed to write a final and poignant message before his beheading:

> We, through torment, were constrained to speake that which we never meant nor once imagined; the which we take upon our deaths and salvation, that tortured with the extreme torment of fire and water, that flesh and blood could not endure … And so farewell. Written in the dark.

This horror ensured the English would not return to the Spice Islands although they retained some sort of legal claim to the island of Run. Under the 1667 Treaty of Breda, the English signed away their rights to the island in exchange for the island of Manhattan, in New Amsterdam. Few would have believed a small trading village on the island of Manhattan was destined to become the modern metropolis of New York and the once valuable nutmeg-growing island of Run would sink into obscurity.

Sometimes known as 'King Coen' or the 'Butcher of Banda', Jan Pieterszoon Coen ruled his realm with an iron fist. Five years after establishing the Dutch monopoly over the growth of nutmeg and cloves, he resigned his post and returned to Holland. Reassigned back to Batavia as governor-general in 1627, he remained there until his death from cholera or malaria three years later, at the age of 42. Stubborn and determined to the bitter end, he is said to have refused to repent his sins and was denied Holy Communion on his death bed.

Coen's lasting legacy was the Dutch monopoly over the growth of nutmeg and cloves in the Spice Islands, which he established by force of arms and the deaths, exile or enslavement of thousands of islanders. A statue stands in the town square of Hoorn in honour of its most famous son, but whatever honours and reputation as an empire builder Jan Pieterszoon Coen enjoyed during his lifetime, these were always accompanied by charges of barbarity and inhumanity.

Sultan Said died in exile in Manila and his grandson, Mandarsjah, became the Sultan of Ternate. A weak ruler, he was considered too compliant with the Dutch and many of his people opposed him. In November 1651, the Dutch governor of Ambon, Admiral Arnold de Vlamingh van Oudtshoorn, invited the Sultan to visit Batavia. The Dutch gave Sultan Mandarsjah and his entourage the full royal treatment—a parade from the landing place to Kastel Batavia, a suite of rooms within the castle walls, a continuous display of military guards and escorts and a magnificent reception in the state council chambers followed by music and dancing. The governor-general then presented Sultan Mandarsjah with a contract for him to sign that was to spell disaster for his people. He had to give his consent to withdraw all his people from the islands he controlled around Ambon and Ceram, and agree to the extirpation of clove trees from within any part of his realm that remained unruly. In return, the Dutch promised he would receive a fixed annual stipend for himself and other members of his court.

Sultan Mandarsjah signed the infamous contract on 31 January 1652 and immediately took an advance on his stipend. As far as the Dutch were concerned, he had ceded his territory around Ambon and Ceram to them and had effectively agreed to the removal of clove trees from the remaining areas under his control. The legacy of this agreement was the slow destruction of the remaining clove trees in the Spice Islands, the impoverishment of its people, and the gilding of the Sultan's throne with Dutch guilders.

An insight into the amount of wealth being transferred from the East Indies to Holland came when the English captured two heavily laden Dutch vessels, or East Indiamen, in 1665. The vessels were seized as part of reparations demanded by the English after the Amboyna Massacre. At that time, the English diarist Samuel Pepys was surveyor-victualler to the Royal Navy. After his inspection of the Dutch ships he wrote in his famous diary:

> They took me down into the hold of the India shipp, and there did show me the greatest wealth that a man can see in the world. Pepper scattered through every chink. You trod upon it, and in cloves and nutmegs, I walked above the knees, whole rooms full. As noble a sight as I ever saw in my life.

Pepys was also a gourmand, and his diary describes all the meals he enjoyed. He hosted many dinner parties including one for his wealthy patron, the Earl of Sandwich, who served as First Lord of the Admiralty. For this he acquired the finest china dinner service and employed the services of a 'man-cook', which seemed to be a novelty at the time. According to Pepys and his diary, the dinner was a great success, the social company and food were the finest he had experienced and even compared with banquets at court.

It was a dinner of about 6 or 8 dishes, as noble as any man need to have, I think; at least all was done in the noblest manner that ever I have had, and have rarely seen in my life, better than anywhere else, even at the court.

According to prevailing social custom, the higher the rank of the household, the greater its use of spices. This menu might give an idea of the spices used in the kitchens of the period:

Entrée — Tongue and Fresh Udder Stoffado (*The French Cook*, 1653).
     Take your Tongues, and season them with Pepper, Salt and Nutmeg, then lard them with great lard, and steep them all night in Claret-wine, Wine-Vinegar, grated Nutmegs and Ginger, whole Cloves, beaten Pepper and Salt: let them be put in an earthen pot or pan, covered up close and bake them, serve them with French bread and the Spices over them with some sliced lemon.

Main Course — Venison Stew (*The Accomplisht Lady's Delight*, 1675).
     Put the sliced venison in a stewing dish and set it on a heap of coals with a little claret wine, a sprigg or two of Rosemary, half a dozen Cloves, a little grated bread, Sugar, and Vinegar, so let it stew together awhile, then grate on Nutmeg and dish it up.

Dessert — Cheesecake (*The Court and Kitchen of Elizabeth*, 1664)
     Take two quarts of milk curd, one quart of thick cream, one pound of butter, twelve eggs, one and one half pounds of currants, and with cloves, nutmeg and mace beaten, half a pound of good sugar, one quarter pint of rosewater, so mingle it well together and put it into puff paste. Grate on nutmeg before serving.

Ambon and its surrounding islands, Haruku, Saparua and Nusa Laut, were now the only islands where the Dutch allowed cloves to grow in any quantity. These islands produced an estimated annual crop of two million kilograms of cloves, there being about 500,000 trees, each easily producing two kilogram of cloves. The Dutch East India Company was able to sell cloves in Amsterdam for 25 times the contract price paid in Ambon and attempted to balance production with world demand in order to keep prices high. Sometimes drastic measures needed to be taken, and in 1677 the most fragrant scent spread over all of Amsterdam—the VOC was burning a huge quantity of cloves to reduce an oversupply on the market.

     Minor trade continued outside the Dutch monopoly, with cloves from Ternate and Tidore as well as those transplanted into the interior of Halmahera and Ceram and outside Dutch control, being smuggled to markets in Macassar, Manila and Portuguese

The frontispiece and title page of *The French Cook*, Charles Adams, 1653

Timor. Whenever possible, the Ambonese growers diverted their cloves to these markets, which were often offering twice as much as the Dutch. The port of Macassar, in South Sulawesi, greatly increased its trade, and Javanese, Arab, Chinese, Portuguese, Spanish and English merchants flocked there because the Sultan of Macassar permitted them to trade freely, openly and beyond Dutch control. As described by the Dominican Friar Domingo Navarette when he visited the city in 1657:

> Fourscore years ago it was an inconsiderable country but since then has throve mightily by reason of the fairs kept there, for ships met there from Manila, Goa, Macao, English and Portuguese so that the abundance of rich commodities were brought thither from all parts of the archipelago, and trade enriched the country, making its Sovereign powerful … No man paid anchorage or any other duty there and saving the presents that captains of ships and merchants of note made to the Sumbane, all the trade was free. This made it the universal mart of these parts of the world.

The Dutch East India Company was not impressed at having a rival to the trade it controlled from Batavia and at first sought to influence Sultan Hasanuddin by diplomacy and generous gifts. The Sultan had an interest in the sciences, and the VOC presented him with the latest in scientific knowledge—a set of terrestrial and celestial globes by Joan

Blaeu, as well as a world atlas and a telescope. However, this strategy did not convince him to ban the traders from his port, and war appeared to be inevitable. For obvious reasons the Sultan developed an interest in the techniques of modern warfare and, with the help of foreign advisers, set about fortifying his city against attack. George Cockayne, the English factor in Macassar, wrote in a letter to the English East India Company that he was:

> Called every day to the King or else he comes to our house to have me resolve him as well as I can of such questions as he doth propound unto me. The King is much grieved in mind and maketh much preparation for war: all the whole land is making of bricks for two castles this summer to be finished; in the armoury is laid 10,000 lances, 10,000 kris with bucklers for them, and 2422 pieces [guns] … Yesterday in my sight the King, to see his force and how many men he could make, at an instant were mustered 36,000 able men.

After diplomacy had failed, the Dutch demanded that the Sultan expel all foreign traders from his port and stop his own merchants from trading with those in the Moluccas who were defying the VOC-imposed monopoly. Sultan Hasanuddin was no fool and shrewdly responded:

> Such prohibition runs counter to the commandment of God, who created the world in order that all people should have the enjoyment thereof. Or do you believe that God has reserved these islands, so far away from the place of your nation, for only your trade alone?

The Dutch first attacked Macassar in 1660. Their soldiers landed in the southern part of Macassar and successfully seized Fort Panakkukang but were unable to overcome the Sultan's troops and capture the rest of the city. In 1667, the VOC formed an alliance with Aru Palakka, the Ruler of Bone, in South Sulawesi, and with the aid of his Bugis warriors laid siege again to the city. Two years later the Dutch and their Bugis allies were finally able to force the surrender of Macassar, after some of the fiercest fighting they had ever experienced in the Indies. The lithograph celebrating the victory shows portraits of Dutch General Cornelis Speelman and his Bugis ally Aru Palakka above a vast scene of the battle for Macassar.

The Dutch East India Company was now the richest private company the world had ever seen. It owned 150 merchant ships, 40 warships and had 30,000 employees, including an army of 15,000 soldiers. Its stranglehold on the Spice Islands was complete and all believed there was no power in the world that could break its monopoly over the trade in cloves and nutmeg.

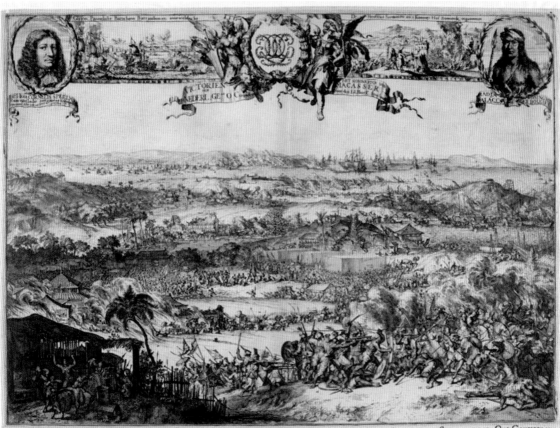

The Dutch victory at Macassar in 1669, Romeyn de Hooge (Netherlands Maritime Museum, Amsterdam)

18 Pierre Poivre

I then realized that the possession of spice which is the basis of Dutch power in the Indies was grounded on the ignorance and cowardice of the other trading nations of Europe. One only had to know this and be daring enough to share with them, this never-failing source of wealth which they possess in one corner of the globe.

—Pierre Poivre, *Voyages of a Philosopher*, 1760

After thousands of years of free commercial trade by Austronesian, Greek, Roman, Arab, Persian, Indian, Javanese and Chinese traders, and ineffective attempts at monopoly by the Portuguese and Spanish crowns, the all-powerful Dutch East India Company had now established a complete monopoly over the spice trade from the Moluccas.

It took the efforts of only one individual, an ingenious and remarkably persistent Frenchman, to break that monopoly.

Born in 1719 in Lyon, Pierre Poivre (Peter Pepper) had a name that curiously showed his predestination. At the age of fourteen he joined the Missionary Brothers of Saint Joseph. He later became a novice with the Paris Society of Foreign Missions and at 21 years of age left France to become a missionary in China.

Foreign missionaries were no longer welcome in China and upon disembarking in Canton he was placed under house arrest. Poivre used his confinement to master Cantonese, in which he was successfully able to plead his case for release. He then spent a year travelling through China and two years at the imperial court of Cochin-China—now known as Vietnam. Although a gifted linguist, he was not nearly as successful as a missionary and made very few conversions. After his three years in the Orient, the Paris Society of Foreign Missions decided he lacked the required missionary zeal and should return to France.

Poivre left for home on a ship belonging to the French East India Company, the Compagnie des Indes, laden with Chinese silks, porcelain and other oriental goods. Jean-Baptiste Colbert, the Minister of Finance under Louis XIV, had founded the company in 1664 with the aim of challenging the English and Dutch trading companies. It received exclusive rights from the King to trade with all lands beyond the Cape of Good Hope, and by the eighteenth century it was rivalling the English in India and had established trading interests in Vietnam and China.

At this time, England was at war with France, and an English naval vessel attacked his ship while it was heading towards the Sunda Strait. Standing on the bridge, the young Frenchman had his right arm smashed by cannon fire and then had to endure the ensuing battle without proper medical attention. He was taken prisoner by the English who amputated his lower right arm to prevent the spread of gangrene. Poivre spent five months in Batavia recovering from his wounds and took the opportunity to learn yet another language. Batavia was the headquarters of the Dutch East India Company, and Poivre had plenty of time to observe the continuous commerce of its spice-laden ships as they entered and left the harbour. He frequented the warehouse district where the spices were stored before being loaded on to the VOC East Indiamen that would transport then to Holland.

A painting by Adam Willaerts in the Netherlands Maritime Museum shows Asian and Dutch ships at anchor off Batavia, with smaller vessels ferrying goods up and down the main canal.

Asian and Dutch ships at anchor off Fort Batavia, Adam Willaerts, 1649 (Netherlands Maritime Museum, Amsterdam)

Pierre Poivre had time to stroll along Batavia's wide shaded boulevards observing the colonial mansions, the fine horse-drawn carriages and the beautifully dressed women, with their retinues of servants, including the parasol bearers and the fan bearers. The women of Batavia were renowned for these displays of the wealth derived from the spice trade. As one visitor described it:

> The most amazing thing in Batavia is the great and marvellous show and splendour which is shown there not just by the Dutch women but also by the Mestise and Kastise women … because everyone is more expensively attired than the next, and dressed in Silk and Satin, in Damask and Gold Alesys, or in all sorts of costly gold coloured, striped or flowery material, with golden embroidery.

Poivre would speak with anyone, Dutch or Indonesian, who might provide information about the conditions in the Moluccas, where the spices grew, and details of the trade. He came to realize that the French could capture part of this trade from the Dutch East India Company if only they could smuggle nutmeg and clove seedlings out of the Spice Islands.

The Dutch jealously protected their trade monopoly by imposing a death sentence on anybody caught smuggling seedlings out of the Spice Islands, and by rendering the seed infertile. Clove spice is a dried flower bud, so there was no risk it could be planted and grown elsewhere, but the nutmeg is a seed and, to prevent its germination and propagation the Dutch first shelled and roasted the seed and then coated it with lime before export and sale on the commercial market.

The Dutch had been successful in transplanting clove seedlings from Ternate and Tidore to the islands around Ambon, but all these had very similar environmental conditions, and it remained to be seen whether clove and nutmeg seedlings could be grown in other parts of the world.

His time recuperating in Batavia also allowed Poivre to reflect on his future. Deciding to abandon his missionary calling and take up botany, he wrote: 'The accident which befell me appeared as an unmistakeable sign that God had not destined me for the calling which I had first followed'.

On the return voyage to France, his ship stopped at the French colony of Mauritius, where Pierre Poivre discussed his idea of transplanting cloves and nutmeg with government officials on the island. They recommended he make a proposal directly to the French East India Company on his return to France. For Poivre, even after the tragedy of losing his arm, returning to France was never going to be easy. In Angola his vessel received orders to sail to the Caribbean island of Martinique and from there he took passage on a Dutch vessel returning to Europe. Off the coast of Brittany, French corsairs attacked and plundered the Dutch vessel. Poivre arranged to return with them to France, but the corsairs were apprehended by an English naval vessel before they could reach

St Malo. Poivre again found himself a prisoner of the English, this time on the island of Guernsey in the English Channel.

After his eventual return to France, Poivre studied botany and then was appointed to return to the Orient as a representative of the French East India Company. His mission was to carry out botanical studies for the company in Vietnam, but he also had a secret mission—to attempt to smuggle clove and nutmeg seedlings from the Spice Islands.

French East India Company officials in India were reluctant to fund Pierre Poivre because of internal jealousies and fear of antagonizing the Dutch. However, in 1751 Poivre received funding to charter a vessel in Macao which he loaded with trade goods before sailing to Manila disguised as a merchant. In Manila he dealt with traders who carried out a secret spice trade from the Moluccas and waited eighteen months before finally acquiring nine rooted nutmeg seedlings. He sailed immediately for Mauritius, not knowing if his precious seedlings would survive the journey across the Indian Ocean. Carefully planting the seedlings, he hoped the tropical climate, proximity to the sea and similar latitude would all be conducive to their survival.

Determined to obtain more seedlings, Poivre sought help from the French governor of Mauritius and obtained another vessel, which although barely seaworthy, allowed him to return to Manila in 1753. It was during this absence that a rival, Jean-Baptiste Aublet, arrived in Mauritius as the recently appointed apothecary-botanist responsible for the development of a botanical garden for medicinal plants on the island.

Pierre Poivre found that seedlings were now even more difficult to obtain in Manila, as none of his traders and their contacts was willing to risk the severe penalties imposed by the Dutch. Undeterred, he decided the only solution was to risk arrest and execution by sailing directly to the islands himself. However, nearing the Moluccas, his crew became increasingly nervous and, fearing mutiny, he was unable to make landfall until they reached the safety of Portuguese Timor. There Poivre confided his plan to the Portuguese governor, and with his support obtained eleven nutmeg seedlings and a handful of clove seedlings, with a promise of more on his return.

Again Poivre set off across the Indian Ocean to Mauritius only to find to his great disappointment that his initial nutmeg seedlings had withered and died. At this point he developed an intense antipathy towards Jean-Baptiste Aublet, whom he suspected of sabotaging his efforts to grow the transplanted spice trees. Undeterred, he planted his new seedlings. Leaving strict instructions for their care, he departed for France in an attempt to obtain funding for another expedition.

The loss of a powerful patron and what seemed to be the imminent collapse of the corruption-ridden French East India Company delayed his plans. Poivre settled down in his home town of Lyon for ten years. He continued his academic pursuits, and was elected president of the Royal Agricultural Society of Lyon and became a member of the Royal Society of Paris. He even had time to write his memoirs,

Voyages of a Philosopher, in which he combined his experiences in the Far East with his ideas on botany.

Poivre's dispute with Jean-Baptiste Aublet became increasingly virulent. In 1758 he accused his fellow botanist of pouring boiling water on the germinating nutmeg seedlings and of being an agent of the Dutch East India Company. This controversy continued to rage, with Poivre's supporters promoting him as a heroic patriot who risked his life attempting to break the Dutch spice monopoly, and his opponents believing he was a self-aggrandizing adventurer wasting public funds.

In 1767, after the eventual collapse of the French East India Company, the Foreign Minister appointed Poivre as intendent, or civil governor, of the islands of Mauritius and Bourbon. His sponsor, the Duke of Praslin, wrote of him:

> Monsieur Poivre will immortalize his administration if he were able to make the colony compete with the Moluccas in the production of spices. Cinnamon is already established at the Isle de France but it is not of good quality … It is easy to obtain pepper for trials, but with nutmegs and cloves there are great difficulties to overcome.

His career rejuvenated, Poivre returned to Mauritius to take up his official position, only to find that his second garden of transplanted nutmegs and cloves had died of neglect. Disappointed, Poivre dedicated his energies to transforming the island into a model agricultural community and to building a magnificent botanical garden, full of tropical plants and fruits from all over the world including mango, durian, mangosteen, avocado and breadfruit. But his desire to break the Dutch spice monopoly had not diminished and with considerable determination he set about gaining funding for a third expedition to the Spice Islands.

In 1769 two French vessels, the *Vigilant* and the *Morning Star*, set sail from Mauritius for the Moluccas. For this mission Poivre entrusted his assistant, Mathieu-Simon Provost, to succeed where he himself had failed. Over the years Poivre had continued to collect intelligence on the Spice Islands and had became aware of a small island north of Ternate where the Dutch might not be especially vigilant. But when the French ships dropped anchor there they discovered that as a result of the Dutch policy of extirpation, every clove tree had been cut down. Bitterly disappointed, Provost decided that the *Morning Star* should sail directly to Portuguese Timor while the *Vigilant* would sail for Ceram in a last attempt to obtain seedlings. At Ceram, Provost learnt that all the spice trees growing there had also been destroyed by the Dutch. Somehow luck was with him and he found his way to the island of Gebe off the east coast of Halmahera. There the local chiefs declared their allegiance to the King of France and led Provost to the Patani peninsula, where there were supposed to be transplanted spice trees, unknown to the Dutch. Parties were sent out to comb the peninsula. Days later a party returned with hundreds of nutmeg seedlings which were carefully loaded on to the *Vigilant*, and as Provost was about to leave a second party arrived with clove seedlings.

The *Vigilant* made the rendezvous in Timor with the *Morning Star* and, dividing the precious cargo between them, they set off across the Indian Ocean. On 24 June 1770, Provost made his triumphant return to Mauritius and presented Pierre Poivre with a cargo of 400 rooted nutmeg seedlings and 70 rooted clove seedlings.

Mindful of the failure of his previous attempts to grow the seedlings in Mauritius, Poivre arranged to have them distributed throughout France's tropical colonies— Reunion, the Seychelles and Cayenne in French Guiana. His efforts to encourage their cultivation by local planters on Mauritius met with little success, and he wrote:

> I observed with deep chagrin that most of our cultivators have calculated the time required by the seedlings to grow, for the plants to bear fruit and provide rich cargoes of commerce, and have shown the greatest indifference for the cultivation of the spices.

In moments of despair, he even expressed a fear that the nutmegs he distributed for seeding had found their way into the planters' kitchens rather than their gardens.

In 1773, after five years in Mauritius, Pierre Poivre returned to France and Lyon with his wife and two children, leaving behind the famous botanical gardens he had established. He left a former neighbour, Jean-Nicolas Céré, in charge of his precious clove and nutmeg trees but seems to have received little encouragement from local officials.

Poivre's written pleas to the new governor on behalf of his spice trees only aroused the following response:

> For you M. le Poivre, the first and foremost care as Intendant of the Ile de France seems to have been to look after your precious spice trees. I have wider and more important things to consider. It is evidently not enough for you to have spoken to me about cloves and nutmegs for days, but now you continue to harp on the same subject. Let me tell you frankly, I am sick of the words 'spice tree'.

However, thanks to Céré's efforts, the clove and nutmeg seedlings survived to bear fruit. He picked the first harvest of French cloves in 1776 and the governor of Mauritius carried them to France to present to Louis XVI. The first harvest of French nutmegs occurred two years later, in 1778, and a brilliant reception was held in Government House to celebrate the event. A lithograph of Pierre Poivre showing him holding cloves and nutmegs, hangs in the State House, Le Chateau de Réduit in Mauritius.

By the 1790s the islands of Reunion, Madagascar, Zanzibar, and the Seychelles in the Indian Ocean, as well as Grenada and Martinique in the Caribbean, had commercial plantations of Indonesian spices. Cloves thrived on the islands of Zanzibar and Pemba off the east coast of Africa, and nutmeg thrived on the Caribbean island of Grenada.

Pierre Poivre, Le Château de Réduit, Mauritius

Thanks to the determination of one man, cloves and nutmeg were now being cultivated throughout the tropical zones of the world and the Dutch monopoly of the Moluccan spice trade, imposed so brutally by Jan Pieterszoon Coen, was over.

For two centuries the Dutch East India Company had been the most powerful trading company in the world, but this huge multinational enterprise was now in financial difficulties caused by fixed overheads and declining prices. The VOC had become a victim of its own success. As the spices it supplied became more readily available they also became less desirable and were no longer considered such a symbol of luxury and prestige. Spices also had to compete with new stimulants such as tea, coffee, chocolate and tobacco. Culinary tastes were also changing. Vegetables from the New World such as corn, potatoes, tomatoes and chilli peppers were adding variety to people's diets.

The competition from new sources of cloves and nutmeg entering the market from the French tropical colonies, courtesy of the persistence of Pierre Poivre, was the last straw for the Dutch East India Company. It went into a slow decline until it came to rely on short-term loans to continue operations. Eventually unable to roll over these loans or raise more funds from banks or shareholders, it was forced into bankruptcy.

In 1798 the Dutch government nationalized the VOC, taking over all its debts and assets, and the overseas possessions of the once all-powerful Dutch East India Company became part of the Dutch colonial empire.

19   *Prince Nuku*

Lord, we place our honour under your foot and trust that everything in the land of Tidore will be in a state of readiness and strengthened, and that the cannon will again be placed in the old fort.

Send the Dutch away from Tidore before our arrival, which will be in September.

—Prince Nuku in a letter to the Sultan of Tidore, 1782

The livelihood of the Sultans of Ternate and Tidore, their courts and many of their people depended entirely on the annual stipend they received from the Dutch East India Company. For this reason the people of the Moluccas came to regard their sultans as hostages to VOC policy and mere mouthpieces for it.

Trouble began with the arrest and exile of Sultan Jamaluddin of Tidore after he acted against Dutch interests. This was followed by the usual dispute over a successor. Unwisely ignoring the advice of the Royal Council, the Dutch passed over the potentially powerful Prince Nuku and nominated a powerless council of regents.

In 1780 Prince Nuku, supported by hundreds of followers, rebelled against the VOC, which then fought a bloody campaign against the rebels, forcing Prince Nuku and 400 of his most faithful fighters to flee to a base on Ceram. From there they organized raids against the VOC, who branded Nuku 'The Bloodthirsty Pirate', but his people saw him as a charismatic leader and a righteous ruler who could force the Dutch out of the Moluccas and restore their past wealth and independence.

The VOC put a price on Prince Nuku's head, sending a fleet of 29 kora-kora and 1100 men to capture him and his supporters. This expedition turned into a disaster for the VOC when rebels within the fleet killed their commanders and then defected to Prince Nuku on Ceram. The rebels secretly sent a letter to the Dutch-appointed sultan explaining their motives and requesting his support for their plan to take action against the Dutch East India Company:

We ask forgiveness, but we will not return until you abandon the Company. If you do not, the land of Tidore will be destroyed because truly the might of your 'father' Nuku in Ceram is very great. His followers are many because the kings of the north, the south, and the entire east are assisting your 'father' and sending warriors, all inclined to fight against the Company.

This led to an uprising in 1783 during which Prince Nuku's supporters seized the fort on Tidore and murdered all the Dutch on the island, including the twenty Dutch soldiers assigned to protect the Sultan. Prince Nuku had travelled from his base in Ceram to the island of Bacan to wait for the uprising. He then returned in triumph to Tidore accompanied by 200 kora-kora filled with his warriors chanting war songs.

As expected, the Dutch gathered their forces from across the archipelago and prepared to wreak vengeance. Later that year a joint Dutch and Ternatean force crossed the narrow strait between the two islands and began wreaking havoc on the people of Tidore. They burnt entire villages to the ground and more than 1800 people were killed in the fighting. Governor Cornabé proudly reported to his superiors in Batavia that so many of the supporters of Prince Nuku were killed, including women and children, that spilled Dutch blood had been repaid a hundredfold.

Prince Nuku and his remaining forces again retreated to their bases in Ceram and Papua, where he found himself a new and surprising ally—the British East India Company. The captains of vessels sent by the British to trade surreptitiously for cloves and nutmegs in Ceram began to supply Prince Nuku with arms and support him in his war against the Dutch. They even drew up a manifesto committing all parties to the British–Moluccan alliance and the expulsion of the Dutch from the region. With new-found confidence, Prince Nuku sent a letter to the next Sultan of Tidore nominated by the Dutch:

I have the honour, Your Highness, to inform you that the English Company and I are in agreement. I therefore await your intention towards me, and I beseech Your Highness to not be afraid; govern Tidore and its people quietly and with all caution so that no evil can befall you from the Dutch Company … We hope and wish for nothing other than that our Brother the Sultan and the Tidorean noblemen will ally themselves with us to expel the Dutch, and should you have nutmeg, mace, and cloves for sale, the English Company will pay you handsomely in cash or munitions, or whatever wares you require.

The British had a renewed interest the Moluccas, not only because of cloves and nutmegs but because of their involvement in the highly lucrative China trade. Tea from China had become the single most important commodity in the portfolio of the British East India Company. The so-called Eastern Passage between the Papuan islands of Batanta and Salawati allowed the British to sail directly from the Cape of Good Hope to China, even when the countervailing winds of the north-west monsoon were blowing. Prince Nuku had declared himself Sultan over the Moluccas, Papua and Ceram, and his control of the Eastern Passage, together with his long and successful opposition to the

Dutch, made him a natural ally of the British. They had long coveted a position in the Moluccas and the opportunity to displace the Dutch and establish a base close to their new trade route between Britain and China was too tempting to resist.

In 1795, forces of the French Revolution invaded Holland and King Willem escaped to London. Consultations with the British government and the British East India Company resulted in him calling upon the Dutch governors of all overseas territories to surrender to the British expeditionary forces that might soon be expected to appear.

In 1796, Admiral Rainer sailed from Penang in Malaya with a British fleet of ten ships and a force of 1000 men. Sailing into the protected harbour of Ambon, the fleet anchored off Fort Victoria and fired off its cannon. Although the British had expected some resistance, Governor Cornabé, the same man responsible for the vengeful murder of woman and children during the VOC attack on Tidore, quickly capitulated. Almost 175 years after the Massacre of Amboyna and the humiliating departure forced on them by the Dutch East India Company, the British and the Company of Merchants Trading to the East Indies had officially returned to the Spice Islands.

As soon as he learnt of the seizure of Fort Victoria by the British, Prince Nuku sent an 'embassy' to Ambon consisting of his nephew, Ibrahim, accompanied by a fleet of 100 kora-kora and 3000 men. Admiral Ranier received 'ambassador' Ibrahim with all the honour and respect due to his rank and the 'sultan' he represented. In his audience with the admiral, Ibrahim informed him that his uncle was the true sovereign of Tidore, Ternate and all of the Moluccas, and if the British could restore him his rights he would ensure they had exclusive trading privileges throughout the islands. Ranier, in a typical colonial judgment, described Ibrahim as dignified and well acquainted with European ways and table manners but was less impressed with his fleet of kora-kora, which he considered trifling vessels.

Admiral Ranier explained to Ibrahim that he did not have the authority to reinstate Sultan Nuku and that his orders extended only to taking possession of those territories held by the Dutch until the end of the war in Europe, when a treaty would determine whether the Moluccas would remain in permanent British possession. Captain Walter Lennon, the secretary to the admiral, wrote of the meeting in his admirably titled *Journal of an Expedition to the Molucca Islands under the command of Admiral Ranier with Some Account of Those Islands at the Time of Their Falling into Our Hands, and Likewise Suggestions Relative to their Future Better Management in Case of Being Retained in Our Permanent Possession*:

> Ibrahim did not seem to think the Admiral quite sincere in saying he did not have the authority to reinstate his uncle in the sovereignty of Tidore, but rather that he made this as sort of an excuse, observing that he could not help thinking him invested with unlimited powers. He also seemed to imagine that our taking of Amboina and Banda was entirely owing to the intimacy between Sultan Nuku and the captains of the country-ships, who have had an intercourse with him for some times past; and who, probably, to gain his

Kora-kora from Gebe Island, Alphonse Pellion, 1817 (State Library of NSW, MRB/Q980/F)

support, were liberal in their promises on the part of the English, to second his views against the Dutch. To set him right in this particular the Admiral endeavoured to explain the difference between the King of England and the East India Company, which was a distinction, that even with the assistance of a perfect knowledge of the language would be very difficult to make him understand.

It was not until 1799, when Robert Farquhar became the British Resident in Ambon, that this policy changed and the British supported the rebels more directly. Prince Nuku and his warriors prepared for a second invasion of Tidore, this time with the use of British arms and support. He gathered his forces off Tidore, consisting of 70 kora-kora filled with his warriors, as well as a British support vessel carrying a group of fierce Bugis fighters paid for by the British and recruited from Macassar. Prince Nuku found enough local support on the island to overthrow the Sultan, who fled to Ternate. The Tidorean royal council then proclaimed him as the new Sultan and he and his English allies made plans for the invasion of Ternate.

Capturing Fort Oranje from the Dutch would be a much more difficult operation and would require British troops, so the first option was to try diplomacy. The British sent a ship from Penang and Captain Packenham went ashore to pay a diplomatic call on Governor Budach, inviting him to accept British protection. But the Dutch were not facing any overwhelming force of arms and Governor Budach probably used some colourful language when suggesting that Captain Packenham leave the island.

The British waited until 1801, when they dispatched a more formidable force of six vessels and hundreds of troops to Ternate. Anchoring off Fort Oranje, they gave the Dutch time to assess the situation before sending two officers ashore to hand Governor Cransssen an ultimatum calling for the capitulation of the fort within two hours. The Dutch governor's response was a round of cannon fire from the fort, forcing the British vessels to withdraw to a safe distance. The next day the British fleet began to assemble troops ashore for an attack on Fort Oranje, reinforced by a large body of Sultan Nuku's fighting men who had crossed over from Tidore. A long blockade of Fort Oranje followed, giving the members of the governor's council time to debate the advisability of further resistance and for Dutch morale to collapse. One evening, as the governor sat down for his dinner, conspirators within the fort overpowered him and began negotiations with the British. A Dutch surrender was soon signed, which allowed for the governor and his garrison to return unharmed to Batavia.

The culmination of Prince Nuku's long rebellion was his formal installation as Sultan of Tidore, which Robert Farquhar describes:

> On the 12th of November 1801, Nuku was solemnly crowned in Fort Oranje, Sultan of Tidore, an honour which he had been fighting the Dutch to obtain for twenty years. It must have been an inexpressible satisfaction to the old man sixty years of age, perfectly decrepit from persecution and continual hardships, to have still accomplished the darling object of his heart before death and the pleasing reflection will no doubt contribute in a powerful degree to render his latter days, a scene of happiness to himself and grateful thanksgiving to the British.

The British and Sultan Nuku signed a treaty that unlike those with the Dutch stressed respect and mutual trust, hinting only vaguely at Tidore's dependence on the British. Significantly, the British abandoned the Dutch extirpation policy, for the destruction of their precious clove trees had been the greatest source of resentment for the Moluccans. The British East India Company was now in control of all of the Moluccas, with responsibility for administering the corrupt and exploitative monopoly system that the Dutch had created and the British had promised to dismantle. Reality soon came face to face with liberal rhetoric, and those of a cynical disposition already know what the result would be. The British quickly convinced themselves they needed to maintain the monopoly in order to offset their own expenses and provide an income for the local people. It only remained for the steadfast Captain Walter Lennon to justify the change in policy:

> It may be argued as more generally advantageous to the English to throw open the trade altogether and suffer private adventurers to carry merchandise and provisions there and be at liberty to purchase the

spices on the spot. But it is only on the principle of an absolute monopoly of the spices that it could ever be an objective to form settlements in so detached a situation and there is little doubt but this monopoly under proper regulations would not only be extremely productive to the State but also more beneficial to the people themselves, than if they were left without control, as their violent tempers and the competition that would immediately take place among the different islands would inevitably lead them into endless wars and anarchy, to which they are already too much addicted.

Unfortunately for Sultan Nuku the British rule was short lived. The Treaty of Amiens signed in 1802 brought peace to Europe and control of the Moluccas was handed back to the Dutch a year later. Nuku's brief reign of glory had ended and his health declined until his death in 1805.

In 1807 Napoleon appointed Willem Daendels, a well-known leader of the Dutch revolution, as governor-general of the East Indies. Arriving in Java, Daendels proclaimed the annexation of the Dutch East Indies to the French Empire and raised the French flag over Batavia. This was waving a red flag at John Bull. The British mobilized their forces in India and launched a successful invasion of Java in 1811. The British East India Company took control of the Dutch Colonial Empire in all of the East Indies and Stamford Raffles was elevated to governor-general. Raffles never visited the Moluccas, and the British administration there was characterized more by benign neglect than any enlightened liberalization of the former Dutch policies. In 1816, after the Battle of Waterloo, followed by Napoleon's exile to the South Atlantic island of St Helena and the Peace of Paris, the British returned to Holland their colony in the East Indies.

We have a good idea of what the settlement of Ternate looked like at this time from a map and profile drawn by the Dutch in 1818. It shows the massive stone walls of Fort Oranje, with the Dutch administrative buildings secure inside. To the right of the fort is the town of Malayo, laid out along two long streets following the waterfront, with cross streets leading to the port. Next is the Royal Mosque, with its minaret, and further north is the Sultan's Palace, a Western-style building recently built by the British. To the left of the fort are native houses and groves of clove trees growing in the hills, and above the town Mount Gamalama can be seen belching smoke in the background. At this time the population of the town was about 4000, including 1000 Macassarese, 417 Europeans or Eurasians, 396 Chinese, 250 Ambonese and 19 Arabs, as well as 100 Papuan slaves who were granted their freedom in the latter half of the century.

The once-splendid sultanates of Ternate and Tidore had already begun their decline. The Dutch maintained a Resident who had few responsibilities, and the islands that were once the centre of the world's attention slowly sank into obscurity. The only excitement came from the sudden rumblings of Mount Gamalama, which in the 1840s began spewing ash and then violently erupted, throwing rocks into the air and issuing a stream of molten lava that flowed down its slopes into the steaming sea. John Dill Ross, returning from Papua on a coastal trading vessel, described the eruption:

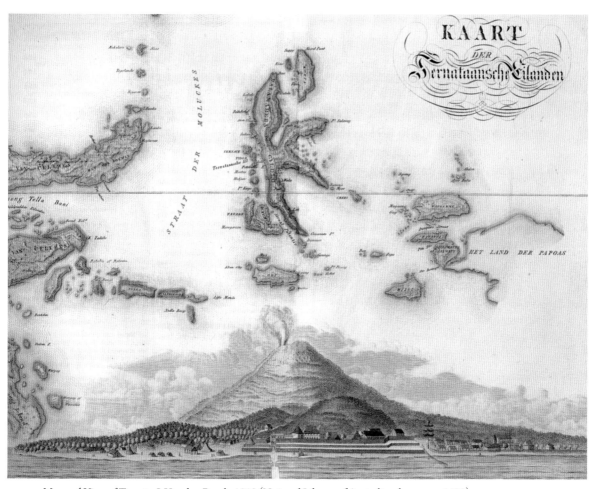

Map and View of Ternate, J. Van den Bosch, 1818 (National Library of Australia, nla.map-rm1439)

Presently a red glare flamed on the black sky, it was Ternate in eruption … The sky was like black marble veined with a fiery network of lightning flashes. Vast columns of flame roared at the summit of the volcano, a gleaming river of molten lava flowed from the crater through blazing forests and plantations, until it ended its course in the sea amidst stupendous clouds of steam. The sounds of the storm were dominated by the awful roar of the volcano. The sea was rolling in huge never-ending waves of flame and blood … a couple of buildings totter and come crashing to the ground amidst clouds of dust. Ternate was being racked by an earthquake.

In ten hours, Ternate had been reduced to rubble and those inhabitants wealthy enough to live in brick houses had become homeless. The massive walls of Fort Oranje, which had stood firm for almost two centuries, mainly withstood the tremor, but its brick barracks became uninhabitable. For a while the Dutch considered leaving Ternate but eventually committed themselves to rebuilding the government buildings that had been destroyed.

The protocol and rituals of empire were still important in this remote colonial outpost. The Dutch Resident paid special deference to the Sultan, who in his turn was subservient to the Resident. When there was need for a formal visit, these took the form of political theatre. The Sultan and his courtiers would travel the few hundred metres to the Dutch Residency in his state carriage, pulled not by horses but by sixteen palace servants. The Resident's deputy met the Sultan and his courtiers on arrival and led them to the reception hall through two rows of servants holding tall candelabra. The Resident would greet the Sultan respectfully as 'Your Highness', and he in turn would address the Resident in the Indonesian language as 'Father'. After the Sultan was seated in a heavily carved and gilded chair he would be offered tea and cakes before any polite discussion of one's health and the weather could commence. Invariably any political issues had already been settled by intermediaries, with the Sultan's visit to the Resident signifying a form of consent. After a respectful period of polite discussion, it was customary for the Resident to inquire if the Sultan was perhaps feeling fatigued, to which he would respond in the affirmative. The ceremonial goodbyes then began and the ritual of the return of the Sultan to his palace was set in motion.

When necessary, the Dutch Resident made his visit to the Sultan's Palace dressed in full ceremonial uniform, on horseback or by carriage, with his aides and military escort. After he had made his way up the curved stone steps to the palace, the same formal greetings would take place before the Resident and the Sultan were seated together on a canopied dais. Lining the reception room would be the members of the royal court dressed in their traditional costumes, with princes on one side and princesses on the other. After refreshments and the usual polite conversation, music and traditional dances were provided for the entertainment of the guests. Most probably there would be a warrior's dance performed by the princes, to celebrate the surrender of the Portuguese to Sultan Baabullah in 1575, followed by a graceful dance by the princesses to the rhythmic melody of a gong orchestra.

For the remainder of the century the main towns on Ternate and Tidore continued their roles as colonial anachronisms, little known and seldom visited. As one Dutch observer noted, agriculture languishes, fisheries do not flourish, trade declines and society is moribund.

For the Dutch Resident this was an ideal situation. He could report to his superiors in Batavia that, 'throughout the Residency tranquillity now prevails'.

Dutch officials being entertained at the Sultan's Palace, Ver Huell, 1820 (Maritime Museum, Rotterdam)

Epilogue

The major clove producing countries in the world today are Indonesia, Zanzibar, Madagascar and Sri Lanka. In Indonesia the main production is from large plantations in North Sulawesi, Central Java and Sumatra, with only a small contribution coming from the former Spice Islands. Most of the world's nutmeg is grown in various parts of Indonesia, followed by Grenada in the West Indies.

Indonesia is also the world's largest consumer of cloves and most of that goes up in smoke because of the Indonesians' love of kretek, the clove-flavoured cigarettes. These are about 60 percent tobacco and 40 percent ground cloves, the name coming from the cracking sound made when the volatile oil in a piece of ground clove explodes. Inveterate kretek smokers can be identified by the small burn marks on the front of their shirts. Anyone who has visited Indonesia can tell of the pungent aroma of these cigarettes, usually smelt as soon as you exit from immigration and customs at the airport. The cigarettes were initially popular among farmers in Central and East Java as well as lower income workers in the cities and towns, but clever marketing and packaging has created a more sophisticated image for a new generation of kretek smokers. With a large population and an expanding market, the big international tobacco companies have bought into the market and even the Marlboro Man now smokes kretek.

Clove oil is recovered from the crushed buds using a water distillation process and is a premium product used to flavour seasonings and as an aroma in high quality perfumes. The hint of clove gives an exotic scent to L'air du Temp by Nina Ricci and Armani pour Homme. Calvin Klein's Obsession contains the scent of both nutmeg and clove.

Cloves are an essential ingredient in many spice mixtures such as the French quatre épices, Chinese five-spice powder, Mogul Indian garam masala, the Arabic baharat, Moroccan ras el hanout, Tunisian galat dagga, Ethiopian berebera and many others. Rice is also frequently aromatized with cloves in Indian and Indonesian cooking, and cloves are also used to flavour Indian Chai teas.

Cloves are not as much part of European cooking as in the past, but are still used to flavour meats such as ham and corned beef, as well as the sauerkraut that accompanies them. Traditional meat hot pots flavoured with cloves are the French pot-au-feu and baëckeofe from the Alsace. Cloves and cinnamon still flavour traditional European spiced teabread or pain d'épices. Cloves and nutmeg flavour stewed fruits, add a dash of flavour to an apple pie, and are an essential ingredient in chutneys, relishes and sauces such as Worcestershire sauce.

Nutmeg flavours the traditional Christmas drink known as eggnog, while nutmeg and cinnamon are believed to be some of the secret ingredients that go into the Coca-Cola, the world's most popular soft drink.

The history of the Spice Islands can be read in the crumbling Portuguese, Spanish and Dutch forts that dot the islands. Fort Oranje, in the centre of Ternate town, has been restored to attract tourists and the ancient cannon on its bulwarks still point out to sea. I hired a car and driver to take me on the 40 kilometre circuit around the island. The narrow paved road passes Fort Toloko which stands in a commanding position on a rocky outcrop north of town, its circular walls stand tall and it still has a sixteenth century Portuguese seal over the entrance. The road then crosses the barren black lava rock which flowed from an erupting Mount Gamalama in the 1840s. Looking up towards the volcano I could see the trail left by the molten lava as it flowed down the mountain, burning the forest and destroying everything in its path as it flowed to the sea. On the other side of the island in the village appropriately called Kastela, the outline of Fort Gamalama can be seen from the remnants of its crumbling walls, but only one segment of the 500-year-old wall still stands tall, tenuously held up by the roots and vines that encircle its stones. Nearby, a memorial topped by a large clove bud shows the sequence of events leading from the murder of Sultan Hairun to the surrender of the Portuguese and their departure from the island. Returning towards Ternate town, a well-preserved fort, begun by the Portuguese and completed by the Dutch, lies on the waterfront south of Ternate harbour at the nearest crossing to the island of Tidore, and was probably meant to guard against any attack from the twin island.

History does have a habit of repeating itself, often with tragic consequences. While exploring Ternate town I saw evidence of the recent conflict on the island, with many mosques and churches being rebuilt, and the remnants of burnt-out houses. A roadside statue erected in one of the worst affected areas commemorates the human victims of Ramadan Berdarah, or Bloody Ramadan, a result of the violence that ravaged Ternate during November 1999.

The conflict started far away in Central Maluku, when communal fighting between Christians and Muslims broke out in the city of Ambon in January 1999. Conflict in North Maluku occurred the following August in the predominantly Christian area of Kao, on the north-east coast of Halmahera. Refugees from the mainly Muslim island of

Makian had been resettled in Kao after the 1975 eruption of the volcano that dominates their island. A government plan to create a new sub-district on traditional Kao land would effectively change the status of these people from refugees to permanent settlers and was highly controversial. The conflict started with the burning of a single house. The following day refugees from the minority Muslim and Christian communities in both districts streamed from one area to the other, as full-scale fighting broke out involving the use of locally made machetes and spears.

The influence of the Sultan of Ternate still extended to Halmahera. He was able to intervene and convince the Christian Kao, still loyal to their Muslim sultan, to lay down their arms. However, the underlying cause of the conflict was never resolved and fighting broke out again in October, when the Kao destroyed the village of Malifut, burning homes, schools and mosques with the loss of 100 lives. The local police and the military seemed unable or unwilling to control the situation, and Muslim refugees from Kao fled to Ternate and Tidore.

After the outbreak of the religious violence in Ambon, a Muslim militia group known as Laskar Jihad had been able to send thousands of armed jihadists from Java to Maluku without any intervention by the Indonesian government or the military. This militia added an even more violent dimension to the conflict as they were primed for holy war against the Christians in the community. Some of the Laskar Jihad reached Tidore in November 1999, inciting conflict there which resulted in the murder of a priest, the burning of a church and the loss of 35 lives.

On Ternate, the Sultan and his supporters activated a local militia group to protect the minority Christian community. Wearing the Sultan's colours and known as the 'yellow militia', they were able to work with the police and army to prevent the conflict spreading to Ternate. Muslim refugees who had fled to Ternate from Kao formed an opposing 'white militia'. After the religious violence on Tidore, they were joined by members of Laskar Jihad and their supporters who had crossed over from Tidore with evil intent.

Fighting soon broke out in Ternate between the yellow and white militias, resulting in 38 deaths and the destruction and burning of houses, churches and mosques. The white militia were able to occupy the grounds of the Sultan's Palace, forcing him to reach an agreement with the Sultan of Tidore, which allowed for the white militia to withdraw from the palace grounds if the yellow militia withdrew from the streets and resumed their former role of protecting the palace. It was the driver on my circuit around the island who told me about the militias, and until then I had thought this was a strictly Christian–Muslim conflict.

By far the most death and destruction had occurred on the north-east coast of Northern Halmahera in the Moro area of Tolebo and Galela. This area had been a Christian stronghold since the visit to the area by Francis Xavier in 1547, when he had tended to the abandoned Christians there, strengthened the converts in their faith and described the area as the Islands of Hope in God.

In February 2002, the Christian and Muslim groups signed a peace accord in the town of Malino in South Sulawesi. The Malino Peace Accord calls for the disarming of all militias, the creation of joint security patrols and establishes a framework for the return of refugees to their villages. It will take a long time for the communities to return to normal and forget the killings, but the peace accord seems to be working and there has been no further outbreak of full scale fighting in North Maluku.

Returning to Ternate town I visited the Sultan's Palace. It is a substantial building within large grounds that looks similar to an English country mansion, mainly because it was built by the British East India Company in the early 1800s. The palace is graced by two adjacent flights of stone steps leading to a wide verandah overlooking the harbour. Here, I was greeted by the Sultan's sister who very graciously showed me around the palace and explained the family history. There is a small museum area in the palace which displays the Sultan's throne and the royal banners, as well as a collection of relics from the Portuguese, Spanish and Dutch occupation of the island.

The Sultan of Ternate's sister and her son with the author (Ian Burnet)

Before leaving the island, I decided to climb Mount Gamalama and make a pilgrimage to the Afo clove tree. My guidebook told me it was the oldest clove tree in the world, standing 36 metres tall, having a circumference of more than three metres and having lived for four centuries. The track up the mountain started from a small village located on the highest slopes accessible by road. It was a steady upward climb through the cool verdant forest and groves of clove trees to a point halfway up the mountain. There I learnt the object of my pilgrimage had finally died of old age. This was a disappointment, but the fragrant aroma of the forest and the views of the sea glimpsed through the trees had made the climb worthwhile.

Before descending, I rested in a small clearing overlooking the chain of volcanic peaks rising from the sea to the south. I thought of the extraordinary story of these forgotten islands and the tiny clove buds that made them wealthy. It hardly seemed possible that these dramatic events could really have taken place on the peaceful shores below me. Relaxing, I crushed a clove bud between my thumb and forefinger and inhaled the rich spicy aroma of the 'scent of paradise', the scent that helped discover the world.

Timeline

1721 BC Dating of cloves found in a kitchen in Terqa, Syria

235 BC Eratosthenes is able to accurately measure the circumference of the earth

200 BC Earliest written reference to cloves during the Han Dynasty

138 BC Opening of Silk Road across Central Asia

50 BC Start of Greco-Roman trade with India

77 Pliny refers to cloves in his *Naturalis Historia*

140 Ptolemy publishes his *Geographia*

350 Earliest evidence of Hindu Sanskrit inscriptions in Indonesia

525 Cosmas Indicopleustes visits Ethiopia

600 The Qu'ran is revealed to Mohammed

618 Beginning of the Tang Dynasty and 300 years of stability along the Silk Road

661 Damascus becomes the centre of influence in the Islamic world

671 Earliest evidence of Arab seaborne traders in Guangzhou

711 Muslim occupation of Portugal

750 Baghdad becomes the centre of influence in the Islamic world

800 Construction of the Borobodur Monument

969 Cairo becomes the centre of influence in the Islamic world

1099 The Christian Crusaders capture Jerusalem

1165 A letter supposedly sent by the legendary Prester John reaches Europe

1187 Jerusalem is captured by the Muslim leader Saladin

1227 Northern China is captured by the Mongols

1249 End of the Muslim occupation of Portugal

1266 Polo brothers reach the court of Kublai Khan

1271 Polo brothers with Marco Polo depart on their second journey across the Silk Road

1275 Polo brothers reach Shangdu and introduce Marco to Kublai Khan

1291 First evidence of Islam in North Sumatra

1293 Polo brothers with Marco Polo sail on return journey to Venice

1298 Polo brothers and Marco Polo finally return to Venice

1325 Ibn Battutah departs Tangier

1368	Mongols toppled by a peasant revolt
1405	First voyages of the Chinese Treasure Fleets commanded by Admiral Zheng He
1405	Mission from Malacca to the Ming court
1419	Prince Henry the Navigator founds his school of navigation
1454	Papal Decree gives the Portuguese trading rights as far as India
1480	Portuguese explorers reach as far as the Gulf of Guinea in West Africa
1484	Evidence of Islam reaching Ternate
1488	Christopher Columbus proposes a westward voyage to the Orient to the Portuguese court
1489	Bartholomeu Dias rounds the Cape of Good Hope
1489	Portuguese spy Pero da Covilhão reaches Calicut in India
1492	Christopher Columbus sails west to the Orient
1493	Portuguese spy Pero da Covilhão reaches Axum in Ethiopia
1494	The Treaty of Tordesillas divides the world between the Portuguese and Spanish
1498	The fleet of Vasco da Gama reaches India
1500	The fleet of Pedro Alvares Cabral reaches India
1508	The Portuguese defeat a Turkish-Gujurati fleet off Diu in India, in a decisive battle
1510	Admiral Alfonso de Albuquerque captures Goa
1511	Admiral Alfonso de Albuquerque captures Malacca
1512	Antonio de Abreu reaches Banda
1512	Francisco Serrão reaches Ternate
1513	Portuguese fleet from Malacca reaches Banda to trade for nutmeg
1515	Admiral Alfonso de Albuquerque captures Hormuz
1515	Portuguese fleet from Malacca reaches Banda and Ternate to trade for nutmeg and cloves
1517	Ferdinand Magellan brings to Spain his plans for a westward journey to the Moluccas
1519	The Armada de Molucca sails from Seville under the command of Ferdinand Magellan
1521	Ferdinand Magellan killed at Mactan in the Philippines
1521	The Armada de Molucca reaches Ternate
1522	Juan Sebastian el Cano in the *Victoria* completes the first circumnavigation of the world
1523	The Portuguese build Fort Gamalama on Ternate
1529	The Spanish sign the Treaty of Saragossa, selling their rights over the Moluccas to the Portuguese
1536	Antonio Galvao becomes Governor of Ternate
1540	Sultan Hairun of Ternate comes to power
1546	The Jesuit priest Francis Xavier arrives in Ternate
1552	Francis Xavier dies of fever in the Bay of Canton
1570	Sultan Hairun of Ternate is murdered by the Portuguese
1575	Portuguese surrender to Sultan Baabullah and leave Ternate

1579	Francis Drake reaches Ternate and meets with Sultan Baabullah
1580	Francis Drake in the *Golden Hind* completes the second circumnavigation of the world
1581	The union of the crowns of Spain and Portugal
1581	Dutch rebel against the Spanish to form the United Provinces of the Netherlands
1583	Sultan Baabullah of Ternate dies
1596	Jan Huygens van Linschoten publishes his book *Itinerario*
1596	The first Dutch fleet to the Indies led by Van Houtman arrives in Banten
1600	Vessels of the second Dutch fleet reach Ternate and meet with Sultan Said
1601	The English East India Company is formed
1601	The first English fleet to the Indies led by James Lancaster arrives in Banten
1602	The Dutch East India Company (VOC) is formed
1604	The second English fleet to the Indies led by Henry Middleton
1605	The Portuguese fort in Tidore is captured by the Dutch
1607	The Spanish capture Fort Gamalama on Ternate and exile Sultan Said to Manila
1609	Spain and the Netherlands sign a truce
1618	Jan Pieterszoon Coen becomes Governor-General of the Dutch East India Company
1619	The Dutch capture the town of Jayakarta and found Batavia
1621	Dutch Forces under Jan Pieterszoon Coen commit the Banda Massacre
1623	The English East India Company departs from the East Indies after the Ambon Massacre
1652	Sultan Mandarsjah of Ternate signs the extirpation contract with the Dutch
1667	In the Treaty of Breda the English exchange the island of Run for the island of Manhattan
1663	The Spanish abandon Fort Gamalama in Ternate
1669	Dutch capture Macassar, completing their monopoly of the spice trade in the Moluccas
1754	Pierre Poivre plants his first nutmeg seedlings in Mauritius
1755	Pierre Poivre plants his second nutmeg and clove seedlings in Mauritius
1770	Pierre Poivre plants his third nutmeg and clove seedlings in Mauritius
1780	Prince Nuku of Tidore rebels against the Dutch East India Company
1795	Clove and Nutmeg trees thrive in the French dependencies of the Indian Ocean and the Caribbean
1798	The Dutch East India Company is forced into bankruptcy
1801	The English East India Company installs Prince Nuku as the Sultan of Tidore
1802	After the Treaty of Amiens, the English hand the Moluccas back to the Dutch
1808	Marshal Daendels raises the French flag over Batavia
1811	The British invasion of Java, Stamford Raffles becomes Governor-General of the British East Indies
1816	The British hand control of the East Indies back to the Dutch

Bibliography

Akveld, Leo, and E.M. Jacobs, *The Colourful World of the VOC*, THOTH, Amsterdam, 2002

Alwi, Des, *Sejarah Maluku*, Dian Rakyat, Jakarta, 2005

Andaya, Leonard, *The World of Maluku*, University of Hawaii, 1943

Benda, Harry J., and John A. Larkin, *The World of Southeast Asia*, Harper & Row, New York, 1967

Bergreen, Laurence, *Over the Edge of the World*, HarperCollins, New York, 2004

Blackburn, Susan, *Jakarta: A History*, Oxford University Press, Singapore, 1990

Boulnois, Luce, *Silk Road*, Odyssey, Hong Kong, 2004

Boxer, Charles R., *The Portuguese Seaborne Empire*, Penguin Books, London, 1969

Brierley, Joanna, *Spices: The Story of Indonesia's Spice Trade*, Oxford University Press, Kuala Lumpur, 1994

Brotton, Jerry, *Trading Territories*, Reaktion Books, London, 1997

Brotton, Jerry, *The Renaissance Bazaar*, Oxford University Press, New York, 2002

Camões, Luis Vaz de, *The Lusiads*, Oxford University Press, New York, 1997

Corn, Charles, *The Scents of Eden*, Kodansha America, New York, 1998

Cortesao, Armando, *The Suma Oriental of Tome Pires*, The Hakluyt Society, London, 1967

Dalby, Andrew, *Dangerous Tastes: The Story of Spices*, British Museum Press, London, 2000

De Clercq, F.S.A., *Ternate: The Residency and its Sultanate*, The Irian Jaya (Papua) Fund, 2001

Disney, Anthony, and Emily Booth, *Vasco da Gama and the Linking of Europe and Asia*, Oxford University Press, New Delhi and New York, 2000

Dodge, Bertha, *Quest for Spices and New Worlds*, Archon Books, Hamden, Connecticut, 1988

Forster, William, *The Voyage of Sir Henry Middleton to Banten and the Maluco Islands*, The Hakluyt Society, London, 1855

Gaastra, Femme S., *The Dutch East India Company*, Walberg Pers, Zutphen, 2003

Galvao, Antonio, *A Treatise on the Moluccas*, Jesuit Historical Institute, Rome, 1970

Grove, Richard, *Green Imperialism*, Cambridge University Press, Melbourne, 1996

Hakluyt, Richard, *Voyages and Discoveries*, Penguin Classics, London, 1972

Hampden, John, *Francis Drake, Privateer*, Eyre Methuen, London, 1972

Hanna, Willard, *Turbulent Times Past in Ternate and Tidore*, Rumah Budaya Banda Naira, 1990

Hanusz, Mark, *Kretek*, Equinox Publishing, Jakarta, 2000

Heuken, Alfred, *Portuguese Sources for the History of Jakarta*, Yayasan Cipta Loka Caraka, Jakarta, 2002

Heuken, Alfred, *Be my Witness to the Ends of the Earth*, Yayasan Cipta Loka Caraka, Jakarta, 2002

Hobhouse, Henry, *Seeds of Change*, Counterpoint, Berkeley, 2005

Hourani, George, *Arab Seafaring*, Princeton University Press, Princeton, NJ, 1951

Jacobs, Els, *In Pursuit of Pepper and Tea*, Walberg Pers, Zutphen, 1991

Jane, Cecil, *The Journal of Christopher Columbus*, Clarkson Potter, New York, 1966

Jardine, Lisa, *Worldly Goods*, Doubleday, New York, 1996

Joyner, Tim, *Magellan*, International Marine Publishing, Camden, Maine, 1994

Kearney, Milo, *The Indian Ocean in World History*, Routledge, New York, 2004

Keay, John, *The Spice Route: A History*, University of California Press, Berkeley, 2007

Keen, Benjamin, *The Life of the Admiral Christopher Columbus*, Rutgers University Press, New Brunswick,
    NJ, 1992

Lane, Frederic C., *Venice: A Maritime Republic*, Johns Hopkins University Press, Baltimore, 1973

Levathes, Louise, *When China Ruled the Seas*, Simon & Schuster, New York, 1994

Ly-Tio-Fane, Madeleine, *Mauritius and the Spice Trade*, Mauritius Archives Publication, 1958

Mackintosh-Smith, Tim, *The Travels of Ibn Battutah*, Picador, London, 2002

Menzies, Gavin, *1421: The Year China Discovered the World*, Bantam Press, London, 2002

Miksic, John, *Borobodur*, Periplus Editions, Hong Kong, 1990

Miller, George, *To the Spice Islands and Beyond*, Oxford University Press, Kuala Lumpur, 1996

Miller, James Innes, *The Spice Trade of the Roman Empire*, Clarendon Press, Oxford, 1969

Milton, Giles, *Nathaniel's Nutmeg*, Sceptre, London, 1999

Monk, Kathryn, *The Ecology of Nusa Tenggara and Maluku*, Periplus Editions, Hong Kong, 1997

Muller, Kal, *Maluku: Indonesian Spice Islands*, Periplus Editions, Hong Kong, 1997

Panikkar, K.M., *Asia and Western Dominance*, George Allen & Unwin, London, 1959

Pepys, Samuel, *The Diary of Samuel Pepys*, Modern Library, London, 2001

Pigafetta, Antonio, *Magellan's Voyage*, Dover, New York, 1969

Polo, Marco, *The Travels*, Penguin Books, London, 1958

Raby, Peter, *Alfred Russel Wallace: A Life*, Pimlico, London, 2002

Reid, Anthony, *Southeast Asia in the Age of Commerce*, Volumes 1 and 2, Yale University Press, New
    Haven, Connecticut, 1993

Reid, Anthony, *Charting the Shape of Early Modern Southeast Asia*, Silkworm Books, Bangkok, 1999

Rizzo, Susanna Grazia, *From Paradise Lost to Paradise Found*, PhD, University of Wollongong, 2004

Rodrigues, Francisco, *The Book of Francisco Rodrigues*, The Hakluyt Society, London, 1944

Schiebinger, Londa, and Claudia Swan, *Colonial Botany*, University of Pennsylvania Press, Philadelphia,
    2005

Sherry, Frank, *Pacific Passions*, William Morrow, New York, 1994

Snitwongse, Kusuma, *Ethnic Conflicts in Southeast Asia*, ISEAS Publications, Singapore, 2005

Stella, Alain, *The Book of Spices*, Flammarion, Paris, 1999

Thorn, Major William, *The Conquest of Java*, Periplus, Hong Kong, 2004

Turner, Jack, Spice: The History of Temptation, HarperCollins, London, 2004

Wallace, Alfred Russel, The Malay Archipelago, Oxford University Press, Singapore and New York, 1986

Watkins, Ronald, Unknown Seas: How Vasco da Gama Opened the East, John Murray, London, 2003

Wilson, Derek, The World Encompassed: Drake's Great Voyage, 1577–1580, Alison & Busby, London,
    1998

Yanuarti, Sri, Konflik Maluku Utara, LIPI, Jakarta, 2004

Index